DISCARDED

RADIO PLAYS
for
YOUNG PEOPLE

Radio Plays
for
Young People

*Fifteen Great Stories Adapted
For Royalty-Free Performance*

by

WALTER HACKETT

With an introduction by Norman Corwin

Boston
PLAYS, INC.
Publishers

Copyright 1950 by
WALTER HACKETT

All Rights Reserved

Reprinted 1968

CAUTION

The plays in this volume are fully protected by copyright law. All rights, including motion picture, recitation, television, public reading, radio broadcasting, and rights of translation into foreign languages are strictly reserved.

NOTICE FOR AMATEUR PRODUCTION

Any strictly amateur group may produce as a non-commercial radio broadcast, without permission or royalty payment, any of the plays contained in this volume. And permission is granted to any amateur group to make copies of any play in this book for use as acting scripts for its own amateur production.

NOTICE FOR PROFESSIONAL PRODUCTION

For any form of non-amateur presentation (sustaining or commercial radio), permission must be obtained in writing from the publisher. Inquiries regarding royalty fees should be addressed to PLAYS, INC., 8 Arlington Street, Boston 16, Massachusetts.

MANUFACTURED IN THE UNITED STATES OF AMERICA

INTRODUCTION

For some time I have had a growing fear that the minds of young people in this country will be atrophied by what they hear on the radio and see on television. The diet of adults is in danger of becoming mental chewing gum; that of children already consists of the hopelessly condescending pap of standard juvenilia, the bang-bang of whodunits and the endless chasings of hoss opera.

Where, from one end of the radio-TV listings to another, does one find any intimation that such writers as Mark Twain, Robert Louis Stevenson, Nathaniel Hawthorne and Anatole France ever lived? There are no programs representing their work; for they have apparently not made the grade. Their stories are seldom, if ever, chosen for adaptation. And that is curious, because this is the Age of Adaptation.

Radio, films, and television are far richer and more powerful than any form of Theater in all history. Yet they express the most abject poverty of creative ideas, and are unblushing about it. Hollywood generally adapts only contemporary plays and books, being afraid to trust the tastes of bygone generations; from Hollywood's borrowings, radio then borrows further. At this writing, the two most prosperous dramatic programs in radio and television exclude *all* original drama, and present *only* adaptations of movies and stage plays. This is fixed policy.

Because of the disinclination of networks and stations to bring James Fenimore Cooper and De Maupassant to their listeners, because they prefer *Hopalong Cassidy* and *John's Other Wife* to Oscar Wilde and Louisa May Alcott, because *Mr. District Attorney* has a higher rating than Washington Irving and Charles Dickens, little of the work of these masters gets to be adapted and heard. The literature of such scripts is very small indeed, and will fill barely two inches of bookshelf.

The collection of scripts in these pages, marks at least another inch of progress in the right direction. Here are adaptations of essentially excellent basic material. It may well be that through such vehicles, the names of the great writers here represented are introduced to many young people for the first time—names which should be at least as well known to growing Americans as the names of shortstops and catchers for the Boston Red Sox and Brooklyn Dodgers.

Some, if not most of these scripts were broadcast before Hucksterism moved in and brought ceiling zero over good source material. I understand that Mr. Hackett has reduced and simplified the scripts in order to facilitate performance by school or home groups, in the absence of regular radio outlets.

Whatever else may be said, it is pleasant to meet Twain and Hawthorne again, after listening for so long to the sales conventions and the twaddle of *Captain Video*. *Vive* Anatole France! And I only hope the legends of Sleepy Hollow and Canterville Chase help to fill the vacuum that is now Radio for young America.

Norman Corwin

Lake Success, N. Y.
January 15, 1950.

PREFACE

Radio has proved itself to be a powerful educational tool. Its value as an addition to classroom work was made particularly evident to me during the years when I wrote scripts for the Columbia Broadcasting System's *School of the Air*. Its importance as a medium that can be used effectively by young actors has been shown by the many thousands of free air-hours granted schools throughout the country and the innumerable broadcasts by students over school public address systems and in assembly programs.

The scripts in this book have been produced over the air by both professionals and amateurs. Some of them have been done on local stations, some on regional networks and others on major networks. A radio play, like a stage play, benefits from rehearsal and actual performance. The combination irons out any plot, dialogue, scene transition or other general production snags that exist in a script fresh from the duplicating machine. Improvements made during the course of broadcasts have been incorporated into these scripts so that, in their present form, they run smoothly both production-wise and dramatically.

The layout of the scripts is the pattern followed by the Columbia Broadcasting System. For example, each sound and music cue is set out by itself instead of being hidden between chunks of dialogue and narration.

It is possible that some of the technical terms may not be clear to all directors. *B. G.* is one that comes to mind. It means *Background*. For example: *Fade music to B. G.* Another term is *Segue*. Suppose that during a scene you hear in the background a nostalgic theme of music. The scene ends, and the music, acting as a bridge, suddenly changes from the background theme to one suggesting anger, or war, or trouble. In short, insofar as radio drama is concerned, it represents a quick switch in mood or tempo.

In several places you will note a bit of radio jargon: BIZ. As far as I know it is a term used mostly by the CBS genre of script writers and goes back to the era of Max Wylie. BIZ means something that neither SOUND nor MUSIC, singly or together, can describe properly. Here is a bit of BIZ from an original *Joe Powers of Oakville* script I wrote for CBS several years ago.

BIZ: *Piano playing, males singing last bars of "When Irish Eyes Are Smiling." Voice yells, "Hey, shut that door!" At conclusion of song, patrons ad lib happily and applaud. This weaves up and down through balance of scene.*

In effect, you might say that BIZ is a unified combination of music and voices blending into a single pattern, a pattern into which sound may be woven.

As for the music cues, naturally it must be supposed that when you produce these scripts you will use either the transcribed or recorded variety which will be carefully selected for mood and length and then fitted into the script.

Following production, these scripts were published in *Plays, the Drama Magazine for Young People,* which was a pleasure to me; otherwise they would have remained housed in that utterly useless limbo of forgotten radio scripts—the author's filing cabinet.

I trust you will find as much pleasure in producing, acting in, or reading these scripts as I did in writing them.

Walter Hackett

Boston, February, 1950

TABLE OF CONTENTS

		page
Introduction	*Norman Corwin*	v
Preface		vii
THE MAN WITHOUT A COUNTRY	*Edward Everett Hale*	3
THE MILLION-POUND BANK NOTE	*Mark Twain*	23
THE CANTERVILLE GHOST	*Oscar Wilde*	44
THE NECKLACE	*Guy de Maupassant*	62
A TALE OF TWO CITIES	*Charles Dickens*	83
RIP VAN WINKLE	*Washington Irving*	105
THE YOUNG MAN WITH THE CREAM TARTS	*Robert Louis Stevenson*	124
THE SPY	*James Fenimore Cooper*	143
THE GREAT STONE FACE	*Nathaniel Hawthorne*	165
THE LAURENCE BOY (from LITTLE WOMEN)	*Louisa May Alcott*	182
THE JUGGLER	*Anatole France*	199
THE LEGEND OF SLEEPY HOLLOW	*Washington Irving*	208
MY DOUBLE AND HOW HE UNDID ME	*Edward Everett Hale*	228
THE SIRE DE MALETROIT'S DOOR	*Robert Louis Stevenson*	246
THE CHRISTMAS CAROL	*Charles Dickens*	261

RADIO PLAYS
for
YOUNG PEOPLE

The Man Without a Country
by Edward Everett Hale

MUSIC: *A strong Americana theme. Forte and fade under.*
VOICE 1: I understand he's comin' aboard tomorrow. I've never seen him. I wonder what he looks like?
VOICE 2: Who you talkin' about?
VOICE 1: The Man without a Country.
MUSIC: *Forte briefly and under again.*
NARRATOR: Fort Massac is a small yet strategic United States Army outpost that stands on the muddy banks of the lower Mississippi River. In this year of 1805, its officers and men are none too happy concerning their lonely detail. But on this particular day there is in evidence a more-than-average amount of excitement. A famous guest has come to visit them. At the evening mess he sits in the place of honor, at the commanding officer's right. As the meal progresses the officers stare at the newcomer: Aaron Burr! Aaron Burr, former Vice-President of the United States, rabid Federalist, master politician, smooth-tongued orator; Aaron Burr, the man who had killed Alexander Hamilton in a duel. (*Fading*) The Colonel turns to Burr and says.
MUSIC: *Out.*
COLONEL: Are you sure I can't get you to change your mind, Mr. Burr? You're welcome to remain here as long as you wish.
BURR: Thank you, Colonel, but I'm afraid I must be leaving within the next day or so.
COLONEL: Pressing business, I imagine.

BURR: Yes, of a sort.

OFFICER (*Away*): Mr. Burr, we had rather imagined that this journey of yours was one of pleasure.

BURR: Suppose we call it a journey of observation. You see, gentlemen, my career has never allowed me to relax long enough to seek pleasure. By the way, I hope to talk more with some of you gentlemen before I leave.

COLONEL: That is a pleasure all of us will look forward to, sir.

BURR: I hope so. And now if you will excuse me, (*Fading*) I'll go to my quarters. I'm rather tired by my journey. (*A pause, then:*)

SOUND: *Knock on door.*

BURR (*Muffled tone*): Yes?

NOLAN (*A young voice*): It's Lieutenant Nolan, sir. I have the tobacco you asked for this morning.

SOUND: *Door open—closed.*

NOLAN: Here you are, sir, a pound of fine burley.

BURR: Thank you, er—

NOLAN: Lieutenant Nolan.

BURR: First name?

NOLAN: Philip, sir.

BURR: Thank you for the tobacco. (*Pause*) Sit down.

NOLAN: Thank you, Mr. Burr.

BURR: You haven't been in service too long, I take it.

NOLAN: No, sir. Going on four years.

BURR: Like the Army?

NOLAN (*Slowly*): Why, yes, sir.

BURR: The pay of a junior officer isn't very much, eh?

NOLAN: No, sir.

BURR: Ever get tired of this duty? (*Beat*) Don't be afraid to speak up, Nolan. Remember I once was in the Army, too. I was very young when I enlisted. So I have an idea how you younger officers think.

NOLAN (*Hesitantly*): Well, Mr. Burr, to be frank . . . (*He shoots it out*) . . . to be very frank, life on a frontier post like this is just about the most boring existence in the world. (*Beat*) Of course I wouldn't want the Colonel to hear me say that.

BURR (*Laughs easily*): Of course you wouldn't.

NOLAN: Then another thing—(*He hesitates.*)

BURR: Go on.

NOLAN: I happen to be in debt. As you just said: an Army lieutenant's pay isn't very much.

BURR (*Smoothly*): I'm sorry to hear that.

NOLAN: I've been thinking of applying for a transfer.

BURR: Perhaps I could help you on that, Nolan.

NOLAN (*Eagerly*): Oh, if only you would, Mr. Burr—

BURR: It wouldn't mean you would be transferred to another post.

NOLAN (*Puzzled*): No?

BURR: No! It would mean a great chance for you. A chance for fame and position and money—a great deal of money.

NOLAN: And where is this place, sir?

BURR: In a new country.

NOLAN: A new country?

BURR: A new glorious empire. Nolan, there is a place for you in that empire. But before I tell you more, you must swear to say nothing to anyone. Understand—not a word! Will you swear it?

NOLAN: Yes . . . I swear it.

MUSIC: *A theme of excitement. Forte and fade under for:*

VOICE (*Reading rapidly*): "Washington, D. C., July 3, 1807. To all commanding officers of United States Army posts in the Mississippi River sector: You are hereby commanded to apprehend and secure the persons of Aaron Burr, General James Wilkinson, and any other such conspirators guilty of attempting treason and plotting to seize a portion of these United States, on which to fashion a new country of their own. . . . Signed, John Clarke, Secretary of War."

MUSIC: *Up and out.*

PROSECUTOR: To sum up my case as prosecution on this board of court-martial: gentlemen, I accuse the defendant, Lieutenant Philip Nolan, of the crime of treason against the United States of America.

BIZ: *A buzz of voices.*

SOUND: *Gavel on wood.*

JUDGE: Silence! The prosecution will proceed.

PROSECUTOR: This man sitting here is guilty of actively abetting the most odious political plot in the entire history of our beloved country—and I am including the one another gentleman participated in—Mr. Benedict Arnold.

COUNSEL: Objection.

JUDGE: Objection overruled.

COUNSEL: But, sir, I can present conclusive evidence that will prove that Philip Nolan—

SOUND: *Gavel rapped.*

PROSECUTOR: There is not a bit of doubt that Philip Nolan knowingly entered into a secret and infamous agreement with Aaron Burr; an agreement to undermine the safety of his own native land. You have heard me question him concerning his dealings with Burr. And what has been his reply? That he is under oath to say nothing of what transpired between them.

COUNSEL: Objection.

JUDGE: Objection overruled.

PROSECUTOR: And why did this Judas sell himself? The answer: for the empty promises of an egotistical dreamer, who promised him money and fame. That is why Philip Nolan sold his soul; that is why he broke the solemn oath of fidelity

to country that he swore to abide by at the time of his enlistment.
NOLAN (*Away*): You're a liar.
SOUND: *Gavel in sharply.*
JUDGE: I might warn the prisoner that any such further remarks might result in adversely swaying the members of this board of court-martial. The prosecution may proceed.
PROSECUTOR: I simply repeat what is obvious: Lieutenant Nolan should be adjudged guilty.
JUDGE: Has the defense anything to say?
COUNSEL: Sir, Lieutenant Nolan wishes to speak for himself.
JUDGE: Let *Mr.* Nolan proceed.
NOLAN (*Quietly*): For two days I have sat here and listened as the charges piled up against me. I have heard the prosecution deliberately distort every statement, every answer I gave.
PROSECUTOR: I object.
JUDGE: Sustained.
NOLAN: I readily admit that I listened to Burr's offer to join him.
PROSECUTOR: Then why didn't you come forward and unmask him?
NOLAN: Because I was under oath to say nothing.
DEFENSE: I object. Lieutenant Nolan is not now being cross-examined. I request the court that he be allowed to finish uninterrupted.
JUDGE: Continue, Mr. Nolan.
NOLAN: I swear that I rejected Burr's offer. (*Beat*) I realize that military justice is of a necessity swift and sometimes unjust.
PROSECUTOR: Objection.
JUDGE: Sustained. The defendant will reword his line of reasoning.
NOLAN: I realize that in any court of justice it is possible for

an innocent man to be falsely accused of the wrongs done by others. (*His voice rises*) For the past two weeks I have seen other officers—men actually guilty of the same crime I allegedly committed—go free. Free because this board wished to find them free.
BIZ: *Angry ad libs from members.*
SOUND: *Gavel.*
JUDGE: Are you finished, Mr. Nolan?
NOLAN: No! I know well what the verdict will be. I know I will be made an example of the fate in store for others.
JUDGE: Mr. Nolan, I believe it has been easily established that you have been unfaithful to your country, that you have committed against the United States—
NOLAN (*Angrily*): Damn the United States. I wish I may never hear of the United States again!
MUSIC: *Angry theme. Up and out into:*
SOUND: *Gavel on wood: three times.*
JUDGE: The prisoner will rise and face the board. (*Beat*) Philip Nolan, hear the sentence of this board. The board of court martial, subject to the approval of the President, decrees that you shall never again hear the name of the United States!
MUSIC: *Up and fade under.*
JUDGE: Mr. Nolan is to be taken to New Orleans and delivered to Lieutenant Mitchell, Acting Naval Commander. You will request that no one will ever mention the United States to the prisoner while he is on board ship. Mr. Nolan is to be confined until further orders.
MUSIC: *Up briefly and under.*
JEFFERSON: "Washington, D. C., October 28, 1807. To Secretary of Navy Crowninshield. Your deposition relative to the case of Philip Nolan received and noted. You are hereby empowered to turn the prisoner over to Captain Ethan Shaw, commander of the *Nautilus,* now in New Orleans. Sincerely

yours, Your obedient Servant, Thomas Jefferson, President of the United States."

MUSIC: *Up and out into:*

SOUND (*Away*): *Ship's bell striking six.*

SHAW (*On fourth stroke*): Lieutenant Mitchell, I can't say I like this duty.

MITCHELL: Sorry, Captain Shaw, but I'm just carrying out my orders.

SHAW: I understand. Go on and read the rest of the order.

MITCHELL: "You will provide him with such quarters, rations, and clothing as would be proper for an officer of his late rank. The officers on board your ship will make arrangements agreeable to themselves regarding his society."

SHAW (*Gloomily*): That is going to be a pleasant situation. Go on.

MITCHELL: "He is to be exposed to no indignity of any kind, nor is he ever unnecessarily to be reminded that he is a prisoner . . ."

SHAW: And I suppose that is going to be an easy order to obey.

MITCHELL: "But under no circumstances is Philip Nolan ever to hear of his country again, nor to see any information regarding it; and you will caution all your officers that these rules are not to be broken. It is the unswerving intention of the government that he shall never again see the country which he has disowned. Before the end of your cruise you will receive orders with regard to transferring the prisoner. Respectfully yours, W. Southard, Assistant to the Secretary of the Navy."

SHAW (*As though shrugging*): Well—! (*Beat*) How does he take it?

MITCHELL: I don't think he realizes what is going to happen.

SHAW: He'll soon learn. (*Abruptly*) Where is he now?

MITCHELL: Waiting outside, sir.

SHAW: Bring him in.
SOUND: *Chair scraping on floor. Hatch door slid open.*
SHAW (*Calling out*): Guard, bring the prisoner here.
GUARD (*Off*): Aye, sir. (*As an aside to* NOLAN) Step lively, you.
SHAW: You can leave us now, Lieutenant Mitchell.
MITCHELL: Thank you, sir.
SOUND: *Hatch slid closed.*
SHAW: Well, Mr. Nolan, I suppose you're wondering quite a few things at the moment.
NOLAN: I am.
SHAW: You're to be given quarters. You'll be fairly comfortable. The ship's commissary will supply anything you lack. Your meals will be served to you in your cabin.
NOLAN: About my uniforms, the insignia has been removed.
SHAW: You are to be allowed to wear your uniforms minus all insignia.
NOLAN: But—
SHAW: Orders.
NOLAN: I see. (Pause) Captain Shaw, exactly what is my position aboard your ship?
SHAW (*Fumbling*): Why—why, er—(*Quickly recovering himself*) You may consider your position as that of a guest—a slightly underprivileged guest.
NOLAN: Am I to sail with you?
SHAW: Naturally.
NOLAN: Where?
SHAW: Around the Horn, into the Pacific, and across to Tahiti.
NOLAN: Tahiti? That's a long way from the United States.
SHAW: A very long way.
NOLAN: How long are we to be gone?
SHAW: Two years!
MUSIC: *A dramatic theme. Forte and out.*

THE MAN WITHOUT A COUNTRY 11

OFFICER 1 (*Lazily*): I sometimes wonder why I joined the Navy, rather than the Army. This idea of roaming the seven seas can be tiresome. When we get back to the States, I'm going to put in for shore duty.

OFFICER 2: I rather like it here in Tahiti. It's warm and peaceful; a nice lazy life.

OFFICER 1: It's been almost two years since I last saw my parents. In fact, it's been nine months since we sailed from New Orleans. A couple of nomads, you and I, men without a home.

OFFICER 2: Much better than being a man without a country.

OFFICER 1: What's that? Oh, yes. Poor Nolan! At times I feel sorry for him.

OFFICER 2: Too bad he lost his head. Wonder if the government will ever rescind his sentence?

OFFICER 1: Hard to say.

OFFICER 2: It would have been a more merciful thing to have hanged him. Anything in place of being a floating derelict.

OFFICER 1 (*He lowers his voice*): Quiet! Here he comes now. Watch what you say.

NOLAN: Good afternoon, gentlemen. Grand day, isn't it? (OFFICERS *ad lib greetings*) Mind if I join you?

OFFICER 1: Plenty of deck space.

OFFICER 2: Sit down.

NOLAN (*Sighs deeply*): Ahh! That sun feels good. Thought I would do a bit of reading. The surgeon passed on this old newspaper to me—an English newspaper.

OFFICER 2: You're a great reader, Mr. Nolan.

NOLAN: Oh, yes. Helps pass away the time, you know. Keeps me in touch with what is taking place. (*Pause*) Would you gentlemen tell me something?

OFFICER 1 (*Cautiously*): Why . . . yes.

NOLAN: I notice that these newspapers that are passed on to me

have certain paragraphs cut out. For example, this one here.
SOUND: *Newspaper unfolded.*
NOLAN: Here! Now here is a story dealing with Napoleon's campaign, and just as it apparently starts to relate the policy of the United States toward The Little Corporal, I discover that the rest of the account has been sheared out. Peculiar, isn't it? Er, could you tell me why?
OFFICER 1: No.
OFFICER 2: Hadn't noticed.
NOLAN: Well, I guess it doesn't matter. By the way, what is the latest news from our country?
OFFICER 2: We have no news.
NOLAN: But last night in the wardroom you were talking over the dispatches received from the States. As soon as I came in, you stopped. Why?
OFFICER 2: I wish you wouldn't ask, Mr. Nolan.
NOLAN (*As though shrugging*): Very well. I realize you're not supposed to talk about the United States to me. I thought I could worm some information from you.
OFFICER 2: We're honor-bound not to discuss the matter with you.
OFFICER 1: You should understand.
NOLAN (*Dully*): Yes, I understand.
OFFICER 1: What about your parents, Mr. Nolan, or your relatives? Couldn't they—?
NOLAN: My parents are dead. As for my relatives, they don't know, and I doubt if they'd help. (*A simple dignity*) Now, if you don't mind, I'll go to my quarters.
OFFICER 1: Nolan.
NOLAN: Yes?
OFFICER 1: If I were in your position, I wouldn't show the courage you're displaying.
MUSIC: *Up dramatically and under.*

VOICE: "Belfast, Ireland, June 14, 1810. To Captain James Wyatt, U.S.S. *General Greene.* You will receive the person of Philip Nolan, who will accompany you on your voyage to the Straits of Gibraltar and through the Mediterranean."

MUSIC: *Up briefly and under.*

VOICE 2: "From the log of the U.S.S. *Enterprise.* November 11, 1814. Havana, Cuba. Today we took on fresh supplies for our cruise to the Far East. Also received as passenger Mr. Philip Nolan."

MUSIC: *Up and out into:*

SOUND: *Knock on door.*

LANE: Enter.

SOUND: *Hatch slid open.*

SAILOR: Mr. Nolan, sir. He would like to speak with you.

LANE: Show him in.

SAILOR: Aye, aye, sir. (*Slightly away*) The captain will see you.

SOUND (*After a beat*): *Hatch slid shut.*

LANE: Yes, Mr. Nolan?

NOLAN: Captain Lane, I have heard scuttlebutt that we may engage the enemy at any moment.

LANE: That's no great secret. What about it?

NOLAN: Well, Captain, I have heard you're a bit shorthanded. I'm wondering if you can use me.

LANE (*Surprised*): Hmmm?

NOLAN: I know ship's routine well. Any detail would be welcome, sir, even that of a powder monkey.

LANE: You mean you desire combat duty?

NOLAN: Exactly, sir.

LANE (*Not unkindly*): That's generous of you, Nolan, but I'm afraid it's impossible. Your position . . . my orders concerning you, they're very strict.

NOLAN: Couldn't you forget them, just this once?

LANE: In the Navy you don't wink an eye at orders. In fact,

Mr. Nolan, when and if we do engage the enemy, I must ask that you go below and remain there until the action has stopped.

MUSIC: *Up briefly and out into:*

BIZ: *Group of men singing a Christmas Carol. They sing one chorus. As they stop:*

OFFICER 3: A toast, gentlemen.

BIZ: *Voices: "A toast."*

OFFICER 3: A toast to our ship, the mighty *Constitution*.

BIZ: *"Hear, hear." "A great fighting ship."*

OFFICER 3: A toast. To this Christmas Day in the year of our Lord, 1821.

BIZ: *"Merry Christmas." "A great day."*

NOLAN: Gentlemen, may I propose a toast? (*There is an awkward pause.*)

OFFICER 3: Go ahead, Mr. Nolan.

NOLAN: I propose a toast to the United States. (*Another pause.*)

OFFICER 3: Sorry, Mr. Nolan, but that toast will have to be drunk later, when you are not present.

SOUND: *Glass broken, as though dropped from* NOLAN'S *hand.*

MUSIC: *Up dramatically and out.*

CAPTAIN: Well, gentlemen, who would like to read next? Dr. Bates?

BATES: Thank you, Captain, but I'll remain just a ship's doctor.

CAPTAIN: Lieutenant Harper, how about you?

HARPER: I'm not much of a hand at reading, but I'll try.

CAPTAIN: Try this. It's a new book of poems by that Scotsman, Walter Scott. Let me see. Ah, here's what seems to be a good poem: "The Lay of the Last Minstrel." Right here.

HARPER (*He reads poorly*):

"After due pause, they bade him tell
Why he, who touched the harp so well,

Should thus, with ill-rewarded toil,
Wander a poor and thankless soil,
When the most generous Southern Land
Would well requite his skillful hand . . ."
NOLAN (*Slightly away*): Stop! Stop!
CAPTAIN: What's wrong, Mr. Nolan?
NOLAN: With all due respect to Lieutenant Harper, Captain, he's not doing justice to that poem.
BIZ: *A few surprised ad libs from others.*
HARPER: At least I thought I was reading intelligently.
NOLAN: Perhaps! But with no feeling.
CAPTAIN: Are you an expert on Sir Walter Scott's works?
NOLAN: As a matter of fact, I've never read this poem, but I do know enough to realize that it isn't being read the way it should.
HARPER: Why don't you read it, Mr. Nolan?
CAPTAIN: You're at liberty to do so.
NOLAN:
"The aged harper, howsoe'er
His friend, his harp, was dear,
Liked not to hear it, ranked so high
Above his flowing poesy:
Less liked he that still that scornful jeer
Misprized the land he loved so dear;
High was the sound as thus again
The bard resumed his minstrel strain.
Breathes there the man, with soul so dead, (*A bit emotionally*)
Who never to himself hath said—
This is my own, my native land!
Whose heart hath ne'er within him burned
As home (*Stumbling a bit*) his footsteps he hath turned
From wandering on a foreign strand?

If such there breathe, go, mark him well.
For him no minstrel raptures swell; (*His voice starts to break.*)
High though his titles, proud his name,
Boundless his wealth as wish can claim,
Despite these titles, power and pelf, (*He shouts*) The wretch, concentred all in self . . ."

SOUND: *Book dropped to floor.*

NOLAN (*A beaten voice*): I . . . I guess I'm not such a fine reader, after all.

MUSIC: *A theme of motion. Forte and under for:*

VOICE 1 (*Calling out, as though speaking through a speaking trumpet*): Hooo there, *Constellation*. Stand by to receive our longboat.

VOICE 2 (*Off in distance*): What have you for us? Any mail?

VOICE 1: No mail. We are transferring Philip Nolan.

MUSIC: *Up and out.*

RANKIN: It's certainly a pleasure to have you aboard, Anna. Let me see, I haven't seen you in four—no, in five years.

ANNA: As soon as I heard word at the Consulate that your ship was coming here, I said to myself: "I'll be the very first American to welcome Ben Rankin."

RANKIN: And you kept your word. Your husband sent a message that he'd come aboard late this afternoon. You know, Anna, you don't seem to have aged one bit since I last saw you.

ANNA: And I can return the compliment. Ben, you look just the same as you did thirty years ago. Yes, that's when we first met, thirty years ago in Charleston. You were just a plain midshipman then. And now look at you—a captain of a man-o-war.

RANKIN: And here you are, married.

ANNA: I'm a grandmother.

RANKIN: How do you like Naples?
ANNA: I like everything but the odors. (*Both laugh*) You know, Ben, I haven't been home in seven years, not since 1840. (*Sighs*) Being wife to an American Consul isn't all sunshine. Right now, I'd give a pretty penny for one good whiff of Charleston Harbor.
RANKIN (*Suddenly*): Have you ever heard of Philip Nolan?
ANNA: Nolan, Nolan!
RANKIN: Perhaps you know him better under his other name . . . The Man without a Country.
ANNA: Don't tell me that he's—?
RANKIN: Yes, I have him aboard.
ANNA: When my husband was stationed at Marseilles—which was six years back—the *Constellation* came in for repairs. Nolan was aboard, but I didn't see him.
BIZ (*Off in distance*): *Some of the crew ad libbing.*
RANKIN: I've heard of him ever since I was a midshipman, but until fifteen months ago, I had never as much as laid eyes upon him.
ANNA: He's become something of a legend.
RANKIN: Practically a Navy tradition. Shifted from one ship to another. Poor man, he's the nearest thing to perpetual motion I have ever encountered.
ANNA: Does he give you any trouble?
RANKIN: No. I've heard that during the early days, he was quite aggressive, but he's lost all that. Getting fairly old. Must be around, oh, I'd say at least sixty-five. Minds his own business and keeps pretty much to himself. (*He lowers his voice*) Look! There he is walking toward us. Poor old devil!
ANNA: I'm afraid I don't share your sympathy. In my opinion, Nolan deserves to suffer.
NOLAN (*Fading in*): Captain Rankin, sir.
RANKIN: Yes, Mr. Nolan?

NOLAN: The second officer wants to know if you have any instructions before the liberty party goes ashore.
RANKIN: Anna, will you excuse me for several minutes?
ANNA: Certainly.
RANKIN: By the way, Anna, this is Mr. Nolan. Mr. Nolan this is Mrs. Rutledge.
ANNA: Good afternoon.
RANKIN (*Fading*): Mr. Jenks, I wish to see you before you go ashore. Have a detail for you. (*Ad lib voices in background gradually die out.*)
NOLAN: This is a nice day, don't you think, Mrs. Rutledge?
ANNA (*Coldly*): Quite comfortable.
NOLAN: The last port we touched was Havre. Very interesting place. I wasn't allowed ashore, but I heard the crew talking. These foreign places are fine enough, but not like home. Mrs. Rutledge, what is the news from the United States?
ANNA: I thought you were the man who once said he never wanted to hear that name again.
MUSIC: *A tragic theme. Up and out into:*
SOUND: *Clock striking five strokes.*
RANKIN (*His voice has grown older. He speaks on the third stroke of the clock*): Mr. Secretary, it seems to me that you doubt the truth of my story. I assure you, sir, that I am speaking the truth.
NAVY SECRETARY: I—I don't know what to think. I know your word is good, but hang it all, Rankin, the Navy Department's records show absolutely no trace of this man you speak of . . . this Philip Nolan.
RANKIN: Naturally not, Mr. Secretary. Those records were destroyed by fire when the British seized Washington during the War of 1812.
SECRETARY: It all sounds like a fairy tale, like a nightmare.
RANKIN: Whether you want to believe it or not, Philip Nolan

was sentenced back in 1807, and this is 1859. Mind you, Mr. Secretary, for 52 years Philip Nolan has been shifted from one ship to another. For 52 years he has never set foot on American soil. For 52 years he has not heard the name of the United States even mentioned by anyone. For over a half-century this unfortunate derelict has experienced a living death.

SECRETARY: Captain Rankin, why do you concern yourself with this matter?

RANKIN: Because I like Nolan. He has been committed to my care on two occasions, and each time I found him to be a kind, mild gentleman. (*Pleadingly*) Mr. Secretary, won't you investigate his case? The man has only a few years of life ahead of him. Why not let him enjoy them?

SECRETARY: With the possibility of war with the South growing stronger this department hasn't time for such an investigation.

RANKIN: Aren't you trying to tell me that you don't care to unearth any skeletons?

SECRETARY: An unfortunate choice of words, Captain. (*Coldly*) Taking for granted there is such a man as Philip Nolan, he will have to remain an unknown; a legend, if you like.

RANKIN (*Casually*): Suppose the newspapers got hold of this story? The national election is only a year off.

SECRETARY (*Significantly*): It is entirely within my power to depose you from your command. Then there is the Far East. That is a long voyage. (*Fading*) You know how many days a voyage to Japan takes, do you not, Captain Rankin? Or don't you? (*A pause, then*)

SOUND: *Telegraph buzzer. Sending message.*

VOICE 1: "Washington, D. C., January 12, 1860. To Captain Benjamin Rankin, Newport News, Virginia. . . . Prepare to sail on 27th for extended tour of Far East, including China and Japan. Detailed orders following."

SOUND: *Buzzer up briefly and under again.*
VOICE 2: "Shanghai, China, May 11, 1862. To Captain Benjamin Rankin, aboard U.S.S. *Levant*. . . . Captain Chalmers of the *Ohio* will deliver into your hands the person of Philip Nolan. From past contact with him, you will know how to receive and handle his case."
MUSIC: *Washes in over sound. Hold briefly and out.*
RANKIN (*Low voice*): You think the end is in sight, doctor?
DOCTOR: He's liable to go off any minute.
RANKIN: Suppose you leave me alone with him?
DOCTOR: Very well. (*Slight fade*) If you need me, I'll be outside.
SOUND (*Slightly away*): *Hatch slid open, then closed.*
RANKIN: Philip. (*Beat*) Philip, it's Rankin.
NOLAN: Hello, Captain.
RANKIN: Is there anything you wish?
NOLAN: Just sit here and talk to me. (*Beat*) I know I'm dying. Perhaps now you will tell me what I want to know.
RANKIN: Anything you wish.
NOLAN (*Breathing heavily*): I want you to know that there is not a man on this ship—that there is not in America, God bless her!—a more loyal man than I. How like a wretched night's dream a boy's idea of personal fame or of separate sovereignty seems, when one looks back on it after such a life as mine.
RANKIN (*After pause*): Now what would you like to hear?
NOLAN: Is our country larger?
RANKIN: A good many states have been added. Ohio, Kentucky, Michigan, Indiana, and Mississippi; and California and Texas and Oregon.
NOLAN: What of America's progress?
RANKIN: Our country has made tremendous strides. Her cotton manufacturing is the greatest in the world. We have made great improvements on the steam train.

NOLAN: Steam train?

RANKIN: Yes. A form of carriage propelled by steam. Then a Naval Academy has been established at Annapolis and a Military Academy at West Point in New York. A great piece of literature has been written by a woman named Stowe— "Uncle Tom's Cabin."

NOLAN: Are we at peace?

RANKIN: There was a war with England.

NOLAN: In 1812. I heard rumors of it at the time. I have also heard there is trouble between the North and the South. (*Hastily*) No! Don't tell me. I prefer not to know. Who is our President now?

RANKIN: A great man named Abraham Lincoln. He's from the state of Illinois, a man who worked his way up from the ranks.

NOLAN: Good for him.

RANKIN: The United States is fast growing into the greatest democracy in the world.

NOLAN (*Weakly*): Wonderful . . . wonderful news.

RANKIN (*Alarmed*): Philip, are you—?

NOLAN: Better than I have ever been. You see that old flag against the wall?

RANKIN: Yes.

NOLAN: I want to be wrapped in it. You'll see to that?

RANKIN: I promise.

NOLAN: God bless you! (*His voice becomes weaker*) On the table is a Bible.

RANKIN: I have it.

NOLAN: Open it. (*Pause*) Now read what is written on the fly leaf.

RANKIN (*Slowly and with simple dignity*): "Bury me in the sea. It has been my home, and I love it. But will not someone set up a stone for my memory somewhere on my native soil, that my disgrace may not be more than I ought to bear? Say on it: 'In memory of Philip Nolan, Lieutenant in the Army of the United States. He loved his country as no other man has loved her; but no man deserved less at her hands.'"

MUSIC: *Up to curtain.*

THE END

The Million-Pound Bank Note

by Mark Twain

HENRY: When I was twenty-seven years old, I was a mining broker's clerk in San Francisco. I was alone in the world, and had nothing to depend upon but my wits and a clean reputation. These were setting my feet in the road to eventual fortune, and I was content with the prospect. During my spare time, I did outside work. One of my part-time employers was Lloyd Hastings, a mining broker. During this period I was helping Hastings to verify the Gould and Curry Extension papers, covering what seemed to be a highly valuable gold mine. One morning at two, after six hard hours of work on these papers, Lloyd Hastings and I went to the What Cheer restaurant in Frisco. As we lingered over our coffee, he offered me a proposition.

HASTINGS: Henry, how would you like to go to London?

HENRY: Thank you, no.

HASTINGS: Listen to me. I'm thinking of taking a month's option on the Gould and Curry Extension for the locators.

HENRY: And—?

HASTINGS: They want one million dollars for it.

HENRY: Not too much—if the claim works out the way it appears it may.

HASTINGS: I'm going to try to sell it to London interests, which means a trip there, and I want you to go with me, because you know more about these papers than I.

HENRY: No, thanks.

HASTINGS: I'll make it well worth your while. I'll pay all your expenses, and give you something over if I make the sale.

HENRY: I have a job.

HASTINGS: I'll arrange for you to get a leave of absence. What do you say?

HENRY: No.

HASTINGS: Why?

HENRY: If I go to London, I'll get out of touch with my work and with mining conditions here, and that means months getting the hang of things again.

HASTINGS: That's a pretty slim excuse, Henry.

HENRY: More important, perhaps, I think you're doomed to failure.

HASTINGS: But you just said the claim is valuable.

HENRY: It may well turn out that way, but right now its real value can't be proved. And even so, a month's option may leave you too little time to sell it; unless you sell it within the option time, you'll go stone broke.

HASTINGS: I'm willing to gamble.

HENRY: Well, I'm not.

HASTINGS: Think—a free trip to London.

HENRY: I've no desire to go to London. I'll remain right here in Frisco.

HASTINGS (*Fading*): Very well, but I know you're making a mistake, Henry.

HENRY: One of my few diversions was sailing in the bay. One day I ventured too far, and was carried out to sea. Late that night, I was picked up by a freighter which was bound for London. It was a long voyage, and the captain made me work my passage without pay, as a common sailor. When I stepped ashore at London my clothes were ragged and shabby, and I had only a dollar in my pocket. This money fed and sheltered me for twenty-four hours. During the next twenty-four I went without food and shelter. I tried to get a job, doing manual labor. But the reply was always the same.

COCKNEY: I'm not sure you'd do. You ain't the sort. (*Suspiciously*) Look, 'ere, you're a Yank, ain't you?

HENRY: The next morning, seedy and hungry, I was dragging myself along Portland Place, when my desiring eye fell on a tempting treasure lying in the gutter. It was a luscious big pear—minus one bite. My mouth watered for it. But every time I made a move to get it, some passing eye detected my purpose. I was just getting desperate enough to brave all the shame, when a window behind me was raised.

GORDON (*Away*): I say, you there, will you step in here, please?

HENRY: It was a very sumptuous house and an equally sumptuous room into which I was ushered by a servant. A couple of elderly gentlemen were sitting by the window. At that moment if I had known what they had in mind, undoubtedly I would have bolted for the door. They looked me over very thoroughly.

GORDON: He looks poor enough, don't you think, brother?

ABEL: Very. Er, young man, you are poor?

HENRY: Extremely!

ABEL: Good! And honest, too?

HENRY: Honesty is about all I have left; that, and character.

ABEL: Splendid!

GORDON: If my brother and I are judges of people, we'd say you are just the man for whom we have been searching. By the way, you are also intelligent, I would say.

HENRY: Yes, sir, I am. But what do you mean by saying that I appear to be just the man for whom you have been searching?

GORDON: And we don't know you. You're a perfect stranger. And better still, an American.

HENRY: It's very kind of you gentlemen to call me into your

home, but I'm a bit puzzled. Could you tell me what you have in mind?
ABEL: Might we inquire into your background?
HENRY: Pretty soon they had my full story. Their questions were complete and searching, and I gave them straight-forward answers. Finally one said:
GORDON: Oh, yes, we're certain you will do, eh, brother?
ABEL: Definitely! He is elected.
HENRY: To what am I elected, please?
GORDON: This envelope will explain everything. Here, take it. (*Hastily*) No, don't open it now. Take it to your lodgings and look it over carefully.
ABEL: Being sure not to be rash or hasty.
HENRY: I'd like to discuss the matter.
GORDON: There is nothing to discuss at the moment.
HENRY: Is this a joke?
ABEL: Not at all. And now good day.
GORDON: And good luck.
ABEL: Cheerio!
HENRY: As soon as I was out of sight of the house I opened my envelope and saw it contained money. I lost not a moment, but shoved note and money into my pocket, and broke for the nearest cheap eating house. How I did eat! Finished, I took out my money and unfolded it. I took one glimpse and nearly fainted. It was a single million-pound bank note. Five millions of dollars! It made my head swim. The next thing I noticed was the owner of the eating house. His eyes were on the note, and he was petrified. He couldn't stir hand or foot. I tossed the note toward him in careless fashion.
HAWKINS: I-is it real, sir? A million-pound note?
HENRY (*Casually*): Certainly. Let me have my change, please.
HAWKINS: Oh, I'm very sorry, sir, but I can't break the bill.
HENRY: Look here—
HAWKINS: Hawkins is the name, Albert Hawkins, proprietor.

It's only a matter of two shillings you owe, a trifling sum. Please owe it to me.
HENRY: I may not be in this neighborhood again for a good time.
HAWKINS: It's of no consequence, sir. And you can have anything you want, any time you choose, and let the account run as long as you please. I'm not afraid to trust as rich a gentleman as you, just because you choose to play larks by dressing as a tramp.
HENRY: Well, thank you. I shall take advantage of your kindness.
HAWKINS: Not at all, sir, (*Fading*) and please, sir, enter my humble restaurant place any time you wish. I shall be honored to receive you.
HENRY: I was frightened, afraid that the police might pick me up. I was afraid of the two brothers' reaction when they discovered they had given me a million-pound note instead of what they must have intended giving—a one-pound note. I hurried to their house and rang the bell. The same servant appeared. I asked for the brothers.
SERVANT: They are gone.
HENRY: Gone! Where?
SERVANT: On a journey.
HENRY: But whereabouts?
SERVANT: To the Continent, I think.
HENRY: The Continent?
SERVANT: Yes, sir.
HENRY: Which way—by what route?
SERVANT: I can't say, sir.
HENRY: When will they be back?
SERVANT: In a month, they said.
HENRY: A month! This is awful! Tell me how to get word to them. It's of great importance.
SERVANT: I can't, indeed. I've no idea where they've gone, sir.

HENRY: Then I must see some member of the family.
SERVANT: Family's been away too; been abroad months—in Egypt and India, I think.
HENRY: There's been an immense mistake made. They'll be back before night. Tell them I've been here, and that I'll keep coming till it's all made right, and they needn't worry.
SERVANT: I'll tell them, if they come back, but I'm not expecting them. They said you'd be here in an hour to make inquiries, but I must tell you it's all right, they'll be here on time to meet you. (*Fading*) And that's all they said.
HENRY (*Slowly*): I had to give it up and go away. What a riddle it all was! They would be here "on time." What could that mean? Then I thought of the letter. I got it out and read it. It said: "You are an intelligent and honest man, as one can see by your face. We conceive you to be poor and a stranger. Enclosed you will find a sum of money. It is lent to you for thirty days, without interest. Report to this house at the end of that time. I have a bet on you. If I win it you shall have any situation that is in my gift, any, that is, that you shall be able to prove yourself familiar with and competent to fill." That was all. No signature, no address, no date. I hadn't the least idea what the game was, nor whether harm was meant me or kindness. The letter said there was a bet on me. What kind of a bet? Was the bet that I would abscond with the million-pound bank note? Which brother was betting on my honesty? I reasoned this way: if I ask the Bank of England to deposit it to the credit of the man it belongs to, they'll ask me how I came by it, and if I tell the truth, they'll put me in the asylum; on the other hand, if I lie, they'll put me in jail. The same result would follow if I try to bank it anywhere or borrow money on it. Therefore, I have to carry this burden around until those men come back. A month's suffering without wages or profit—unless I help win that bet, whatever it

may be. If I do, I will get the situation I am promised. My hopes began to rise high. Then I looked at my rags. Could I afford a new suit? No, for I had nothing in the world but a million pounds. Finally I gave in and entered a fashionable tailor shop. The clerk looked at me very arrogantly.

Tod (*Icily*): No chores to be done here. Get out!

Henry: Perhaps you have a misfit suit.

Tod: We don't give away suits, even misfits.

Henry: I can pay for it.

Tod: Follow me.

Henry: He took me into a back room, and overhauled a pile of rejected suits. He tossed the rattiest looking one at me. I put it on. It didn't fit. It wasn't in any way attractive.

Tod: You may have that for four pounds, cash.

Henry: It would be an accommodation to me if you could wait some days for the money. I haven't any small change about me.

Tod (*Sarcastically*): Oh, you haven't? Well, of course, I didn't expect it. I'd only expect gentlemen like you to carry large change.

Henry (*Nettled*): My friend, you shouldn't judge a stranger always by the clothes he wears. I am quite able to pay for this suit.

Tod: Hah!

Henry: I simply don't wish to put you to the trouble of changing a large note.

Tod: As long as rebukes are going around, I might say that it wasn't quite your affair to infer that we couldn't change any note that you might happen to be carrying around. On the contrary, we *can*.

Henry: Oh, very well. I apologize. Here you are.

Tod: Thank you. (*A complete change. He stutters and fumbles.*) Ah—it's—ah—that is—we—ah—you see— It's—

(*Quickly*) take it back, please. (*Raising voice*) Mr. Smedley! Mr. Smedley! Help! Oh, Mr. Smedley.

SMEDLEY (*Coming in. A fussy man*): What is it, Tod, what is it? Stop shouting!

TOD: Oh, but Mr. Smedley, I can't control myself.

SMEDLEY: What's up? What's the trouble? What's wanting? Who's this?

HENRY: I am a customer and I am waiting for my change.

SMEDLEY: Change, change! Tod, give him his change. Get it for him.

TOD: Get him his change! It's easy for you to say that, Mr. Smedley, but look at the bill yourself.

SMEDLEY: Bill, bill! Let me see it! (*Pause*) Tod, you ass, selling an eccentric millionaire such an unspeakable suit as that. Tod, you're a fool—a born fool! Drives every millionaire away from this place, because he can't tell a millionaire from a tramp. Here, sir, are some suits more in keeping with your position.

HENRY: Thank you, but this one will do.

SMEDLEY: Of course it won't do! I shall burn it. Tod, burn this suit at once.

TOD: Yes, Mr. Smedley.

SMEDLEY: We shall be honored to outfit you completely, sir . . . morning clothes, evening dress, sack suits, tweeds, shetlands—everything you need. Come, Tod, book and pen. Now—length of leg, 32 inches; sleeve—

HENRY: But look here, I can't give you an order for suits, unless you can wait indefinitely, or change this bill.

SMEDLEY: Indefinitely, sir. It's a weak word, a weak word. *Eternally, that's* the word, sir. Tod, rush these things through. Let the minor customers wait. Set down the gentleman's address and—

HENRY: I'm changing my quarters. I'll drop in and leave the new address.

SMEDLEY: Quite right, sir, quite right. One moment—allow me to show you out, sir. And don't worry about paying us. (*Fading*) Your credit is the highest. Good day, sir, good day. You honor us greatly, sir.

HENRY (*As though sighing*): Well, don't you see what was bound to happen? I drifted naturally into whatever I wanted. Take my hotel, for example. I merely showed the resident manager my million-pound note, and he said:

MANAGER: We are honored to have you as a guest, sir. Now, I have just the suite for you. It consists of a bedroom, sitting room, a dressing room, a dining room, two baths and—

HENRY: I'll pay you a month in advance with this.

MANAGER (*Laughing*): You honor our simple hotel, sir. Pray, don't worry about the bill.

HENRY: But it may be several months before I can pay you.

MANAGER: We're not worried, Mr.—er—

HENRY: Henry Adams.

MANAGER: Mr. Adams, you are a most distinguished guest. (*Fading*) Anything you desire, please name it and we shall procure it for you immediately. Thank you, sir.

HENRY: And there I was, sumptuously housed in an expensive hotel in Hanover Square. I took my dinners there, but for breakfast I stuck by Hawkins' humble feeding-house, where I had got my first meal on my million-pound bank note. I was the making of Hawkins.

SOUND: *Rattle of dishes and silver, customers' voices ad libbing in background.*

HAWKINS: Business is brisk, sir, very brisk, indeed, and has been ever since you and your million-pound bank note became patrons of my humble establishment. I've had to hire extra help, put in additional tables. Look for yourself, sir. There's a long queue waiting to get in. Why, I'm famous and fair on my way to becoming wealthy.

COCKNEY 2: Pardon me, Guv'ner, but aren't you the gentleman what owns the million-pound bank note?
HAWKINS: Look here, you, go away and stop bothering Mr.— Mr.—
HENRY: Adams.
HAWKINS: Mr. Adams.
COCKNEY 2: I was just anxious to get a look at him.
HAWKINS: Who? Mr. Adams?
COCKNEY 2: No. The bank note.
HENRY: Glad to oblige. There you are.
COCKNEY 2: By George, it *is* real. (*Fading*) Now I can go home and tell me old lady I've seen it with me own eyes. I hopes she believes me, but she won't.
HAWKINS: Mr. Adams, I wonder if I couldn't force upon you a small loan—even a large one.
HENRY: Oh, no.
HAWKINS: Please allow me, sir.
HENRY (*Relenting*): Well, as a matter of fact, I haven't gotten around to changing this note.
HAWKINS: Fifty pounds might help tide you over. You know, a little spending money?
HENRY: It would help, a bit.
HAWKINS: I consider it a great honor. (*Fading*) Indeed, a very great honor. Here you are, Mr. Adams, fifty pounds it is. (*Fading*) And don't worry about repaying me.
HENRY: I was in, now, and must sink or swim. I walked on air. And it was natural, for I had become one of the notorieties of London. It turned my head, not just a little, but a great deal. The newspapers referred to me as the "Vest-Pocket Millionaire." Then came the climaxing stroke: "Punch" caricatured me! Wherever I went, people cried:
MAN 1: There he goes!
MAN 2: That's him!

Woman 1: Morning, Guv'ner.

Man 3: He's a bit of all right, he is.

Henry: Why, I just swam in glory all day long. About the tenth day of my fame I fulfilled my duty to my country by calling upon the American Ambassador. He received me with enthusiasm, and insisted that I attend a dinner party he was giving the following night. Two important things happened at that dinner. I met two people who were to play important roles in the little drama I was living. Among the guests was a lovely English girl, named Portia Langham, whom I fell in love with in two minutes, and she with me; I could see it without glasses. And just before dinner, the butler announced:

Biz: *Guests ad libbing in background, very politely.*

Butler (*Calling out*): Mr. Lloyd Hastings.

Henry: I stared at Hastings and he at me, his mouth open in surprise.

Hastings: I, er—pardon me, but are you? No, of course you can't be.

Henry (*Chuckling*): But I am, Lloyd.

Hastings: Henry, I'm speechless. (*Suddenly*) Don't tell me that you're also the Vest-Pocket Millionaire?

Henry: Correct!

Hastings: I've seen your own name coupled with the nickname, but it never occurred to me you were *the* Henry Adams. Why, it isn't six months since you were clerking in Frisco, and sitting up nights helping me verify the Gould and Curry Extension papers. The idea of your being in London, and a vast millionaire, and a colossal celebrity! It's out of the Arabian Nights!

Henry: I can't realize it myself.

Hastings: It was just three months ago that we were eating together, and I tried to persuade you to come to London with me. You turned me down and now here you are. How did

you happen to come, and what gave you this incredible start?
HENRY: I'll tell you all about it, but not now.
HASTINGS: When?
HENRY: The end of this month.
HASTINGS: Make it a week.
HENRY: I can't. How's your business venture coming along?
HASTINGS (*Sighing*): You were a true prophet, Henry. I wish I hadn't come.
HENRY: Stop with me, when we leave here, and tell me all about it. I want to hear the whole story.
HASTINGS: You'll hear it, every last dismal word. (*Fading a bit*) I'm so grateful to find a willing and sympathetic ear.
BIZ: *Background ad libbing out. A pause, then:*
PIANO: *Playing semi-classical tune in background.*
HENRY: After dinner there was coffee and an informal piano recital and dear Miss Langham—lovely Portia Langham, the English girl. I eased her away from the music and the guests, to the library, where we talked.
PIANO: *Out.*
PORTIA: I'm really quite excited, Mr. Adams, meeting you like this. A millionaire!
HENRY: But I'm not one.
PORTIA: B-but of course you are.
HENRY: You're wrong.
PORTIA: I don't understand.
HENRY: You will! You will, that is, if you allow me to see you tomorrow.
PORTIA (*As though smiling*): Well, Mr. Adams—
HENRY: Henry.
PORTIA: Henry, then. I will give the invitation serious thought.
HENRY: Tomorrow is going to be a sunny day, just right for a picnic in the country. Yes?
PORTIA: Yes.

HENRY: I'll tell you the whole story then.
PORTIA: Do you think you should?
HENRY: Certainly! After all, we're going to be married.
PORTIA (*Amazed*): We—we're—going to—marry!
HENRY: Absolutely! I'll call for you at noon. Where?
PORTIA: Meet me here.
HENRY: You're a guest here?
PORTIA: N—no, but it will be more convenient.
HENRY: Do you like me?
PORTIA: Yes, Henry. (*Fading*) You're a very unusual young man, even if you are a millionaire, and even if you claim you aren't.
HENRY: All the way home I was in the clouds, Hastings talking, and I not hearing a word. When we reached my suite, he said to me:
HASTINGS: This luxury makes me realize how poor, how defeated I am. Even the drippings of your daily income would seem like a tremendous fortune to me.
HENRY: Unreel your story, Lloyd.
HASTINGS: I told you the whole story on the way over here.
HENRY: You did?
HASTINGS: Yes.
HENRY: I'll be hanged if I heard a word of it.
HASTINGS: Are you well?
HENRY: Yes. I'm in love.
HASTINGS: That English girl you were speaking to?
HENRY: Yes. I'm going to marry her.
HASTINGS: Small wonder you didn't hear a word I said.
HENRY: Now I'm all attention.
HASTINGS: I came here with what I thought was a grand opportunity. I have an option to sell the Gould and Curry Mine and keep all I can get over a million dollars.
HENRY: Sounds like a good proposition.

HASTINGS: Yes, it's a fine claim.

HENRY: Well?

HASTINGS: The parties here whom I tried to interest have backed down. And so here I am trying to peddle a gold mine, but with nary a buyer in sight. In addition, I am almost penniless.

HENRY: Surely you'll find a buyer.

HASTINGS: My option on the mine expires in a matter of days; in fact, at the end of this month.

HENRY: You *are* in a fix.

HASTINGS: Henry, you can save me. Will you do it?

HENRY: I? How?

HASTINGS: Give me a million dollars and my passage home for my option.

HENRY: I can't.

HASTINGS: But you're wealthy.

HENRY: I—I—not really.

HASTINGS: You have a million pounds—five millions of dollars. Buy the mine and you'll double, maybe triple your investment.

HENRY: I'd like to help, but I can't.

HASTINGS: You know the value of this mine, as well as I do.

HENRY (*Tired*): Oh, Lloyd, I wish I could explain, but I can't. What you ask is impossible.

HASTINGS: That's quite all right. I'm sorry to have bothered you, Henry. (*Fading*) You must have a good reason in turning me down, I'm sure.

HENRY: It hurt me to have to refuse Lloyd, but it made me comprehend my delicate and precarious position. Here I was, deep in debt, not a cent in the world, in love with a lovely girl, and nothing in front of me but a promise of a position, if, *if* I won the bet for the nameless brother. Nothing could save me. The next day, Portia and I went on our picnic in the country. I told her the whole story, down to the last detail. Her reaction wasn't exactly what I thought it would be.

Sound: *Bird singing in background. Weave in and out of this scene.*
Portia (*Laughs*): Oh, Henry, that's priceless.
Henry (*A bit stiffly*): I fail to see the humor.
Portia: But I do, more than you can imagine.
Henry: Here I am mixed up in a bet between two eccentric old men, and for all they care I might well be in jail.
Portia (*Still laughing*): Wonderful, the funniest thing I've ever heard.
Henry: Pardon me if I don't laugh.
Portia (*Stops laughing*): Sorry, but it is both funny and pathetic. But you say that one of the men is going to offer you a position?
Henry: If I win the bet.
Portia: Which one is he?
Henry: I don't know. But I have one solution. If I win, I get the position. Now, I've kept a very careful track of every cent I either owe or have borrowed, and I'm going to pay it back from my salary. If the position pays me six hundred pounds a year, I'll—I'll—
Portia: You'll what?
Henry: I'll— (*He whistles.*) To date I owe exactly six hundred pounds, my whole year's salary.
Portia: And the month isn't ended.
Henry: If I'm careful, my second year's salary may carry me through. Oh, dear, that *is* going to make it difficult for us to get married immediately, isn't it?
Portia (*Dreamily*): Yes, it is. (*Suddenly*) Henry, what are you talking about? Marriage! You don't know me.
Henry: I know your name, your nationality, your age, and, most important, I know that I love you. I also know that you love me.
Portia: Please be sensible.

HENRY: I can't. I'm in love.
PORTIA: All this sounds like a play.
HENRY: It is—a wonderful one. I'll admit my owing my first two years' pay is going to pose a problem insofar as our getting married is concerned. (*Suddenly*) I have it! The day I confront those two old gentlemen, I'll take you with me.
PORTIA: Oh, no. It wouldn't be proper.
HENRY: But so much depends upon that meeting. With you there, I can get the old boys to raise my salary—say, to a thousand pounds a year. Perhaps fifteen hundred. Say you'll go with me.
PORTIA: I'll go.
HENRY: In that case, I'll demand two thousand a year, so we can get married immediately.
PORTIA: Henry.
HENRY: Yes?
PORTIA: Keep your expenses down for the balance of the month. Don't dip into your third year's salary.
HENRY: And that is how matters stood at that point. Thoughts raced through my mind. What if I lost the bet for my nameless benefactor? What if he failed to give me a position? Then the answer came to me, like a flash of lightning. I roused Lloyd Hastings from bed. He was a bit bewildered.
HASTINGS: I don't understand you. What are you getting at?
HENRY: Lloyd, I'm going to save you. Save you—understand!
HASTINGS: No.
HENRY: I'll save you, but not in the way you ask, for that wouldn't be fair, after your hard work and the risks you've run. Now, I don't need to buy a mine. I can keep my capital moving without that; it's what I'm doing all the time. I know all about your mine; I know its immense value and can swear to it if anybody wishes it. You shall sell it inside of the fortnight for three million cash.

HASTINGS: Three million!
HENRY: Right!
HASTINGS: But how?
HENRY: By using my name freely—and right now my name is on the tip of everybody's tongue. We'll divide the profits, share and share alike.
HASTINGS (*Overjoyed*): I may use your name! Your name—think of it! Man, they'll flock in droves, these rich English. They'll fight for that stock. I'm a made man, a made man forever. (*Fading*) I'll never forget you as long as I live . . . never, never . . .
HENRY: In less than twenty-four hours London was abuzz! I hadn't anything to do, day after day, but sit home, and wait for calls.
SIR ALFRED: Then I may assume, Mr. Adams, that you consider this mining property a sound investment?
HENRY: A very sound investment, Sir Alfred.
SIR ALFRED: And what of this American chap, Hastings?
HENRY: I know him very well, and he is as sound as the mine.
SIR ALFRED: Then I think I shall invest in this property. Your recommendation does it.
SOUND: *Telephone bell.*
HENRY: Excuse me, Sir Alfred.
SOUND: *Receiver lifted from hook.*
HENRY (*Into phone*): Yes, this is Henry Adams. Who? Sir John Hardcastle. Yes, Sir John. The Gould and Curry Extension? Yes, I know a great deal about it. I certainly would recommend it as a shrewd investment. The mine is worth far more than the asking price. Yes, Mr. Hastings is very well known in the States. Honest as the day is long, as they say. Yes, I suggest you contact Mr. Hastings. Thank you. Not at all. Good day, Sir John.
SOUND: *Receiver replaced onto hook.*

SIR ALFRED: That clinches it. If Sir John is in, so am I. Do you suppose that your Mr. Hastings would mind if I brought in a few discreet friends on this venture?

HENRY: Er, no, in fact I'm sure he wouldn't. Mr. Hastings is a very democratic chap.

SIR ALFRED: Directly I shall go and call upon Mr. Hastings. By the way, exactly where is this mine?

HENRY: California.

SIR ALFRED: Is that near Washington, D. C.?

HENRY: Not exactly.

SIR ALFRED: A pity, for I had thought of asking the British Ambassador to look at it. (*Fading*) Well, I'm off. Thank you for your advice. Good day, Mr. Adams.

HENRY: And that's the way it went—a steady stream of wealthy Londoners asking my advice, which, of course, I gave freely. Meanwhile I said not a word to Portia about the possible sale of the mine. I wanted to save it as a surprise; and then there always was the possibility the sale might fall through. The day the month was up, she and I, dressed in our best, went to the house on Portland Place. As we waited for the two old gentlemen to enter, we talked excitedly.

PORTIA: You're certain you have the bank note with you?

HENRY: Right here. Portia, dearest, the way you look it's a crime to ask for a salary a single penny under three thousand a year.

PORTIA: You'll ruin us.

HENRY: Just trust in me. It'll come out all right.

PORTIA (*Worried*): Please remember if we ask for too much we may get no salary at all; and then what will become of us, with no way in the world to earn our living? (*Fading*) Please handle this delicately, Henry.

HENRY: When the two old gentlemen entered, of course they were surprised to see Portia with me. I asked them to introduce themselves, which they did.

THE MILLION-POUND BANK NOTE

GORDON: I am Gordon Featherstone.

ABEL: And I am Abel Featherstone.

HENRY: Gentlemen, I am ready to report, but first may I ask which of you bet on me?

GORDON: It was I. Have you the million-pound note?

HENRY: Here it is, sir.

GORDON: Ah! I've won. *Now* what do you say, Abel?

ABEL: I say he did survive, and I've lost twenty thousand pounds. I never would have believed it.

HENRY: Perhaps you might enlighten me as to the terms of the bet.

GORDON: Gladly! The Bank of England once issued two notes of a million pounds each. Only one of these had been used and cancelled; the other lay in the vaults. Well, Abel and I got to wondering what would happen to a perfectly honest and intelligent stranger turned adrift in London without a friend and with no money in the world but the million-pound bank note. Abel said he would starve to death, and I claimed he wouldn't. My brother said he would be arrested if he offered the note at a bank. Well, we went on arguing until I bet him twenty thousand pounds that the man would live thirty days, *anyway,* on that million, and keep out of jail, too.

ABEL: And I took him up.

HENRY: How did you know I was the right choice?

ABEL: After talking with you, we decided you had all the qualifications.

GORDON: And that pear incident, if you had picked it up very boldly, it would have proved to us you were nothing but a tramp.

HENRY: You don't know how tempted I was to do just that.

GORDON: And so you shall receive your reward—a choice of any position you can fill.

HENRY: First I ask that you look at this scrap of paper, all of you. You, too, Portia.

GORDON: A certificate of deposit in the London and County Bank—
ABEL: In the sum of—
GORDON: Two hundred thousand pounds.
PORTIA: Henry, is it yours?
HENRY: It is. It represents my share of the sale of a mining property in California, sold by my friend Lloyd Hastings; a sort of commission, as it were. It all came about by thirty days' judicious use of that little loan you gentlemen let me have. And the only use I made of it was to buy trifles and offer the bill in change.
ABEL: Come, this is astonishing.
GORDON: It's incredible.
HENRY (*Laughing*): I can prove it.
PORTIA: Henry, is that really your money? Have you been fibbing to me?
HENRY: I have, indeed. But you'll forgive me, I know.
PORTIA (*Half-smiling*): Don't you be so sure.
HENRY: Oh, you'll get over it. Come, let's be going.
GORDON: Wait! I promised to give you a situation, you know.
HENRY: Thank you, but I really don't want one.
PORTIA: Henry, I'm ashamed of you. You don't even thank the good gentleman. May I do it for you?
HENRY: If you can improve upon it.
PORTIA: I shall. Uncle Abel, first, thank you for making this possible. And, dear Father—
HENRY: Hold on. You're her uncle?
ABEL: I am.
HENRY: And you—
GORDON: Yes, I'm her step-father.
PORTIA: And the dearest one that ever was. You understand now, don't you, Henry, why I was able to laugh when you told me the story of the bet with the two nameless gentlemen.

Of course I couldn't miss knowing that it was this house and that the two men were Father and Uncle Abel.

HENRY: Sir, you *have* got a situation open that I want.

GORDON: Name it.

HENRY: Son-in-law.

GORDON: Well, well, well! But if you haven't ever served in that capacity, you of course can't furnish satisfactory recommendations to satisfy the conditions of the contract.

HENRY: Only just try me for thirty or forty years.

GORDON: What do you think, Abel?

ABEL: Well, he does look to be a satisfactory sort.

GORDON: And you, Portia?

PORTIA: I agree—heartily.

GORDON: Very well. Take her along. If you hurry, you can reach the license bureau before it closes. (*Fading*) Hop to it now.

HENRY: Happy, we two? Indeed, yes! And when London got the whole history of my adventure for a month, how it did talk. My Portia's father took the million-pound bank note to the Bank of England, cashed it, had it cancelled, and he gave it to us at our wedding. Framed, it now hangs in our home. It gave me my Portia, but for it I could not have remained in London, would not have appeared at the American Ambassador's, never should have met her. And so I always say: Yes, it's a million-pounder; but it made but one purchase in its life, and then got the article for only about a tenth part of its value.

THE END

The Canterville Ghost

by Oscar Wilde

MUSIC: *An eerie theme. Up and under.*

NARRATOR: When Mr. Hiram B. Otis, the American Minister to England, bought Canterville Chase, everyone told him he was doing a very foolish thing, as there was no doubt the place was haunted. Indeed, Lord Canterville himself had felt it his duty to mention the fact to Mr. Otis when they came to discuss terms.

MUSIC: *Out.*

CANTERVILLE: As I told you, Mr. Otis, we have not lived in the place in quite some years.

OTIS: Yes, I've been wondering about that, Lord Canterville. From my inspection of Canterville Chase, I'd say it is a remarkably beautiful place, and in good repair.

CANTERVILLE: Oh, indeed it is all you say, and more, too. Make no mistake, you are getting a fine bargain. You see, we have not cared to live in the place since my grandaunt, the Dowager Duchess of Bolton, was frightened into a fit.

OTIS: A fit, you say?

CANTERVILLE: Yes, and a bad one at that. I feel I should tell you this before you sign the papers.

OTIS: I don't quite see the connection, my lord.

CANTERVILLE: It happened some years ago. My grandaunt was dressing for dinner. Suddenly she was frozen to the spot. Two skeleton hands were placed on her shoulders.

OTIS: Oh, come now! Surely you don't expect me to believe that.

CANTERVILLE: It's the truth. The ghost has been seen by several living members of my family. Lady Canterville, for example, often got very little sleep because of the mysterious noises that came from the corridor and the library.

OTIS: The library, eh! Nothing like an intellectual ghost, I say.

CANTERVILLE: It's all well and good to joke about it, but you've probably never encountered a ghost.

OTIS: I come from a country where we don't believe in ghosts.

CANTERVILLE: Whether or not you believe it is your own concern, Mr. Otis, but it does exist. It has been well known for over three centuries. And one peculiar thing: it generally makes its appearance just before the death of any member of our family.

OTIS (*Laughing*): Well, for that matter, so does our family doctor. But there is no such thing as a ghost.

CANTERVILLE: As I say, I feel it only fair to warn you.

OTIS: Thank you for your trouble, Lord Canterville, but it doesn't change my mind. I still want to buy Canterville Chase.

CANTERVILLE: What of your family? Perhaps they may object.

OTIS: I feel certain that the ghost won't bother them. They are a very energetic and hardy group of individuals. In fact, they can handle any situation. Now, if you have the papers ready, I'll sign them and then give you your check.

CANTERVILLE: If you don't mind a ghost in the house, it is all right. Only you must remember, Mr. Otis, I warned you.

MUSIC: *Forte and under.*

NARRATOR: A few weeks later Mr. Otis and his family trained down from London to Ascot, the nearest railroad station to Canterville Chase. The Otises were a rather formidable family of individuals. Mrs. Lucy Otis, for example, had a magnificent constitution and a wonderful amount of animal spirits. Virginia, the daughter, was fifteen, lithe and lovely, and with a fine freedom in her eyes. Then there were the twins, age twelve, christened Washington and Jefferson in a rash moment of parental patriotism. The twins were a bustling law unto themselves.

MUSIC: *Out.*

NARRATOR (*No pause*): As they drove from the station to Canterville Chase, the Otises were in fine spirits. It was a lovely July evening. As they entered the avenue of the Chase, however, the sky suddenly became overcast.

SOUND: *Rolling thunder. It continues under* NARRATOR.

NARRATOR (*No pause*): Before they reached the house, some big drops of rain had fallen. They were greeted by Mrs. Umney, the aged housekeeper, who had remained on. She led them to the library, where tea had been laid out.

SOUND: *Thunder out.*

MRS. UMNEY: This room affords a fine view of the east garden and the meadow. It was Lord Canterville's favorite place for spending a quiet hour.

OTIS: Very fine panelling, Mrs. Umney.

VIRGINIA: And all those wonderful books. Thousands of them.

WASHINGTON: Aw, this room's too dark. Don't you think so, Jeff?

JEFFERSON: Kind of spooky, I'd say, Wash.

MRS. OTIS: Over there by the fireplace, Mrs. Umney; I'm afraid something has been spilt on the floor.

MRS. UMNEY (*A low voice*): Yes, madam, blood has been spilt on that spot.

MRS. OTIS: How horrid! I don't care for blood stains in the library. It must be removed at once.

MRS. UMNEY (*Mysteriously*): It is the blood of Lady Eleanore de Canterville, who was murdered on that very spot by her own husband, Sir Simon de Canterville, in 1575.

OTIS: He wasn't very neat about it, I must say.

MRS. UMNEY: Sir Simon survived her nine years, and disappeared suddenly under very mysterious circumstances. His body has never been discovered, but his guilty spirit still haunts the Chase. That blood stain cannot be removed.

WASHINGTON AND JEFFERSON (*Together*): Gee! A real ghost!

MRS. OTIS: Nonsense! I mean about that stain. I have something right here in my bag that will clean it up in no time. Pinkerton's Champion Stain Remover and Paragon Detergent. Watch closely.

MRS. UMNEY (*Worried*): It can't be removed, Mrs. Otis.

VIRGINIA: You don't know my mother, Mrs. Umney. If she says it can be removed, it can.

MRS. OTIS (*As though scrubbing*): A few . . . brisk . . . rubs and . . . off it comes. There you are! Clean as a whistle.

SOUND: *A peal of thunder.* (MRS. UMNEY *moans. Body hitting floor.*)

VIRGINIA: Mrs. Umney—she's fainted.

OTIS: Here, boys, give me a hand with her. (*Straining a bit*) What a monstrous climate! I guess the old country's so overcrowded that they haven't enough decent weather for everybody. I have always been of the opinion that emigration is the only thing for England.

MRS. OTIS: Hiram, what can we do with a woman who faints?

OTIS (*Calmly*): Charge it to her like breakages. She won't faint after that.

VIRGINIA: She's coming to. (MRS. UMNEY *sighs.*) Are you all right now, Mrs. Umney?

MRS. UMNEY: Yes, all right now. (*Sternly*) But let me warn you. Trouble, it's coming to this house. I have seen it . . . things with my own eyes that would make anyone's hair stand on end. Many a night I have not closed my eyes for the awful things done here.

SOUND: *Peal of thunder.*

MUSIC: *Mysterious. Up and down under.*

JEFFERSON (*Excitedly*): Mother, it's back again, the blood stain on the library floor.

MRS. OTIS: Take the stain remover and wipe it off.

JEFFERSON: But every time Wash and I clean it off, the stain is there again the next morning.

MRS. OTIS: Oh, nonsense!

JEFFERSON: But it's the truth.

MRS. OTIS: Someone's playing a joke on us.

MUSIC: *Up and out into*:

SOUND (*Off*): *Hall clock striking 12 times.*

MRS. OTIS (*On third stroke*): Hiram. (*Pause*) Hiram, are you awake?

OTIS (*Sleepily*): Uhummm!

MRS. OTIS: That stain, I don't understand. It was there again this morning.

SOUND: *As they talk: coming in from distance, clanking of chains. It gets louder.*

OTIS: Not very nice to spoil the floor that way.

MRS. OTIS: You don't suppose—Oh, but that's sheer nonsense. (*She pauses*) Hiram, listen.

SOUND: *Clanking gets louder.*

MRS. OTIS: Sounds like chains being dragged.

OTIS (*Very calmly*): Oh, my! I was afraid of this.

MRS. OTIS: Where are you going? What are you looking for?

OTIS: You'll see. Follow me. And be quiet.

SOUND: *Door open. Rattle of chains.* (GHOST *gives a hollow groan.*)

MRS. OTIS (*Pleasantly*): Why, it's the Canterville Ghost. Good evening. (GHOST *moans.*)

OTIS (*Briskly*): My dear sir, I really must insist upon your oiling those chains, and I have brought you for that purpose a small bottle of Tammany Rising Sun Lubricator. It is said to be completely efficacious upon one application. There are several testimonials to that effect on the wrapper from some of our most eminent native divines. I shall leave it here for you on the table. Should you require more, I shall be happy to supply you.

MRS. OTIS (*Sweetly*): And now good night. If you wish anything, knock.

SOUND: *Door closed.* (GHOST *groans in rage and disappointment. He grunts.*) *Bottle dashed to the floor. Another door opens.*

WASHINGTON: There he is, Jeff. Quick.

JEFFERSON: Come on!

SOUND: GHOST *being hit with pillows.*

JEFFERSON (*Against sound*): Stop trying to duck, Mr. Ghost.

WASHINGTON: Sure! Being hit with pillows shouldn't bother you.

JEFFERSON: Not much, that is. (GHOST *moans in rage.*)

SOUND: *Rattle of chains.*

WASHINGTON: Hold still.

SOUND: *Starts to fade away.*

JEFFERSON: Hey, come back.

SOUND: *Out.*

WASHINGTON: Did you see that?

JEFFERSON: He disappeared right through the wainscoting. He's a pretty poor sport.

WASHINGTON: I can see the Canterville Ghost hasn't any sense of humor.

MUSIC: *Eerie theme. Up briefly and out.*

GHOST (*Fuming*): Never in my brilliant and uninterrupted career of a ghost have I been so grossly insulted. Zounds!

ELEANORE: I pray thee, Sir Simon, to control thyself. If thee should ask me, I would say thou art guilty of exaggeration.

GHOST: M'Lady Eleanore, I did not request your opinion. And furthermore, stop using that archaic English.

ELEANORE: I merely said—
GHOST: As my wife you are not entitled to any opinion. When I murdered you, I thought I was rid of you once and for all. My allowing you to return temporarily from your grave is just a courtesy.
ELEANORE: Concerning these Americans from the Colonies.
GHOST (*Patiently*): The Colonies no longer belong to England. They are now part of the United States. As for these Otises, who offer me lubricator oil for my chains and who throw pillows at my head, I shall be revenged on them.
ELEANORE: What disguise wilt thou—I mean will you wear the next time?
GHOST: Perhaps that of Gaunt Gibeon, the Blood-sucker of Bexley Moor.
ELEANORE (*Eagerly*): May I accompany you?
GHOST: A woman's place is in the home.
MUSIC: *"Hail Britannia." Up and out.*
WASHINGTON (*Sotto*): Can you see him?
JEFFERSON: Yes. Right by the head of the stairs. (*Pause*) What's he doing?
WASHINGTON: Trying to climb into that suit of armor. Let's get closer. Quiet as you can, Jeff.
SOUND: *A crash, as the suit of armor tips over.* (GHOST *yowls in pain.*)
JEFFERSON (*Laughing*): Look—the suit of armor fell over on him. (GHOST *yowls.*)
WASHINGTON: Let's give it to him.
SOUND: *Blowing of breath, as though using a pea shooter.* (GHOST *yowls.*)
JEFFERSON: You got him. Now it's my turn.
SOUND: *Quick blowing of breath.* (GHOST *yowls.*) *Door away opens.*
MRS. OTIS (*Coming in*): What are you two doing out of bed?

THE CANTERVILLE GHOST

JEFFERSON: Look—the ghost.
WASHINGTON: Mother, we're using our pea shooters on him.
SOUND: *Blowing of breath.* (GHOST *yowls.*)
OTIS (*Coming in*): Mr. Canterville Ghost!
MRS. OTIS: Hiram, what *are* you doing, pointing that revolver at the ghost's head?
OTIS: In the name of the United States government, I command you to surrender. (GHOST *gives an echoing, ghostly laugh, like a madman.*)
MRS. OTIS: I am afraid you are far from well. If you will wait, I'll bring you some medicine for that indigestion. You will find it a most excellent remedy.
MUSIC: *"Hail Britannia." Up briefly and out.*
GHOST: If only I could have climbed into that suit of armor before they put in an appearance.
ELEANORE: That suit never did fit you.
GHOST: Lady Eleanore, I wore that same suit of armor at the Kenilworth tournament four hundred years ago. The Queen herself told me what an excellent fit it was. Oh, my shins. Rub some more balm on them.
ELEANORE: Wherever did thou—I mean, where did you get the idea to wear the armor?
GHOST: Oh, from reading a silly poem about a skeleton in armor. Written by some American chap named Longfellow. Ouch! My foot, be careful.
ELEANORE: What is your next step to be?
GHOST: I'll first need a rest after tonight's fiasco. Perhaps the next time I'll take you with me.
ELEANORE (*Happily*): Oh, splendid, Sir Simon! But I haven't a thing to wear. Ah, I have it: I'll not wear any head.
MUSIC: *A ghostly theme. Up and out.*
GHOST (*Nervously*): Now, you're quite positive you know what to do?

ELEANORE: I am to go to Mr. and Mrs. Otis' room and gibber at them from the foot of the bed.

GHOST: At the same time I will go to the twins' bed and sit on their chests. At the same time I will stab myself three times in the throat.

ELEANORE: And what of the girl?

GHOST: Virginia? She has never insulted me. A few hollow groans should do for her.

SOUND (*Away*): *Hall clock strikes twice.*

ELEANORE: Are we off?

GHOST: Not a sound out of you until the right moment. This must come as a grim surprise. (*Pause*) Straight down the hallway.

ELEANORE (*Suddenly*): Sir Simon! Look—straight ahead. (*She screams.*)

GHOST: It's . . . it's a . . . ghost. Holding a sword.

ELEANORE (*Frightened*): We must leave. I'm frightened.

GHOST: You're quite right. (*Quickly gathering himself*) One moment. This ghost has no right to be here. He's trespassing.

ELEANORE: Trespassing or no, I refuse to stand here.

GHOST (*Sternly*): You stay, while I upbraid this . . . this intruder. (*Boldly*) Sir, whoever you may be, I demand you explain your presence. (*Pause*) Well, sir, speak!

ELEANORE (*Nervously*): Don't go any closer, Sir Simon.

GHOST: I shall! Speak or I shall seize you, sir. (*Pause*) Very well! Come here—(*A pause, then in a stunned voice*) Why, it's—

ELEANORE: Not a ghost.

GHOST: Just a white curtain . . . a squash . . . and a sweeping brush.

ELEANORE: That placard on its chest—I mean on the curtain.

GHOST: It says: "Ye Ghost. Ye only true and original spook. Beware of ye imitations. All others are counterfeits." Tricked again by those Americans! Foiled, outwitted! Revenge, oh, sweet revenge!

Music: *A light, humorous theme. Forte and then segue to ghostly, measured theme. Hold under.*

WASHINGTON (*Low voice*): I wish he'd show up.

JEFFERSON: Aw, Wash, let's go back to bed.

WASHINGTON: Wait just another few minutes.

JEFFERSON: All right. (*Pause*) You got everything ready?

WASHINGTON: I think I hear something. Listen.

SOUND: *Slight rattle of door handle. Door opens.*

WASHINGTON: Let him have it, Jeff.

JEFFERSON: Here goes!

SOUND: GHOST *being thumped with a pillow.* (GHOST *yelps.*)

JEFFERSON: Don't . . . like being hit with a pillow, huh!

SOUND: *More thumping.*

WASHINGTON: Stand back, Jeff.

SOUND: *Pail of water being tossed on* GHOST.

WASHINGTON (*With sound*): Nothing like a nice cold pail of water to cool off a ghost. (GHOST *yells.*)

MUSIC: *Up and out.*

ELEANORE: I must say, Sir Simon, that you've mishandled this whole situation, almost from the start.

GHOST: Don't be so annoying. (*He sneezes.*) That water they tossed on me has given me a miserable cold. (*He sneezes*) I wish you would go to Mrs. Otis' medicine chest and see if she has any cold pills.

ELEANORE: I wouldn't dream of stirring from this cell. (*Shuddering*) Getting chased by those awful Americans! (GHOST *sneezes again.*) I certainly am sorry I ever came back.

GHOST (*Irritably*): Then go back to your grave.

ELEANORE: That is just what I intend doing. I have had enough of this mortal life to know when it is time to leave. And if you will heed my advice, I advise you also to do the same.

GHOST: I shall remain.

ELEANORE: You will rue it, mark me.

GHOST: Revenge, revenge is what I seek. I shall drive them from this house, once and for all. (*He sneezes.*)

ELEANORE: Then have it, and be done. I am leaving. And happy I am at my decision. And where I come from, I shall be able once again to revert to a type of speech that is normal. Thee may continue alone. Dost thou understand me, m'lord and late husband?

GHOST (*Glumly*): I dost. (*He sneezes.*)

MUSIC: *A brisk, light bridge. Forte and out.*

MRS. OTIS: It seems to be coming out all right, doesn't it, Mrs. Umney?

MRS. UMNEY (*As though exerting herself*): Yes, just needs a bit of brisk rubbing, that's all, Mrs. Otis. Ah! There we are, clean as a whistle.

MRS. OTIS: Be certain to check the floor again tomorrow morning.

MRS. UMNEY (*Fading*): I will do that, ma'am, the very first thing, rest assured.

MRS. OTIS: I quite fail to understand this. During the past few days the color of the blood on the floor seems to have changed. (*Pause*) Virginia, will you put down that book and listen to me.

VIRGINIA: Yes, mother.

MRS. OTIS: Haven't you noticed? One day the stain was a dull red, the next a vermillion. Yesterday it was purple and today it was a bright emerald green. I never did hear of emerald green blood, did you, dear?

VIRGINIA: Oh, mother, don't fool about it. I don't think it is at all humorous.

MRS. OTIS: Well, I certainly do. Have you seen him lately?

VIRGINIA: The ghost?

Mrs. Otis: Yes.

Virginia: No.

Mrs. Otis: Not a sound out of him. You know, my bottle of Rising Sun Lubricator is missing. I have an idea Mr. Ghost has taken it and is using it to oil his chains. (*She laughs*) He might have left a note thanking me.

Virginia: You're being ridiculous.

Mrs. Otis: No, just to the point. By the way, we're going riding this afternoon. Do you want to join us?

Virginia: No, I believe I'll stay here and read.

Mrs. Otis (*Fading*): If you change your mind, let me know. I'll have the groom saddle your horse. (*A pause, then* Virginia *hums an old English Ballad.*)

Sound: *Door opens.* (Ghost *moans.*)

Virginia (*Singing stops. A gasp of surprise*): Y-you! You're the—

Ghost (*Deep concern*): Yes, I'm the Canterville Ghost. I hope you don't mind my sitting here in the library.

Virginia: No. My brothers are going back to Eton tomorrow, so if you behave yourself, no one will annoy you.

Ghost: It is absurd asking me to behave myself. I must rattle my chains, and groan and walk about at night. It is my only reason for existing.

Virginia: It is no reason at all for existing, and you know you have been very wicked. Murdering your wife!

Ghost (*Petulantly*): Well, I quite admit it, but it was a family affair, and concerned no one else.

Virginia: It is very wrong to kill anyone.

Ghost: Oh, I hate the cheap severity of abstract ethics. My wife was very plain, never had my ruffs properly starched, and she was a bad cook.

Virginia: That is not a proper way to talk.

Ghost: Yes, that's all over. However, I don't think it was very nice of her brothers to starve me to death, even though I did kill her.

VIRGINIA: Oh, Mr. Ghost, I mean Sir Simon, are you hungry? Let me get you a sandwich.

GHOST: No, thank you, I never eat now; but it is very kind of you. You are much nicer than the rest of your horrid, rude, vulgar, dishonest family.

VIRGINIA: It is you who are rude and horrid and vulgar. As for being dishonest, you know you stole the paints out of my box to furbish up that ridiculous blood stain here in the library. Who ever heard of emerald green blood?

GHOST (*Meekly*): What was I to do? Blood is so difficult to get nowadays. As for color, that is a matter of taste: the Cantervilles have blue blood, for instance.

VIRGINIA: The best thing for you to do is to emigrate.

GHOST: Emigrate?

VIRGINIA: My father will be only too happy to give you free passage.

GHOST: But isn't there a heavy duty on spirits of every kind?

VIRGINIA: True! But my father knows all the Customs officers. There are many Americans who would pay any amount of money to have a real live family ghost.

GHOST: I don't think I should like America.

VIRGINIA: I suppose because we have no curiosities.

GHOST: No curiosities! You have your manners.

VIRGINIA (*Stiffly*): Good evening! I will ask poppa to get the twins an extra week's holiday.

GHOST: Please don't go, Miss Virginia. I am so lonely, so unhappy, and I really don't know what to do. I want to go to sleep and I cannot.

VIRGINIA: That's quite absurd. Sleeping isn't difficult.

GHOST: I have not slept for over three hundred years, and I am so tired.

VIRGINIA: Poor ghost, have you no place where you can sleep?
GHOST: Far away beyond the pine woods there is a little garden. There the grass grows long and deep, there are the great white stars of the hemlock flowers, there the nightingale sings all night. And the cold, crystal moon looks down, and the yew tree spreads out its giant arms over the sleepers.
VIRGINIA (*Softly*): You mean the Garden of Death.
GHOST: Yes, Death. Death must be so beautiful. To lie in the soft brown earth, and listen to silence. To have no yesterday and no tomorrow. To forget time, to forgive life, to be at peace. You can help me.
VIRGINIA: How?
GHOST: You can open for me the portals of Death's house, for kindness and love are with you, and they are stronger than Death. (*Pause*) Have you ever read the old prophecy on the library window?
VIRGINIA: Oh, often. I know it quite well. (*She reads*)
"When a golden girl can win
Prayer from out of the lips of sin,
When the barren almond bears,
And a little child gives away its tears,
Then shall all the house be still
And peace come to Canterville."

But I don't know what they mean.
GHOST: They mean that you must weep with me for my sins, because I have no tears, and pray with me for my soul, because I have no faith. Then perhaps the Angel of Death will have mercy on me.
VIRGINIA: I will ask the Angel to have mercy on you.
MUSIC: *A thin, unearthly strain. Sneak in and hold under.*
GHOST: Then take my hand. This wall will open, and we will disappear. I signal once.

Sound: *A rap on the wall.*
Ghost: Twice.
Sound: *Rap on the wall.*
Ghost: The panel slides back, and we disappear.
Music: *Up and out into:*
Sound: *Telephone bell.*
Otis: I'll take it.
Sound: *Receiver lifted from hook.*
Otis: Hello. Yes, this is Mr. Otis. Oh, yes, Inspector. Any news? (*A long pause*) I see. Thank you, and keep in touch with me. Good night.
Sound: *Receiver slowly replaced on hook.*
Otis: That was the local police.
Mrs. Otis: Any word?
Otis: No.
Mrs. Otis: There must be something you can do, Hiram.
Otis: Lucy, I don't know what to do.
Mrs. Otis: Keep on looking.
Otis: But where? The servants have been and still are searching. The police have scoured the country for miles around. We've covered the house and grounds and stable. All we can do now is stay by the telephone and wait.
Mrs. Otis: Where are the twins?
Otis: With Mrs. Umney, looking.
Mrs. Otis: One thing is certain. We know approximately when Virginia disappeared. It was around six o'clock. Mrs. Umney had asked her if she didn't want some tea, and Virginia said no. When Mrs. Umney returned, which was in less than a half-hour, the child was nowhere to be found. (*Pause.*) You've tried the railway station?
Otis: Yes. The police checked. She's not been there. Very mysterious, the whole affair.
Mrs. Otis: I think you should have the pond dragged.

OTIS: Stop talking such nonsense.
MRS. OTIS: I should have insisted that she go riding with us. (*The sound of the twins' voices can be heard ad libbing in the distance. They gradually fade in.*)
OTIS: Here come the boys.
MRS. OTIS: Perhaps they have news. (*Calls out*) Boys, come here.
WASHINGTON (*Fading in*): No, not a sign. Searched everywhere.
JEFFERSON: Even as far as the road to the village.
OTIS: It's late. The pair of you'd better get off to bed.
WASHINGTON: Oh, poppa, we couldn't sleep.
JEFFERSON: Besides, we aren't tired, and we want to wait up with you.
MRS. OTIS: May as well allow them to remain up, Hiram.
OTIS: Very well.
MUSIC: *A thin, unearthly strain* (*the same theme that introduced the disappearance of* VIRGINIA *through the panelling*). *It sneaks in and holds under.*
MRS. OTIS: Listen.
WASHINGTON: To what, mother?
MRS. OTIS: Do you hear music? (*A pause.*)
OTIS: Yes.
WASHINGTON: I hear it, too, mother.
JEFFERSON: So do I.
SOUND (*Muffled*): *Three measured, evenly-spaced raps on the panelling.*
WASHINGTON: What do you—
OTIS (*Tensely*): Quiet.
SOUND: *A section of the panelling flies back with a crash.*
MUSIC: *Out.*
MRS. OTIS: Virginia!
SOUND: *The panel flies shut.*

OTIS (*Almost angrily*): Where have you been?
WASHINGTON: You all right, Virginia?
JEFFERSON: Gee! We're glad you're here.
OTIS: Where have you been?
MRS. OTIS: Don't scold her.
VIRGINIA: Poppa, I have been with the Ghost. He's dead, and you must come and see him, all of you.
OTIS (*Sharply*): Nonsense!
VIRGINIA: You must come and see him. He had been very wicked, but he was really sorry for all he had done.
MRS. OTIS (*Anxiously*): Dear, are you certain you're all right, and not just imagining things?
VIRGINIA: Follow me and you will see what I say is true. Take a light, someone, for it's dark where we are going . . . dark and lonely.
MUSIC: *The sliding panel theme. Sneak in and hold under.*
SOUND: *One knock on panel, then a second, and a third. Panel bangs open.*
MUSIC: *Up full. Hold, then out.*
WASHINGTON: Golly! It's certainly damp down here.
OTIS: Jeff, hold your light up higher.
MRS. OTIS: What is this place, anyhow, Virginia?
VIRGINIA: A secret corridor. (*Pause*) Here we are. (*Straining*) Someone help me swing this door open.
OTIS: Here, I'll do it. (*Grunting*) Here we . . . go. (*Pause*) Ah, there you are.
SOUND: *As he says line, heavy door squeaks open.*
JEFFERSON (*Awed*): It's a cell.
OTIS: Musty smelling.
WASHINGTON: Look—over in the corner. (MRS. OTIS *screams*.)
OTIS: It's only a skeleton.
VIRGINIA: It's our ghost, Sir Simon.
OTIS (*Sharply*): What are you trying to tell us?

VIRGINIA: That skeleton is our ghost.
JEFFERSON: Look, he's chained to the floor.
OTIS: Suppose you explain all this, daughter.
VIRGINIA: The ghost, Sir Simon, murdered his wife, the Lady Eleanore. Her brothers, upon learning of it, overpowered him. They took him here and chained him to the floor.
MRS. OTIS: That trencher and ewer lying just out of his reach, what do they signify?
VIRGINIA: They held water and food, carefully placed *just* out of reach.
JEFFERSON: And that meant he died of hunger and thirst.
VIRGINIA: Yes.
WASHINGTON: What a way to die.
MRS. OTIS: A tragedy.
VIRGINIA: He was wicked then. He asked me to see that his remains are buried in the family graveyard.
OTIS: What happened to him this afternoon?
VIRGINIA: He repented.
MRS. OTIS: Sounds mysterious to me.
VIRGINIA: Never again will he haunt this place.
JEFFERSON (*Suddenly*): Look, just outside of this grated window. That old withered almond tree has blossomed.
WASHINGTON: I can see the flowers quite plainly in the moonlight.
VIRGINIA: The Lord has forgiven him. Poor Sir Simon! I owe him a great deal. He made me see what life is, and what death signifies, and why love is stronger than both.
MUSIC: *Up to final curtain.*

THE END

The Necklace

by Guy de Maupassant

MUSIC: *A theme sombre in nature. Forte and fade under.*

NARRATOR: Mathilde was one of those pretty and charming girls who are sometimes, as if by a mistake of destiny, born in a family of clerks. She had no dowry, no expectations, no means of being known, understood, loved or wedded by any rich and distinguished man. As a consequence she let herself be married to a little clerk at the Ministry of Public Information, a man named Claude Loisel. She dressed plainly because she could not dress well. She suffered unceasingly, feeling herself born for all the delicacies and luxuries of life. She hated the poverty of her dwelling. All these things tortured her and made her angry. She thought of long, gracious salons; she imagined herself being sought after by famous people, who crowded her charming home just to get a glimpse of her. And Mathilde would like to have been sought after. Instead, she had nothing!

MUSIC: *Out.*

NARRATOR: All she had was a simple little husband, who every night sat at the dinner table covered with a cloth three days old.

CLAUDE (*Expectantly*): Ah, what have we to eat this evening?

SOUND: *Cover lifted from soup tureen.*

CLAUDE: Stew! Wonderful, wonderful stew! What more could a man ask for!

SOUND: *Ladle against plate, as stew is dished out.*

CLAUDE: Mathilde, you are a superb chef. Your stew is nectar of the gods. Just enough herbs, a touch of white wine. Here you are, my dear.

MATHILDE: I don't want it.

CLAUDE (*Puzzled*): You don't care for any stew?

MATHILDE (*Listlessly*): I do not care for any stew. That is correct.

CLAUDE: B-but it . . . it's—

MATHILDE: Stew!

CLAUDE: But you made it.

MATHILDE: That is just the trouble. I always make the stew. I always cook everything. I'm beginning to smell like a greasy kitchen.

CLAUDE: Mathilde, I don't understand you.

MATHILDE: I know that.

CLAUDE: But what have I done?

MATHILDE: Nothing, and that is just your trouble.

CLAUDE: What do you want of me?

MATHILDE (*Wearily*): Eat your stew, Claude, and don't ask any questions.

MUSIC: *An unhappy theme. Forte and out into:*

SOUND: *Canary chirping in background.*

JEANNE: Won't you have another cake, Mathilde?

MATHILDE: No, thank you.

JEANNE: Some more chocolate?

MATHILDE: Not a thing, dear Jeanne. Every time I come here, I eat much more than I should.

JEANNE (*Laughing*): I always try to please my guests.

MATHILDE (*A trace of envy*): You are a lucky girl, Jeanne. This lovely home, a rich and handsome husband, servants, lovely clothes and jewels—you have everything any wife could ask for.

JEANNE (*Quietly*): Yes, I am fortunate.

MATHILDE: It is strange how life turns out. Here we are, close friends for many years, schoolmates at the convent, both the same age, equally pretty—

JEANNE: You're prettier than I, Mathilde.

MATHILDE: You marry a rich husband, while I marry a poor clerk.

JEANNE: Claude is a good man.

MATHILDE: He thinks and looks and acts just like what he is—a little man with no imagination or particular ambition. He is happy to come home and eat his stew and then spend the evening smoking his smelly pipe and reading his newspaper. We never go anywhere. We never attend balls or receptions or dinners.

JEANNE: I've never heard you speak quite like this.

MATHILDE: I need excitement and attention and everything that goes with such a life. Instead, I'm nothing but a drudge. (*Suddenly*) Good-bye, Jeanne. Thank you for your kindness.

JEANNE: Do stay a while longer.

MATHILDE: No, for if I do, I shall become more and more envious of your good fortune. Besides, I have to cook dinner for Claude—stew, again, of course.

JEANNE: You'll call again soon?

MATHILDE: Perhaps. Maybe the next time I won't be in such a foul mood—although I do not guarantee it.

MUSIC: *A short bridge. Forte and out into:*

SOUND: *Door open. In background: a small clock strikes six times.*

CLAUDE: Mathilde, Mathilde! Where are you? It is Claude.

MATHILDE (*Fading in*): Good evening, Claude.

CLAUDE: You have a small kiss for your husband?

MATHILDE: I suppose so.

CLAUDE (*A pause, then*): Ah, so! (*Triumphantly*) I have a surprise.

MATHILDE (*Unenthusiastically*): Oh!

CLAUDE: A great surprise. Here! This is for you.
MATHILDE: A letter.
CLAUDE: But what a letter! Well, open it. Read it.
MATHILDE: Probably a bill.
CLAUDE: And whoever heard of a bill being enclosed in such a fine envelope. Go ahead—open it, Mathilde.
SOUND: *Envelope ripped open. Rustle of paper.*
MATHILDE (*Reading*): "The Minister of Public Information and Mme. Georges Ramponneau request the honor of M. and Mme. Loisel's company at the palace of the Ministry on Monday evening, January 18th." (*Disdainfully*) Well, what do you want me to do with that?
CLAUDE: But, my dear, I thought you would be glad. You never go out, and this is such a fine opportunity. I had trouble to get it.
MATHILDE: Really!
CLAUDE: Don't you understand every one wants to go. It is very select, and they are not giving many invitations to clerks. The whole official world will be there.
MATHILDE: And what do you want me to put on my back?
CLAUDE (*Stammering*): W-why the . . . the dress you go to the theatre in. It looks very well to me.
MATHILDE (*Practically in tears*): Oh, oh, Claude!
CLAUDE (*Stuttering*): What's the matter? Tell me.
MATHILDE (*Controlling herself*): Nothing. Only I have no dress, and therefore I can't go to this ball.
CLAUDE: But of course you can.
MATHILDE: I cannot go. Give your card to some colleague whose wife is better equipped than I.
CLAUDE: Come, let us see, Mathilde. How much would it cost for a suitable dress, something you could use on other occasions, something very simple?
MATHILDE: Well, it would—let me think. (*Pause*) I'd say—

I don't know exactly, but I think I could manage it with . . . four hundred francs.

CLAUDE: Four hundred francs.

MATHILDE: See, I told you. It's a great deal of money, too much for us to consider.

CLAUDE: I have four hundred francs laid aside.

MATHILDE: But you've saved that to buy a gun so you can go shooting at Nanterre with your friends.

CLAUDE: That is quite all right.

MATHILDE: I won't hear of it.

CLAUDE: The four hundred francs are for you. And try to have a pretty dress, a very pretty dress.

MATHILDE (*Joyfully*): Oh, Claude, you are so good to me.

MUSIC: *A cheerful theme. Forte and out.*

CLAUDE: Now turn around, more toward the light. (*Admiringly*) Indeed, it is a very pretty dress, Mathilde. You will be the prettiest woman at the ball. People will ask: "Who is that beautiful woman?" And others will answer: "Don't you know that is Mme. Claude Loisel? Is she not lovely, and that exquisite gown she is wearing, it must have been designed exclusively for her." (*Pause*) Mathilde.

MATHILDE: Yes?

CLAUDE: What is the matter?

MATHILDE: Nothing.

CLAUDE: Come, tell me. You've been so queer these past few days. Are you unhappy?

MATHILDE: It annoys me not to have a single jewel, not a single stone, nothing to put on. I shall look like distress. I should almost rather not go at all.

CLAUDE: You might wear flowers.

MATHILDE (*Not convinced*): Flowers! Hmph!

CLAUDE: It's very stylish at this time of the year. For ten francs you can get two or three magnificent roses.

MATHILDE: No! There's nothing more humiliating than to look poor among other women who are rich.
CLAUDE: But how stupid you are!
MATHILDE: It is not stupidity. It is a case of not looking well-groomed.
CLAUDE: But you are stupid! Go to your friend, Jeanne Forestier, and ask her to lend you some jewels. You are friendly enough with her to do that.
MATHILDE (*Joyfully*): It's true. I never thought of it. Oh, but suppose she refuses.
CLAUDE: She won't. You are such close friends, and after all it is merely a loan for the evening.
MATHILDE: I shall go tomorrow. (*Longingly*) She has so many beautiful jewels.
MUSIC: *A short bridge. Forte and out.*
JEANNE: But of course I don't resent your request. You must look well, you know, and I have any number of nice things, and you're welcome to use any of them. Here, let us see what this box holds. (*Pause*) There!
MATHILDE: Bracelets.
JEANNE: I wouldn't wear bracelets, if I were you. Try on this pearl necklace. There! Now look at yourself in the mirror. (*Pause*) Lovely!
MATHILDE (*Reflectively*): Mmm! Perhaps! (*Eagerly*) What is this?
JEANNE: A Venetian cross—heavy gold.
MATHILDE: I don't think it suits me.
JEANNE: Here are rings—diamonds, black pearl, a ruby, two emerald ones. Do you like them?
MATHILDE: Y-yes, they're very beautiful. Haven't you any more?
JEANNE: Why, yes. Look here, in this box. I don't know what you like. Examine them.

MATHILDE (*After a pause*): This . . . this diamond necklace. (*Pause*) How well it looks on me.

JEANNE: It does suit you.

MATHILDE: Can you lend me that, only that?

JEANNE: Why, yes, certainly.

MATHILDE (*Overjoyed*): You're so kind, Jeanne. Such a wonderful friend. Now I shall indeed look my best. Such a gorgeous necklace!

MUSIC: *A light theme. Forte and out into:*

SOUND: *Background of many voices: the people attending the ball. Hold under.*

FOOTMAN (*Calling out in a loud voice*): Monsieur and Madame Claude Loisel.

MATHILDE (*Low voice*): Claude, I'm so excited. Such a beautiful palace and all these beautifully gowned women. And such handsome, distinguished men.

CLAUDE (*Nervously*): Shh! Look, we are to meet the Minister and his wife. He is my superior.

MATHILDE: Have you ever met him?

CLAUDE: No. I have only seen him from a distance. Quiet, now.

MINISTER: Good evening, er—

CLAUDE: Loisel . . . Claude Loisel. And my wife, Your Excellency.

MINISTER: Good evening, Madame Loisel. May I introduce you to my wife, Madame Ramponneau.

MATHILDE: Good evening, Madame Ramponneau.

MADAME: Good evening, my child.

MINISTER: She is very beautiful, is she not, my dear?

MADAME: Very.

MATHILDE: Thank you.

MINISTER: Young and lovely.

MADAME: And such a beautiful diamond necklace. Did you get it in Paris?

MATHILDE: No! Er, that is—yes, in a way. It's er—new, you see.
MADAME: It sets off your beautiful skin to advantage.
MATHILDE: Thank you, Madame.
MINISTER: Monsieur, er—
CLAUDE: Loisel.
MINISTER: Your face is so familiar. Where have we met? Perhaps at Auteuil or Longchamps?
CLAUDE: I never go to the races, Your Excellency.
MINISTER: I wish I could place you.
CLAUDE: I work for you, sir.
MINISTER (*Surprised*): Oh!
CLAUDE: I am an under-clerk in the Ministry.
MINISTER: In any event you (*Stressing this*) and your very lovely wife are welcome. Perhaps Madame Loisel will honor me with a dance later in the evening.
MATHILDE: I shall look forward to it, Your Excellency.
MUSIC: *An orchestra playing a bright waltz of the period. Up full and hold under.*
SOUND: *Background of guests. Weave in and out of scene.*
GUEST 1 (*A man*): That woman dancing—the one with the diamond necklace, who is she?
GUEST 2 (*Man*): I don't know. Such grace. See how well she dances. I should like to meet her.
GUEST 1: As would I. I want to dance with her.
GUEST 2: His Excellency has danced twice with her. It would seem that she is the belle of the evening.
GUEST 1: Notice how the other women glare at her.
GUEST 2: Small wonder. She puts them to shame, what with her youth and beauty.
MUSIC: *Up full and fade out.*
SOUND: *The background of guests' voices continues.*
ATTACHÉ: And mamselle will save this next dance for me?

GUEST 1: No, she's promised it to me.
GUEST 2: You're both quite mistaken. It is I she has promised it to, messieurs.
MATHILDE (*Gay*): Now, now, please do not argue over me, gentlemen.
GUEST 2: And why not? After all, you are by far the most beautiful woman present.
ATTACHÉ: The most beautiful woman in Paris.
GUEST 1: In France, you mean.
MATHILDE: You will turn my head, make me vain.
ATTACHÉ: It is only right that a beautiful woman should be complimented, not once, but over and over.
GUEST 1: Your husband, he will become jealous. (*Anxiously*) You are married?
MATHILDE: Yes.
GUEST 1 (*Disappointed*): Oh, I was hoping otherwise.
MUSIC: *A waltz. Hold under.*
GUEST 2: Ah, we shall dance.
GUEST 1: This is my dance.
ATTACHÉ: You are both mistaken, for this dance is mine.
MATHILDE: And I am afraid that all three of you are mistaken, for I have already promised this dance to that gentleman who is approaching. See—the tall one.
GUEST 2: You are dancing with him?
MATHILDE: Yes, who is he? I did not catch his name when we were introduced.
ATTACHÉ: He is the British Ambassador.
MUSIC: *Waltz up full and fade under to background.*
SOUND: *Clock strikes twice.*
CLAUDE (*Yawns deeply*): Sorry, monsieur. I hope I did not wake you.
HUSBAND (*Wearily*): Not at all. I really was not asleep—just dozing.
CLAUDE: How much longer does this affair last?

HUSBAND: You still have two hours to go.

CLAUDE: But some of the guests have already left.

HUSBAND: That is your wife dancing—the one with the necklace?

CLAUDE: That is she.

HUSBAND: Then you have two hours to go, my friend. The penalty you have to pay for having such a beautiful and popular wife. See how the men cluster about her.

CLAUDE: I gave up at midnight. I tried to make my way to her, but there was such a crush, I could not pierce even the outer ring. (*Pause*) But you must be in the same position. You are not with your partner.

HUSBAND: My partner is my wife.

CLAUDE: She also must be popular.

HUSBAND: Quite to the contrary, she is most unpopular. A remarkably plain woman who receives only barely polite attention from men. You see in my position, we have to attend many such functions. We dare not leave early, and so, according to our custom, my wife retires to the ladies' cloak room on pretence of a headache, while I retire to the gentlemen's cloak room, but on no pretence whatsoever. And after dozing several hours, we rise, thank our host, and take our leave. In the morning both of us are well rested. Clever, don't you think?

CLAUDE: If boring.

HUSBAND: Not at all. In these cloak rooms, one meets such interesting people. One night I met the Dey of Algiers. (*Sighs*) I'm glad I have a plain, uninteresting wife. If I had a beautiful wife like you, I would feel as though I would have to go through some semblance of trying to keep pace with her. But with my dull wife, that is not necessary. Wake me in an hour, please.

MUSIC: *Up full and segue to: Another waltz. Hold under in background.*

SOUND: *Clock strikes four times.*

MATHILDE: Claude, Claude, wake up. Wake up.

CLAUDE (*Sleepily*): Oh, are we leaving?

MATHILDE: Yes, this is the last dance, and I want to sneak out unnoticed. I don't want the other women to see what a miserable wrap I am wearing. We'll leave by the side entrance.

CLAUDE: Have you had a fine time?

MATHILDE: Wonderful! And now I return to ugliness, just like Cinderella.

CLAUDE (*Reproachfully*): Cinderella left the ball at midnight.

MATHILDE: Don't spoil my pleasant memory. Hurry, now, Claude, and hail a cab.

MUSIC: *Up full and fade out.*

CLAUDE (*Yawns*): Oh, and to think I have to be at work in another four hours. I could fall into bed fully clothed.

MATHILDE: And I am going to sleep until early afternoon.

CLAUDE: You're lucky.

MATHILDE: It was such a wonderful ball.

CLAUDE: I wouldn't know.

MATHILDE: I could dance every night of my life. (*She hums a bit of a waltz. Suddenly she stops and gives a sharp cry.*)

CLAUDE: What is the matter?

MATHILDE: I have—I have—I've lost Jeanne's necklace.

CLAUDE: What?

MATHILDE: I have lost Jeanne's necklace.

CLAUDE: How? Impossible!

MATHILDE: Look in my cloak . . . my pockets. (*Pause*) Oh, no.

CLAUDE: See if it's caught in the folds of your dress. (*Pause*) Not there. You're sure you had it when you left the ball?

MATHILDE: Yes, I felt it in the vestibule of the palace. Perhaps I dropped it in the street.

CLAUDE: But if you had we should have heard it fall. It must be in the cab.

THE NECKLACE 73

MATHILDE: Yes, probably. Did you notice his number?
CLAUDE: No. And you, didn't you notice it?
MATHILDE: No. (*Pause*) Whatever will we do?
CLAUDE: I shall go back on foot over the whole route which we have taken. Perhaps I can find it.
MATHILDE: You must find it.
CLAUDE: I will. Now suppose you go to bed.
MATHILDE: Bed! I couldn't sleep. I'll sit up until you return.
MUSIC: *A doleful theme. Forte and out into:*
SOUND: *Small clock strikes seven times. Door open-close.*
MATHILDE (*Anxiously*): Claude, you found it. Tell me you have found it.
CLAUDE (*Wearily*): I went over our route, all the way back to the palace. I didn't find it.
MATHILDE: Perhaps a cleaner will discover it. Whoever does may be honest, and will hold it waiting for us to claim it.
CLAUDE: Perhaps. At least, let us hope so, Mathilde.
MATHILDE: I'm going to bed and see if I can't forget the matter, at least for several hours.
CLAUDE: I'll stay up.
MATHILDE: What good will that do?
CLAUDE: I've got to keep searching.
MUSIC: *Grim. Up and under.*
CLAUDE: Monsieur Sous-Prefect, I've come to report the loss of a valuable diamond necklace.
MUSIC: *Up briefly and under.*
CLAUDE: I wish to place in your newspaper the following advertisement. "Lost . . . a valuable diamond necklace—"
MUSIC: *Up and under.*
CLAUDE: If you are the manager, I wish you to ask each of your cab drivers if they have found a diamond necklace.
MUSIC: *Up full and out.*
MATHILDE: I know you are weary, but there must be some-

thing you can do. Claude, I've got to return that necklace to Jeanne.

CLAUDE: Perhaps someone will answer the advertisement, or maybe some cab driver will turn it in to us.

MATHILDE: That is what you said yesterday.

CLAUDE: Then the only thing we can do is for you to write to Jeanne that you have broken the clasp of the necklace and that you are having it mended. That will give us time to turn around. Here, I will dictate it to you. "My Dear Jeanne: Please forgive the delay in returning your lovely diamond necklace. . . ."

MUSIC: *A short bridge, cuts in over dialogue. Forte and out.*

MATHILDE: We came to you, Monsieur Lavell, because your name is on the box. Right here, it is.

LAVELL: Yes, Madame, that is my box. And it is a diamond necklace you say?

MATHILDE: A very expensive one, too, I fear.

CLAUDE: The name of the purchaser is Forestier, Paul Forestier.

LAVELL: I do not recall having sold a diamond necklace to such a party.

CLAUDE: But you must have, for this is the box it came in. See —your name.

LAVELL: I will consult my books (*Fading*) and see if I cannot find the name of Forestier.

MATHILDE (*Low voice*): Oh, Claude, I hope he finds the record of the sale, for then he will be able to get another just like it.

CLAUDE: We must replace it, and without further delay. Try to look a bit more pleasant. It may not be as expensive as we believe.

MATHILDE: Look pleasant! I'm so weary I could sleep standing up.

CLAUDE: Don't worry. This will straighten out.

MATHILDE: Here he comes.

CLAUDE: What success, Monsieur Lavell?
LAVELL: I have never had a customer named Forestier.
CLAUDE: But your name is on the box.
LAVELL: It was not I who sold the necklace. I must simply have furnished the box. I am sorry I cannot help you.
MATHILDE: Perhaps you can replace the necklace. We can give you an accurate description.
LAVELL: Unfortunately at present, I have no stock of diamond necklaces. I suggest you go to De Remy, the jeweler on the Palais Royal. Undoubtedly there you will find just what you seek. He has a large stock of diamonds of all kinds, including necklaces. (*Fading*) Here, I will give you a card to him. He is a friend of mine for many years. (*A pause then*):
DE REMY (*Fading in*): Would it, perhaps, be one like this.
MATHILDE: N-no, not quite. You agree, Claude?
CLAUDE: It isn't like this.
DE REMY: I have shown you almost everything I have in diamond necklaces. Wait! (*Fading a bit*) I have several others. Perhaps one of them may be that for which you are searching. (*Fading in*) Now, here is one. This one here.
MATHILDE: That's it. Look, Claude.
CLAUDE: Yes, it was just like the one you're holding, Monsieur De Remy.
DE REMY: Success at last, eh!
MATHILDE: Thank Heavens!
CLAUDE: How much?
DE REMY: Let me see the tag. (*Pause*) Mmmm! The price is forty thousand francs.
MATHILDE: Forty—
CLAUDE: Forty thousand!
DE REMY: Expensive, I agree, but remember this is a magnificent necklace. The best of matched diamonds, each one protected by a full guarantee.

MATHILDE: But forty thousand francs, it is a great deal. We are quite poor. My husband is only a clerk.
DE REMY: I wish I could help you, for I appreciate your plight.
CLAUDE: Couldn't you take less, Monsieur De Remy?
MATHILDE: It would help, if you could. Please, Monsieur De Remy. A little less, perhaps.
DE REMY: It would have to be cash, of course. In that case, I could sell you this for thirty-eight thousand francs.
MATHILDE: Thirty-six. Please!
DE REMY: Thirty-six, it is, then.
CLAUDE: I will have to raise the money.
DE REMY: I am not able to hold it, at least not without a deposit. If some other customer wishes it, I must sell it.
CLAUDE: Hold it for three days, just three days. I will be back with the money, I promise.
DE REMY: You look honest. Very well, I shall hold it for three days. And I will do this, in addition: If you find the original before the end of February, I shall buy this one back for thirty-four thousand francs.
CLAUDE: That is fair, Monsieur De Remy. I shall be back inside of three days with the money.
MUSIC: *A bridge. Forte and out.*
MATHILDE: But where are we going to raise such a sum of money in so short a time? It can't be done.
CLAUDE: The money my father left me in bonds, I'll sell them. They are worth, at present, eighteen thousand francs.
MATHILDE: But that is only half.
CLAUDE: My stamp collection, on a quick sale I can get fifteen hundred francs.
MATHILDE: You've spent years collecting it.
CLAUDE: It goes.
MATHILDE: But even with that, we are still far short of the amount we need.

CLAUDE: I'll borrow the rest.

MATHILDE: From whom? All our friends are poor.

CLAUDE (*Wearily*): From anyone who will lend me even a few francs. I can always go to the moneylenders.

MATHILDE: But they're usurers. They'll charge exorbitant interest.

CLAUDE (*Briefly*): It can't be helped. I have to raise the money. We've got to buy that necklace, and you've got to take it to Jeanne before she gets suspicious.

MUSIC: *Up and out.*

JEANNE (*Rather coldly*): Well, my dear Mathilde, I had started wondering what had become of you. I thought perhaps you were ill, or away on a vacation.

MATHILDE: No, I have not been away. I'm too poor for that. You did get my note, I hope.

JEANNE: About the necklace. Yes, I received it some days ago.

MATHILDE: I'm sorry about the clasp, but the jeweler replaced it, and it looks as well as ever.

JEANNE: You've brought it with you?

MATHILDE (*As though fumbling*): Yes, I have it right here. This is it.

JEANNE: It is all right?

MATHILDE: Oh, yes. It is in just as good condition as when I borrowed it.

JEANNE: You seem very ill at ease, Mathilde.

MATHILDE (*Uneasily*): I've been working hard. I'm overtired. Rest will help me. Thank you very much for the loan of the necklace. I—I appreciate the great favor you did me.

JEANNE: You should have returned it sooner. I might have needed it.

MATHILDE: Perhaps I never should have borrowed it.

JEANNE (*Stiffly*): No need to feel that way. You asked a favor and I obliged. That's the difficulty in loaning things to friends;

they take offense if you show any apprehension about their return.

MUSIC: *Up and out.*

CLAUDE: Good morning, Monsieur Cote. I have brought the manuscripts, copied neatly, just as you wished.

COTE: Ah, good! (*Reflectively*) Hm, hm! So!

CLAUDE (*Anxiously*): The copying, it is all right?

COTE: Yes, fine, as usual. Your copying is excellent, Loisel. (*Pause*) Why are you waiting? Oh, to be sure! Your pay. Five sous a page. Let me see, I owe you—

CLAUDE: Seven francs even, Monsieur Cote.

SOUND: *Seven coins separately dropped on table.*

CLAUDE: Thank you, Monsieur Cote.

SOUND: *Clink of coins as* CLAUDE *scoops them up.*

CLAUDE (*Anxiously*): Perhaps you have more work for me?

COTE: Not immediately. Perhaps the week after next. I will let you know.

CLAUDE: I have a new address.

COTE: You have moved again?

CLAUDE: Yes, Monsieur Cote, the rent on the other place was too high for us to pay.

COTE: How long have you been doing copying for me, Loisel?

CLAUDE: Going on three—no, four years it is.

COTE: And during the day you work at your regular position?

CLAUDE: Yes, sir, at the Ministry of Public Information.

COTE: You must need money badly, to sit up half the night copying manuscripts at five sous a page.

CLAUDE: Indeed I do, sir.

COTE: Well, leave your new address and I will have some work for you.

CLAUDE (*Eagerly*): Thank you again, and if you know of anyone else who requires a similar service, perhaps you might recommend me.

MUSIC: *A dreary theme. Forte and out into:*
SOUND: *Street noises. People calling out.* (*Note: this is Paris during the late nineteenth century, so do not use any modern transcribed traffic sounds.*)
MONGER (*Calling out*): Fish! Fresh fish! Nice fresh fish!
MATHILDE (*Her voice is older and harder now*): How much is carp?
MONGER: Carp! Ah, of course! Here is a nice piece.
MATHILDE: Too large. Give me a smaller piece.
MONGER: Here is a fine piece, just right for you and your children.
MATHILDE: I have no children.
MONGER: Ah, they are now grown up and married.
MATHILDE: Stop wagging that tongue long enough to tell me the price of this carp.
MONGER: This piece will cost but three francs.
MATHILDE: Three francs! You are mad! Three francs for this miserable segment of carp. I will give you two francs.
MONGER: But no! It is priced at three francs.
MATHILDE: Here is the money—two francs, you thief. Now wrap it up. Hurry!
MONGER (*Grumbling*): You drive a hard bargain. I am poor—
MATHILDE (*Cutting in*): And so am I, and I have no time to waste arguing with you. I have work to do.
MONGER: If I had many customers like you, I would have to close my fish stall and enter bankruptcy.
MUSIC (*Cuts in over street noises*): *Forte and out into:*
SOUND: *Stiff brush scrubbing floor. It continues at brisk pace.*
MATHILDE (*Over sound and matching the pace of the scrubbing*): I must get this done before Claude comes home . . . must . . . must . . . must.
SOUND: *Scrubbing continues for a few seconds, and then stops.*
MATHILDE: My arms, they are going to drop off. So tired . . .

always tired. Look at me—frowsy hair, red, rough hands just like a scrubwoman . . . lines on my face. Oh, I feel so old, so terribly old and tired. (*Philosophically*) Well, no time to worry about my appearance.

SOUND: *Scrubbing continues faster than ever. Door open slowly and close.* (*Away.*)

CLAUDE: Good evening, Mathilde.

SOUND: *Scrubbing continues.*

CLAUDE: Mathilde!

SOUND: *Scrubbing out.*

MATHILDE (*Listlessly*): Good evening, Claude. Sit down and I will get your dinner.

CLAUDE: No hurry. I'm not very hungry.

MATHILDE: I have a surprise. Tonight we have stew.

CLAUDE: Do you recall when even the mention of the word stew used to anger you? Now stew is a luxury. (*Tenderly*) Oh, Mathilde, it bothers me so to see you looking so tired, so worn out. And why?

MATHILDE: Because of my vanity and heedlessness. Because for one evening eight years ago I had to pretend I was something I was not. What would have happened to us if I had not lost that necklace?

CLAUDE (*Gently*): Who knows.

MATHILDE: Life is so strange. How little a thing is needed for us to be lost or to be saved.

CLAUDE: Only this morning I figured that it will be but another two years before I have completely repaid the money I borrowed.

MATHILDE: Ten years of slavery for both of us. Suffering, no new clothes or holiday journeys; ten long years of doing without even the simple comforts. (*Softly*) And sometimes when I am alone working here, I think. I think of that wonderful, gay evening of long ago when I was so beautiful, and when I danced and danced to that music. (*Crying*) And then I immediately put those thoughts from my mind.

CLAUDE: You're crying, Mathilde.

MATHILDE: Yes, I cry for myself, for having been such a light-headed and foolish woman. But it was such a beautiful evening.

MUSIC: *Up and out into:*

SOUND: *A Sunday in park pattern: children laughing and chattering.*

CLAUDE (*Breathing in*): This air is so clean and the sun so strong. Sunday in the Champs Élysées. A bit of Heaven!

MATHILDE: We should come here more often, Claude. It is good for us to see other people enjoying themselves. See those little boys sailing their boat. How happy they are.

CLAUDE: I hope they never grow up. You know, I feel just like an old man.

MATHILDE: But you are not.

CLAUDE: My hair is thinning and what I have left is gray.

MATHILDE: Time changes all of us, outwardly and inwardly. Ten years ago if you had told me that I would take a Sunday stroll clad in such a gown, I would have hooted at you. Now I wear it and don't care what anyone says about my appearance. I have learned much these past ten years, very much. (*Pause*) Claude, what is the matter?

CLAUDE: That lady approaching.

MATHILDE: It's Jeanne Forestier.

CLAUDE (*Hurriedly*): Come, let us leave.

MATHILDE: Why should we?

CLAUDE: I cannot bear to face her.

MATHILDE: Well, I can. Now I feel perfectly free to speak what is on my mind.

CLAUDE (*Fading a bit*): Mathilde, come back. Mathilde.

MATHILDE: Good day, Jeanne.

JEANNE: But Madame, I do not know you. You must mistake me for someone else.
MATHILDE: No, I have made no mistake. I am Mathilde Loisel.
JEANNE: Oh, my poor Mathilde! How you have changed!
MATHILDE: Yes, I have had days hard enough, since I've seen you, days wretched enough—and all because of you!
JEANNE: Because of me! How so?
MATHILDE: Do you remember that diamond necklace which you lent me to wear at the ministerial ball?
JEANNE: Yes. Well?
MATHILDE: Well, I lost it.
JEANNE: What do you mean? You brought it back.
MATHILDE: I brought you back another just like it. And for this we have been ten years paying. You can understand that it was not easy for us, us who had nothing. At last it is ended, and I am very glad.
JEANNE: You say that you bought a necklace of diamonds to replace mine?
MATHILDE: Yes. You never noticed it, then! They were very like, almost identical.
JEANNE: Oh, my poor Mathilde! Why, my necklace was paste. It was worth at most five hundred francs!
MUSIC: *Curtain theme. Forte and out.*

THE END

A Tale of Two Cities

by Charles Dickens

JUDGE (*Droning loudly*): The prisoner—Charles Evremonde, called Darnay, will rise. Prosecutor, inform this court by whom the prisoner has been openly accused.

PROSECUTOR: By Ernest DeFarge and Therese DeFarge, his wife.

BIZ: *Ad lib of excited voices.*

SOUND: *Gavel on wood. Twice.*

JUDGE: How votes the jury?

JURYMAN: The jury finds the prisoner . . . guilty.

BIZ: *More excited ad libs.*

SOUND: *Gavel. Struck sharply.*

JUDGE: Charles Evremonde, called Darnay, this court condemns you to death by the guillotine!

BIZ: *More excited ad libs.*

MUSIC: *An ominous theme. It cuts in over ad libs, washing them out, and holds under in background.*

NARRATOR: The French Revolution drew into its grasp thousands of victims, many of them innocent people. Among these was Charles Darnay, of the aristocratic French family of Evremonde. Some years previous, young Darnay had taken up residence in London, where he met and married Lucie Manette, daughter of Dr. Alexandre Manette, a Frenchman who had spent many years as a political prisoner in the Bastille. Drawn back to France, Darnay had been seized and falsely accused of acts against the Republic of France, and specifically against the family of DeFarge—Ernest DeFarge, wine vendor, and his wife, Therese, ruthless minor lights in the Revolution. Present at the sentencing of Charles Darnay were Lucie, his wife; Miss Pross, nursemaid to their child; aged Dr. Manette; Mr. Lorry, their banker friend, and Sydney Carton, the lawyer, long hopelessly in love with Lucie. And now the unjust sentence had been passed. Charles Darnay had a meeting with the guillotine. The courtroom quickly emptied. Lucie Darnay rose to her feet, staring at her husband in the grasp of the jailer. Sydney Carton called out.

CARTON: You, jailer. Hold!

JAILER (*Away. He snarls*): What do you want, Englishman?

CARTON: Let them have a few seconds together.

JAILER: Nothing was said to me about it.

CARTON: It can do no harm. Please, just a few seconds.

JAILER (*Growls*): Well, just a few. And hurry.

CARTON: Go ahead, Lucie.

LUCIE: Thank you, Sydney.

SYDNEY: We'll wait in the corridor. (*Fading*) Dr. Manette, Miss Pross, Mr. Lorry, follow me, please.

LUCIE: Oh, Charles!

CHARLES: Lucie, my dearest wife. (*Pause*) I—what can we say?

LUCIE: Nothing except to remember how much we love each other.

CHARLES: Let us take comfort in that wonderful thought.

LUCIE: *We* know you're not guilty. It was not even a trial. You were doomed before you stepped into the prisoner's box.

CHARLES: No need to think about that now.

LUCIE: Perhaps it is not too late. Father will try everything in his power. And Sydney is a lawyer, he is shrewd. Perhaps he can help.

CHARLES: You have our child. Kiss her for me. If ever you need help, lean on our friends—Lorry and Pross and Carton.

JAILER (*Roughly*): You've had long enough. Come along.

LUCIE: Please, jailer, one more second.
JAILER: Time's up.
CHARLES: Good-bye, Lucie.
LUCIE (*Screams*): Charles! Charles! No!
CHARLES (*Fading*): Think of me often.
MUSIC: *Up to climax and out.*
MANETTE: I have influence. The judges, the jury, all these men in power are friendly to me. They knew me many years ago. They know that I am not an enemy, Mr. Lorry.
LORRY (*Troubled*): That is true, Dr. Manette. At least it is well worth trying.
MANETTE: Oh, I intend to try. I will not rest a minute.
LORRY: There is not much time—only twenty-four hours. If only I could aid you.
MANETTE: You're a kind friend, Mr. Lorry.
SOUND: *Door open-close.*
MANETTE: How is my daughter, Mr. Carton?
CARTON: Miss Pross is with her.
MANETTE: My poor Lucie. Perhaps I should go to her.
CARTON: It is best you allow her to rest, Doctor.
LORRY: Dr. Manette is going to appeal to the officials.
MANETTE: Yes, it is not too late, perhaps, for me to ask that they rescind the sentence. I will go to the Prosecutor and the President.
LORRY: Do you wish me to accompany you, Dr. Manette?
MANETTE: Perhaps that might be sound.
CARTON (*Sharply*): It would be a bad idea. Mr. Lorry, as an Englishman, you would only be a drawback.
MANETTE (*Helplessly*): Perhaps you are right, Sydney. Your advice is always sound.
CARTON: Go at once, Doctor. We shall be waiting here.
MANETTE (*Fading slightly*): I may be many hours. But don't despair.
SOUND (*Slightly away*): *Door open-close.*

LORRY (*Hopefully*): Mr. Carton, the officials may look favorably upon Dr. Manette.
CARTON (*Pointedly*): You saw the reaction of the court spectators.
LORRY: Yes. I heard the fall of the axe in that sound.
CARTON (*Gently*): Don't despond. I encouraged Dr. Manette to seek aid, because some day it may be a consolation to Lucie. Otherwise, she might think we failed to try hard enough. (*Abruptly*) Well, I'm off.
LORRY: Shall I join you?
CARTON: No, stay here. You may be needed.
LORRY: Where are you going?
CARTON: To walk and think.
LORRY: Life sometimes takes a peculiar twist.
CARTON (*Musing*): Yes, life is of little worth when we misuse it, but it is always worth the effort to save.
MUSIC: *A dramatic bridge. Forte and fade under.*
NARRATOR: Sydney Carton's steps were aimless as he walked along the Paris streets. Jumbled thoughts tugged at his mind.
CARTON (*Musing*): Shall I show myself? Yes, I think so. It is well that these people should know there is such a man as I here. It is a sound precaution . . . a necessary preparation. But care, care, care! Let me think it out.
NARRATOR: A few minutes later, Carton turned his steps, now brisk, toward the Saint Antoine suburb and the wine shop of the DeFarge's, the pair who had testified against Charles Darnay. There was no one in the wine shop but Ernest DeFarge and Therese, his wife. Madame DeFarge looked at Carton suspiciously. (*Note: in this scene,* CARTON, *feigning lack of knowledge of good French, speaks slowly, and as if in difficulty.*)
MUSIC: *Out.*
THERESE: Your wine, monsieur.

SOUND: *Wine poured into glass.*
CARTON: Thank you.
THERESE: You're English?
CARTON: Yes, Madame, I am English.
ERNEST: You're in Paris on business?
CARTON (*Agreeing*): Yes, Citizen, on business. I drink to the Republic. (*Smacking lips*) Ah, fine wine.
THERESE: Have you attended our greatest spectacle—the Aristos meeting with Madame Guillotine?
CARTON (*Slowly*): My French, Citizeness, it is not the best. I do not quite understand.
THERESE: Small matter, Englishman. Before you leave, you will see the tumbrils rolling through the streets and the old ladies knitting and the heads rolling in the basket.
CARTON: I do not quite understand. Another glass of wine, please.
ERNEST: *That* you understand.
SOUND: *Wine poured into glass.*
CARTON: Your health, Citizen and Citizeness. (*Smacking lips*) Excellent wine. (*Drowsily*) Excellent! Been up since daybreak . . . tired . . . sleepy. (*Yawns*) Close my eyes for . . . few seconds . . . just a . . . few seconds. . . .
ERNEST: Pig of an Englishman. I should toss him into the gutter.
THERESE: Let him sleep. We have more important things to discuss. Did you observe Dr. Manette's face today?
ERNEST: He has suffered much.
THERESE: His face is not that of a true friend of the Republic. Let him take care of his face.
ERNEST: And you have observed his daughter.
THERESE: I have observed his daughter, today and other days. I have observed her on the street and by the prison.
ERNEST: Our wrong is about to be avenged. Tomorrow after-

noon, her husband's head will roll into the basket. I would stop there.

THERESE (*Wrathfully*): Vengeance! That is my goal! Do away with all the Evremondes, or Darnay, as he is now named. His family persecuted mine, and so I say vengeance.

ERNEST: Of course Charles Darnay had nothing to do with the wrong done your family.

THERESE: No matter, he is going to suffer, even though we had to swear falsely in court. And now—

ERNEST: You are going to conspire against Dr. Manette and Darnay's wife.

THERESE: And against their small child. When I am done, none will survive.

ERNEST: And so you propose—

THERESE: You and I will swear that we saw Lucie Darnay signaling her husband in jail. We will produce other witnesses who also have seen this happen, not once but twice. We will produce a note she wrote to him.

ERNEST: Not so loud. This Englishman will hear.

THERESE: He is asleep. Besides, he does not understand. Lucie Darnay, her child and father will follow Charles Darnay to Madame Guillotine. (*Cackling*) She has such a fine, blonde head. I can see the executioner holding it aloft for all to see.

MUSIC: *Suspense. Forte and fade under.*

NARRATOR: Minutes later, Sydney Carton rose from his feigned slumber. He paid his bill and strolled from the wine shop. Back at the Manette home, he found the doctor slumped wearily in a chair, with Mr. Lorry anxiously hovering about.

MANETTE (*Child-like, he whimpers*): Where is my bench? I have been looking for my bench, and I cannot find it. What have you done with my work? I must finish those shoes.

LORRY (*Low voice*): The strain has been too much for him. He thinks he is back in the Bastille.

MANETTE: Please give me my work. Those shoes must be done tonight.
CARTON (*Undertone*): He was unsuccessful?
LORRY: The officials would do nothing. One of them brought him here in this condition. There is nothing to be done.
CARTON: Dr. Manette, you must go to bed. Understand, you must go to bed.
MANETTE: But my shoes, they must be finished.
CARTON: Tomorrow will be time enough. Go to bed, Doctor.
MANETTE (*Fading slightly*): As you say, but my shoes, I must work on them.
SOUND (*Slightly off*): *Door open—close.*
CARTON: Mr. Lorry, I want you to listen closely. Don't ask me why I make the stipulations I am going to make, and exact the promise I'm going to exact. I have a reason—a good one.
LORRY: I do not doubt it. Go on.
CARTON: First take this. It's my certificate which allows me to pass out of the city. You see—Sydney Carton, an Englishman.
LORRY: What am I to do with it?
CARTON: Keep it for me until tomorrow. I am going to see Charles tomorrow.
LORRY: But how will you do so? The prison officials won't allow it.
CARTON: Through Barsad.
LORRY: The spy?
CARTON: Through him, I'll grease a few palms. Leave it to me, but it is better that I don't take my pass with me into prison.
LORRY: What good will your seeing Charles Darnay do?
CARTON: I owe it to him and the others. Now, also take this paper. It belongs to Dr. Manette. It's his certificate, enabling him and his daughter and her child, at any time, to

pass the Barrier and leave the country. Put it with mine and your own.

LORRY: I'll guard it.

CARTON: These passes are good until recalled, and I have good reason to think that the doctor's and Lucie's may soon be cancelled.

LORRY: They are in danger?

CARTON: Great danger. They are in danger of denunciation by Madame DeFarge. I know it from her own lips. It's a plot I've confirmed with Barsad. Don't look so horrified. You will save them all.

LORRY: How?

CARTON: Tomorrow you and the rest are to hurry to the seacoast by private coach. Have your horses ready, so that you can leave by two in the afternoon.

LORRY: But if Lucie objects to leaving before her husband's death, what then?

CARTON: Tell her it was his last wish. Impress that upon her. Tell her more depends upon her leaving than she dares believe or hope. Have all arrangements made in the courtyard here, even to your taking your own seat in the carriage. The moment I come to you, take me in, and drive away.

LORRY: Then I am to wait for you, under all circumstances?

CARTON: Yes. Wait for me! As soon as I am in, nothing is to stop you until you touch foot on England. I must have your solemn word on this.

LORRY: I swear it.

CARTON: And remember if you change your course one bit, a number of lives will surely be lost.

LORRY: I hope to do my part faithfully. (*Suddenly*) You've forgotten one thing. Miss Pross.

CARTON: She'll join you. I'll see her now and make arrangements.

Lorry: I wish you would tell me more, Sydney.
Carton: There is nothing more to tell you.
Lorry: Then I'll say good night.
Carton: Good night.
Lorry (*Fading*): Let us hope everything goes well tomorrow. I don't know what we would have done but for you, Sydney. (*A pause, then fading in*):
Pross: But, Mr. Carton, I do wish I knew what is in back of all this mystery. Why are we leaving so suddenly tomorrow? Please explain.
Carton: Miss Pross, bear with me. There won't be room for you in the coach. More important, there is so much luggage that it would mean a long examination by the guards. Now, I'll make arrangements for a light vehicle to be here tomorrow. Have all effects loaded in. Leave at three o'clock. Traveling as light as you will be, you can overtake the coach at the first stop, when it changes horses. Is that clear? Now you have your pass in order?
Pross: Yes, Mr. Carton.
Carton: Remember you leave at three. Let nothing detain you—nothing. And try to leave here unobserved. I'll see that the horses are drawn up in the courtyard, where they can't be seen from the street. Now, go and try to rest.
Pross: And where will you be tomorrow?
Carton: Don't worry about me. I'll be safe from observation.
Pross: Do you want to say good-bye to Miss Lucie?
Carton: No.
Pross: I believe she's awake.
Carton: You're to say nothing to her about this plan. Nothing, understand? If you do, it will excite her. And, Pross.
Pross: Yes, Mr. Carton.
Carton: Understand, you're to let nothing stand in your way tomorrow. You're to leave at three o'clock.

Pross: You have my word of honor. Mr. Carton. . . .
Carton: Well?
Pross: You've been in love with Lucie for a long time.
Carton: Go to bed, Pross.
Pross: I know you have. And some day she'll realize it, too.
Carton (*Sternly*): You're talking nonsense, Pross. Go to bed.
Pross: You don't pull the wool over my eyes, not one bit, you don't.
Music: *Ominous. Forte and fade under.*
Narrator: The next afternoon at one o'clock, Sydney Carton and Barsad, the spy, made their way to the forbidding looking jail that housed the so-called political prisoners. Barsad muttered a few words into the ear of the guard, and a few minutes later he and Carton were in an anteroom awaiting the arrival of Rambeau, the head jailer.
Music: *Out.*
Barsad: I don't like this, Monsieur Carton. It is too dangerous.
Carton: You're being well paid, Barsad.
Barsad: No matter; it still is dangerous business. And speaking of money, Mr. Carton, we'll need a bit more.
Carton: I paid you last night.
Barsad: The head jailer, he'll want more.
Carton: How much have you told him?
Barsad: Oh, nothing more than I was supposed to tell. I said that you wish a few minutes alone with Darnay.
Carton: See that you say no more.
Barsad: Here he comes now.
Rambeau (*Fading in*): Well, Barsad, what do you wish?
Barsad: Monsieur Rambeau, this is the gentleman I spoke to you about. Monsieur Sydney Carton, the Englishman. You will recall that last night you said you would allow Monsieur Carton to visit his friend for a few minutes.
Rambeau: That was last night.

BARSAD: Just for a few minutes.
RAMBEAU: Evremond or Darnay or whatever his name is—he has an appointment in less than an hour. It is too late.
BARSAD: But it is a simple favor.
RAMBEAU: If I were caught, it might mean my head.
CARTON: Monsieur Rambeau, I appreciate the delicacy of your position, but I am wondering if perhaps a small offering for any purpose you consider worthy might not be well received. Say, ten gold louis.
RAMBEAU: Er, twenty would be more like it.
CARTON: Twenty, then.
SOUND: *Small bag of coins plunked on table.*
RAMBEAU: If you are caught, I know nothing about it, not a thing. You bribed someone else.
CARTON: We understand.
RAMBEAU: Follow me.
MUSIC: *Sneak in a theme of suspense. Hold under.*
NARRATOR: Carton and Barsad followed the head jailer down a flight of stairs and along a corridor lined with locked doors. Carton walked firmly without looking around, with Barsad slinking along in the rear. At last they stopped before a stout door.
MUSIC: *Out.*
RAMBEAU: Here you are. Only a few minutes, now. I'll be up the corridor waiting. Call for me when you need me.
SOUND: *Heavy key in lock. Heavy door swings open.*
RAMBEAU: Step in.
BARSAD: And lose no time.
SOUND: *Door closes.*
CHARLES: Who is it?
CARTON: It is I, Charles.
CHARLES: Sydney Carton.
CARTON: Yes. Don't ask any questions.

Charles: Are you a prisoner?
Carton: No, Darnay. I came from her—your wife. She sent me with a request. A most earnest, emphatic entreaty. You must obey it.
Charles: Of course.
Carton: There is no time to ask me what it means. Here, draw on these boots of mine. Quick!
Charles: No.
Carton (*Commandingly*): Do as I say. Change your cravat for mine. Put on my coat and hat.
Charles: Carton, there is no escaping from this place. It never can be done. You will only die with me.
Carton: I shall not die with you.
Charles: It's madness.
Carton: It would be madness if I asked you to escape, but do I? Here, change and be swift. I'll help you.
Charles (*As though struggling*): It never can be done. It's been tried before and has always failed. Don't add your death to mine.
Carton: Put my coat on. (*Pause*) Now my cloak. There!
Charles: It can't be done.
Carton: Have I asked you to walk through that door? There are pen and paper on this table. Write what I shall dictate. Quick!
Charles: To whom do I address it?
Carton: To no one.
Charles: Do I date it?
Carton: No. Write this.
Charles: I'm ready.
Sound: *Scratching of pen on paper, which stops only when one of the two makes an observation.*
Carton: "If you remember the words that passed between us long ago you will readily comprehend this when you see it.

You do remember them, I know. It is not in your nature to forget them. . . ."

CHARLES: Is that all?

CARTON: No.

CHARLES: Is that a weapon you are holding?

CARTON: No. Write on. "I am thankful that the time has come when I can prove them. That I do so, is no subject for regret or grief. . . ."

CHARLES: What is that odor . . . a vapor?

CARTON: It is nothing. Take up the pen and finish. Hurry! "If it had been otherwise, I never should have used the longer opportunity. If it had been otherwise, I should have so much the more to answer for."

CHARLES (*Groggily*): That vapor . . . my head.

CARTON: I have to do it, Charles.

SOUND: *A slight struggle between the two.*

CARTON: Have . . . to . . . understand . . . have to. . . . A few more whiffs and you'll. . . .

CHARLES: *Breathing heavily for a few seconds. Then out.*

CARTON: Just enough to drug you into unconsciousness. Enough to make you sleep soundly. This note, Charles, I'll leave inside your coat. There! (*Pause*) Barsad. Barsad!

SOUND: *Door creaks open.*

BARSAD: He's all right?

CARTON: Unconscious. No hazard now.

BARSAD: Not if you keep to your bargain.

CARTON: If they do discover the trick, you and he and the rest will be many miles from here. Now, call the jailer and take me to the coach.

BARSAD: *You?*

CARTON: *No*—Darnay. Leave by the same gate we entered.

BARSAD: I understand.

CARTON: I was weak and faint when I came in, and now I am

fainter. This has been too much for me to bear. Such a thing has happened here often. Is that clear? Your life is in your hands.
BARSAD: You promise not to betray me?
CARTON: Yes, now call the jailer.
BARSAD: If we're caught—what then?
CARTON: You won't be if you do exactly as I say. Get him to the coach in the courtyard. Turn him over to Mr. Lorry, and tell him to remember my words of last night to drive away. Now, call the jailer. Here, first get him to his feet. (*Grunting*) I'll help you. There! I'll sit at the table, my back to the door, my head in my hands.
BARSAD (*Calling out*): Monsieur, Monsieur Rambeau.
RAMBEAU (*Away*): Coming.
BARSAD (*To* CARTON): Mr. Carton, don't betray me.
CARTON: I swear I won't.
RAMBEAU (*Fading in*): Well, you were long enough. This is a busy day for me. There are fifty-two visitors to the guillotine today; fifty-two. (*Suddenly*) What has happened to Monsieur Carton?
BARSAD: This has been too much for him to bear. He has fainted. We must get him outside at once into the air.
RAMBEAU: So afflicted to find his friend, Darnay, has drawn a prize in the lottery of the guillotine.
BARSAD: I will support him. You open the door.
RAMBEAU: And Monsieur Evremond, or Darnay, or whatever your name is, why do you hold your head in your hands? Look at me.
BARSAD (*Sharply*): If we are caught, we'll both suffer. Let us go.
RAMBEAU (*Laughing*): A pair of unconscious men. Never worry, Monsieur Darnay, we shall be back for you within a few minutes. Meanwhile, rest well. (*Laughing*)

SOUND: *Door squeaks shut. Key in lock.*
CARTON (*After short pause*): God be with you, Darnay, and you, too, my dearest Lucie.
MUSIC: *Dramatic. Forte and fade under.*
NARRATOR: Sydney Carton was left alone. Minutes ticked away. Then sounds came to his ears. At last his own door was opened. A guard, with a list in his hand, looked in.
GUARD (*Sharply*): Follow me, Evremonde.
NARRATOR: Carton rose and stepped out into the shadows of the damp prison corridor. He was led to a large and windowless room already crowded with other victims waiting to have their arms bound. Carton sat in a dark corner. Meanwhile in the courtyard a few miles away, Mr. Lorry paced nervously back and forth, occasionally consulting his watch. Inside the waiting coach were Lucie Darnay, her child, and Dr. Manette. Suddenly there dashed into the courtyard a small cart driven by Barsad, the spy. Lorry hurried toward him.
MUSIC: *Out.*
LORRY: Thank Heavens you're here.
BARSAD: Hurried as fast as I could. I didn't want to attract too much attention.
LORRY: We should be leaving in a few minutes.
BARSAD: It's ticklish work, and I have no stomach for it.
LORRY: Where is he?
BARSAD: In the back. Give me a hand with him.
LORRY: What happened?
BARSAD: He's overcome.
LORRY: I can well understand.
BARSAD (*Grunting*): Take his feet. Easy now.
LORRY: Hold on! This isn't Carton. It's—it's—
BARSAD: Yes, it's Darnay.
LORRY: But how—
BARSAD: No time to explain. Get him into your carriage.

LORRY: Where's Carton? (*Pause*) Where's Carton? (*It dawns on him.*) Barsad, you mean Carton changed places with him?
BARSAD: Yes.
LORRY: But we can't allow him to do it.
BARSAD: He told me to tell you that you're to keep your promise. He said: tell him to remember my words of last night to drive away.
SOUND: *Coming from distance. A church clock strikes twice.*
BARSAD: There's your signal. Be off!
LORRY (*More to himself*): What a price to pay!
MUSIC: *Sombre, dramatic. Forte and fade under.*
NARRATOR: The strokes of two o'clock reached the ears of Sydney Carton in the prison room. As he sat waiting, a young girl, with a sweet face, came to him.
MUSIC: *Out.*
SEAMSTRESS: Citizen Evremonde. (*Pause*) Or perhaps I should address you as Monsieur Darnay. I am a poor seamstress who was tried the same day as you. Do you remember?
CARTON: Of course I do. I forget what you were accused of.
SEAMSTRESS: Plots. Though Heaven knows I am innocent of any. Is it likely that a poor little creature like me would even think of plotting?
CARTON: I believe you.
SEAMSTRESS: I am not afraid to die, but I have done nothing. Monsieur, if I may ride with you, will you let me hold your hand? I am not afraid, but I am so little and weak, and it will give me more courage.
CARTON: Of course, my child.
SEAMSTRESS: Oh, thank you. (*Astonished*) But you're not him. You're not Charles Evremonde, called Darnay.
CARTON (*Low tone*): Please. Don't say it.
SEAMSTRESS: Are you dying for him?
CARTON: Yes, for him and his wife and child.

Seamstress: Now I can face it with more courage. You are a brave man.
Carton: Hold my hand ... to the last.
Music: *Dramatic. Forte and fade under.*
Narrator: The same shadows that were falling on the prison were falling on the Barrier, the last checking point outside of Paris. A coach going out of Paris drove up. The captain of the guard approached it. Mr. Lorry stepped out.
Music: *Out.*
Captain: Who goes there?
Lorry: Travelers.
Captain: Papers.
Lorry: Here you are, Captain.
Captain: Alexandre Manette. Physician. French. Which is he?
Lorry: The old gentleman.
Captain: Are you Alexandre Manette?
Manette (*Like a child*): My shoes, I must fix them. It is getting late. Where are my shoes?
Captain (*Coarsely*): Apparently the citizen-doctor is not in his right mind. Perhaps the Revolution-fever has been too much for him.
Lorry: He is not well.
Captain: Many suffer from it. Lucie Evremonde, called Darnay. His daughter. French. (*Quizzically*) Evremonde ... Darnay! Ah, so this is the wife of the gentleman who has an engagement with Madame Guillotine.
Lorry: Yes.
Captain: Let her show her face.
Lorry: Please, captain, she is asleep.
Captain (*Grumbling*): Very well. Lucie, her child. This is she?
Lorry: Yes.

CAPTAIN: Sydney Carton. Advocate. Which is he?
LORRY: He is the one in the corner.
CAPTAIN: Apparently the Englishman is in a swoon. You, there, Englishman.
LORRY: He is overcome. At best his health is not good.
CAPTAIN: A sleepy group of companions you have.
LORRY: We have been through much anguish these past few days. It is understandable.
CAPTAIN: It is none of my worry. And the last—Jarvis Lorry. Banker. English.
LORRY: I am he. Necessarily, being the last.
CAPTAIN: This is your whole party?
LORRY: Except for a servant, who is following in another coach.
CAPTAIN: Wait here while I stamp and countersign your papers. (*Fading*) I shall be back.
LUCIE (*Slightly away*): Mr. Lorry.
LORRY: Sshh! Lucie, please. The guards, they will hear you.
LUCIE (*As though trembling with excitement*): He—he's here. Mr. Lorry, it's Charles, my Charles.
LORRY (*Low tone*): Lower your voice.
LUCIE (*Sobbing*): It's my husband. The voices wakened me and I looked, and he is with me. Am I dreaming?
LORRY: No. I'll explain later.
LUCIE: He doesn't stir.
LORRY: He is all right. He'll be awake soon. Don't bother him.
LUCIE: I—I—I'm trembling with excitement. Mr. Lorry. . . .
LORRY: Yes?
LUCIE: This paper tucked into Charles' coat.
LORRY: Read it.
LUCIE: It's in Charles' hand, but it's—the message is not from him. It says—"If you remember the words that passed between us long ago, you will readily comprehend this when you see it—" (*A pause*) It's— (*Sobbing*) it's from—
LORRY: He's a brave man, Lucie.

LUCIE: He did this for us.
LORRY: For you, Lucie. (*Sharply*) Get back into your seat. The captain is returning. (*Calling out*) All in order, Captain?
CAPTAIN: Here they are—stamped and countersigned. You may pass on, Citizen.
LORRY: Thank you.
CAPTAIN: By the way, Citizen Lorry, how many?
LORRY: I do not understand you.
CAPTAIN: How many to the guillotine today?
LORRY: Fifty-two.
CAPTAIN: A good number. The guillotine goes handsomely. And so a pleasant journey, Citizen.
MUSIC: *Up ominously and under.*
NARRATOR: Miss Pross, nursemaid to young Lucie Darnay, watched the coach containing Mr. Lorry and his party depart. Several minutes later the lighter coach that was to take her and the luggage arrived. It was quickly loaded. The driver left to buy some additional straps, with which to secure the load, promising to return shortly. Within the house, Miss Pross busied herself with some last-second details.
MUSIC: *Out.*
NARRATOR: And as she did—
SOUND: *Door open—close.*
THERESE (*Calling out*): Who is here? Who is here, I say?
PROSS (*Quietly*): Who are you, and what do you mean by bursting into a private residence?
THERESE: The wife of Evremonde, where is she?
PROSS: From your appearance, you might be the wife of Lucifer.
THERESE: Where is the wife of Evremonde?
PROSS: You shall not get the better of me. I am an Englishwoman.
THERESE: And I am Therese DeFarge. Does that mean anything to you?
PROSS: Yes, it means the cause of all our trouble. If it were not

for you and your husband, none of this would have taken place.
THERESE (*Mockingly*): In the square my friends are reserving my place for me. We shall knit, without losing a stitch, as we watch the heads fall. I shall see my hated enemy, Evremonde, and shall gloat as the knife falls. And now produce your mistress. I wish to pay my compliments to her.
PROSS: I know your intentions are evil, and you may depend upon it, I'll hold my own against them.
THERESE: Let me see her. Do you hear?
PROSS: I am your match.
THERESE: Imbecile! I take no answer from you. Stand out of the way and let me see her.
PROSS: No.
THERESE: These doors are all open. The confusion here. Odds and ends on the floor. She's—she's gone. Escaped!
PROSS: You cannot touch her.
THERESE: Charges are to be brought against her and her child and father.
PROSS: Preferred by you and your worthy husband, no doubt.
THERESE: Where are they? If they have escaped, they can be pursued and brought back.
PROSS: I don't care a tuppence for myself. I know the longer I keep you here, the greater hope there is for my Ladybird.
THERESE: Stand back from that door. Let me out.
PROSS: Make a move toward me and I'll tear out your hair.
THERESE: I'll give the word, and still have time to see her husband's head roll.
PROSS (*Steadily*): I'll not budge.
THERESE: I'll rip you to pieces.
PROSS: Madame DeFarge, put away that knife.
THERESE: Your last chance. Get away from that door.
PROSS: We are alone. Not a soul around. The courtyard is remote from the street.
THERESE: I'll show you. (*Grunting with exertion*) There!

Sound: *A slight scuffle. A chair overturned.*
Pross: You're not strong enough . . . Madame . . . DeFarge . . . every minute you are here is worth a . . . hundred . . . thousand guineas to . . . my darling.
Therese: I'll . . . I'll—
Pross: But you won't. (*A final desperate effort*) There!
Therese: *A heavy groan.*
Sound: *Body falling to floor.*
Pross (*Breathing heavily*): You turned it against yourself, by accident. You stabbed yourself, Madame DeFarge.
Therese: *Groans.*
Pross: Right under your heart. Your eyes are glazed. You're dying. And I can't say I feel sorry. Now you know what it is like, you who have heaped so much sorrow and anguish on innocent people. Before you close your eyes, let me tell you. (*She whispers*) Charles Darnay escaped. Right now he is riding away from you and your Revolutionists toward England and freedom. (*Pause*) You do understand, don't you? Good! And now good-bye, Madame DeFarge. You will not take your place with the other knitters.
Sound: *Door open-close. Key in lock.*
Driver (*Slightly away*): Ah, mam'selle, we are ready. Yes?
Pross: Yes. I am quite ready, driver.
Driver: Have you forgotten anything?
Pross: No. Everything is taken care of, very nicely. Help me into the coach, and then drive as fast as you can. We have a long journey.
Music: *Ominous theme. Forte and fade under.*
Narrator: Meanwhile the death carts rumble through the streets of Paris, six tumbrils carrying a human cargo. The guillotine looms up, its giant knife shining in the late afternoon sun. Three o'clock has just struck. The crowd looks on, hatred etched on its faces.
Music: *Out.*

NARRATOR: As the tumbrils stop, a roar goes up.

SOUND (*Transcribed*): *Roar of a large crowd. Up and out.*

NARRATOR: One by one, the victims ascend the platform. The little seamstress, her hand still in Sydney Carton's, waits her turn. Then she ascends the steps. There is a pause. The crowd is expectant. The huge knife falls. The crowd goes mad.

SOUND: *Roar of crowd. Up and out.*

MAN (*Calling out*): Number fifty-two! Charles Evremonde, called Darnay! Ascend.

CARTON (*Quietly*): It is a far, far better thing that I do, than I have ever done; it is a far, far better rest that I go to, than I have ever known.

MUSIC: *Triumphant. Forte and out.*

THE END

Rip Van Winkle

by Washington Irving

Sound: *Rolling thunder. Up and hold under.*
Hudson (*Calling*): Rip Van Winkle! Rip Van Winkle! We are waiting for you. The game of nine-pins has started. Hurry, Rip! Hurry!
Sound: *Up briefly and fade out into:*
Music: *A rather ethereal, mystic theme. Forte and fade under.*
Narrator: Whoever has made a voyage up the Hudson must remember the Catskill Mountains. They are seen to the west of the river, lording it over the rest of the country. Every change of season and weather affects the magical hues and shapes of these mountains. When the weather is fair, they are clothed in blue and purple. When the rest of the landscape is cloudless, they will gather a hood of gray vapors about their summits. At the foot of these mountains is a village of great antiquity, founded by the Dutch colonists. In that village there lived a simple, good-natured fellow by the name of Rip Van Winkle. Moreover he was a kind neighbor, and he was married . . . of that there was no doubt.
Music: *Out.*
Mrs. Van Winkle (*Calling out in shrill voice*): Rip Van Winkle! Where *is* that man? Rip, do you hear me?
Rip (*Away. Very meekly*): Yes, I hear you, Mrs. Van Winkle.
Mrs. Van Winkle: What're you doing?
Rip: Just resting.
Mrs. Van Winkle: Resting! What kind of man am I married to? Come in this house. I have a thousand and one chores for you to do. Understand!

RIP: Yes, my dear.

MRS. VAN WINKLE: To think I married you! What a fool I was!

RIP (*A bit more enthusiastically*): Yes, dear!

MUSIC: *Light theme. Forte and fade under.*

NARRATOR: A termagant wife may, in some respects be considered a tolerable blessing; if so, Rip Van Winkle was thrice blessed. Left to himself, Rip would have whistled his life away in perfect contentment. He was a great favorite among all the wives of the village, who took his part in all family squabbles. The children, too, would shout with joy when he approached.

MUSIC: *Out.*

BIZ: *A group of children: "Rip, Rip Van Winkle!" "We're so glad to see you." "Rip, stop and talk to us."*

RIP (*At this point he is about 40*): Now, now, what is it you want?

BOY 1: We've been waiting for you, Rip.

GIRL 1: And for a long time, too.

BOY 2: There's no school today.

GIRL 2: It's a holiday.

RIP: Ah, that is very good. There is nothing I like better than a holiday. (*Laughing*) I have many of them, one each day of the year.

BIZ: *Children laugh.*

BOY 1: We want to go fishing.

RIP: A good day for it. Warm . . . not too much sun.

GIRL 2: But we don't know the good streams, and you do.

GIRL 1: Yes, and we want you to take us.

RIP: Oh, but I can't. You see, Mrs. Van Winkle, my good wife, is sending me to get some shingles. Our roof needs mending.

GIRL 2: But you can always mend a roof.

BOY 2: And it's such a fine day.

Boy 1: You've got to go with us.
Rip (*Weakening*): Well, I shouldn't—
Boy 1: Please, Rip.
Rip: I shouldn't, but—
Boy 2: Then you will go.
Rip: Perhaps for just a few minutes.
Girl 1 (*Disappointed*): Oh!
Rip: Well, for a few hours, then. Let the shingles age a bit more. Let the roof leak a while longer.
Biz: *Children: "Good for Rip." "He's taking us fishing." "Come along, Rip." "Hurry, everybody."*
Music: *Lighthearted theme. Forte and fade under.*
Narrator: That was the great error in Rip's composition: he had an insuperable aversion to all kinds of profitable labor. He would fish all day, with a rod as long and heavy as a Tartar's lance. He would trudge through woods and swamps for hours, carrying his cumbersome fowling piece. He would never refuse to assist a neighbor, even in the roughest toil. He would run errands for neighbors and do little odd jobs. In a word Rip was ready to attend to anybody's business but his own.
Music: *Out.*
Narrator: His wife, her tongue incessantly going, would say to him:
Mrs. Van Winkle: Look at this house. It's falling to pieces. Your fences have collapsed. Your fields are full of weeds. You sit by and watch our cow eat our cabbages.
Rip: But she likes cabbages.
Mrs. Van Winkle: Your father left you many acres, and bit by bit, through your carelessness and laziness, they've dwindled away. And today all we have left is a small patch of corn and potatoes.
Rip (*Meekly*): We had cabbages, until the cow ate them.

Mrs. Van Winkle: And the land we have left, you let go to seed.

Rip: You know our land, it's the worst piece in the village.

Mrs. Van Winkle: And I have the laziest, the worst husband in the village.

Wolf (*The dog*): *He barks from outside the house.*

Rip: It's Wolf.

Mrs. Van Winkle: You and that dog of yours.

Rip: Can I let him in?

Mrs. Van Winkle: No.

Rip: But—

Mrs. Van Winkle: No! Now where are you going?

Rip: For a walk.

Mrs. Van Winkle: You have a wife and two children to feed. Go to work.

Rip: I am. I'm going to help Nicholas Van Vedder mend his barn.

Music: *Humorously doleful. Forte and fade under.*

Narrator: And that is the way it went in the Van Winkle household. The house became more weatherbeaten, the weeds grew thicker and higher, and the cow ate more and more cabbages. Rip's two children—Judith and young Rip—were as wild and ragged as if they belonged to nobody. In fact, young Rip not only inherited his father's old clothes, but his habits as well. As for Wolf, the dog, courageous as he was on a hunting trip, once he entered the house, his tail curled between his legs. Times grew worse. Mrs. Van Winkle kept dinning into her husband's ears the ruin he was bringing on his family. A sharp tongue is the only edged tool that grows keener with constant use. When driven from the house, Rip consoled himself by frequenting a kind of perpetual club, which held its sessions on a bench before the local inn—"The King George the Third." Here gossip was born, here endless sleepy stories about nothing were told. This informal club was presided over by an august personage, the owner of the inn, one Nicholas Van Vedder.

MUSIC: *Out.*

NICHOLAS: As a boy, I can remember my father telling me that the ghostly crew of Hendrick Hudson comes back to this section, and that, led by Hudson, it sails up the river on a voyage.

RIP: You believe that, Nicholas?

NICHOLAS: I do, indeed I do.

RIP: Has anyone in your knowledge ever seen Hudson and his crew from the "Half Moon"?

NICHOLAS (*Grudgingly*): N-no. But it is said that when the thunder echoes through the Catskills, it is his crew playing at bowls.

RIP: It may be as you say, Nicholas. I have tramped all through these mountains, in all kinds of weather, but never have I seen this ghostly crew. (*Shuddering*) I don't think I would enjoy the experience one bit.

NICHOLAS: Nor would I. I much prefer to sit here in the shade, where it is quiet and peaceful, with no interfering noise.

MRS. VAN WINKLE (*Away*): Rip! Rip Van Winkle! So this is where you are, you lazy good for nothing.

RIP (*Wearily*): Nicholas, what did you say about peace and quiet?

MRS. VAN WINKLE (*Fading in*): Don't you dare run away. I've been looking for you.

RIP: Is something wrong, my dear?

MRS. VAN WINKLE: Wrong! The roof over the woodshed collapsed, just as I was about to enter it.

RIP (*Hopefully*): It didn't strike you?

MRS. VAN WINKLE: Luckily, no.

RIP: Too bad.

MRS. VAN WINKLE (*Sharply*): What did you say?

Rip: Nothing, nothing.
Mrs. Van Winkle: You're to come home at once and clean it up.
Rip: I will do it tomorrow.
Mrs. Van Winkle: Now! Understand! Now!
Rip (*Groans*): Very well.
Nicholas: Mrs. Van Winkle, Rip and I were enjoying ourselves. There is no harm in talking.
Mrs. Van Winkle (*As though turning on him*): Talk, talk, talk—that's all you two do. Sit here in the shade and talk, and about what! Nothing!
Nicholas (*With dignity*): Mrs. Van Winkle, you are not to address me in such a voice. I am a man of importance.
Mrs. Van Winkle: Indeed, Nicholas Van Vedder! It's you who encourages this lazy husband of mine. It's you who helps make him lazy and idle. Not that he needs encouraging. And don't answer me back. (*To* Rip) And now you, my shiftless husband, come home and fix that roof. (*Fading*) If you aren't there inside another five minutes, I'll be back, and this time I'll not be so easy on you.
Nicholas: Rip, as the years go by, your wife becomes worse and worse.
Rip (*Hopelessly*): If only I could get away from her tongue! That's impossible, but I like to think about it.
Nicholas: I would not stand for it. You're the head of your family.
Rip: I wonder.
Nicholas: And therefore you have a right to be shiftless and lazy, if you wish.
Rip: Thank you, Nicholas. In you, I have a good friend. (*Sighing*) Well, I suppose I should be going. But tomorrow, Wolf and I will get up early and spend the day in the woods hunting; anything to escape her tongue.

Music: *A theme of outdoors. Forte and fade under.*
Narrator: The next morning's sun had barely blossomed before Rip and his dog were in the woods. It was a warm Indian Summer day, an ideal one in which to ramble. Rip was engaged in his favorite sport of squirrel hunting. Unknowingly he and Wolf had scrambled to one of the highest parts of the Catskills. Late afternoon, panting and fatigued, Rip threw himself on a green knoll. Far below him was the lordly Hudson River. On the other side he looked down into a deep mountain glen—wild, lonely, and dark, the bottom scarcely lighted by the rays of the setting sun. For some time Rip lay musing on this scene. Evening was gradually advancing. The mountains began to throw their long blue shadows over the valleys. Rip addressed Wolf, who lay at his feet.
Music: *Out.*
Rip: It will be dark long before we reach home, Wolf.
Wolf: *Gives a short bark, as if to say, "I agree."*
Rip (*Sighs*): Mrs. Van Winkle, she is going to be very displeased with us. She'll scold me until my head spins. And you, Wolf, she may take the broom to you.
Wolf: *Growls unhappily.*
Rip: She doesn't understand us. She leads us both a dog's life. But never mind, while I live you'll never want a friend to stand by you.
Wolf: *Gives several short barks.*
Rip: Well, I suppose we should start back. Come on, Wolf.
Sound (*Recorded*): *Distant rumble of thunder.*
Rip: Oh, Oh! Thunder.
Sound: *Thunder repeated.*
Rip: Just our luck to get caught in a mountain storm. Up we go, Wolf. We have a long way to travel.
Crew Member (*Off in distance, calling out*): Rip Van Winkle! Rip Van Winkle!

RIP: Peculiar! I thought I heard a voice.
WOLF: *Barks excitedly.*
RIP: Must have been a passing crow.
CREW MEMBER (*Still away*): Rip Van Winkle! Rip Van Winkle!
RIP (*Apprehensively*): That *is* a voice, Wolf. Look—climbing over the rocks. A man! It may be a neighbor, who needs a hand.
WOLF: *Yowls.*
RIP: Now, now, Wolf, that is no way to act. Remember, we are always glad to help anyone who needs it. (*Calling out*) Hello, there! Can we help you? Perhaps you are lost!
MUSIC: *Mysterious theme. Sneak under and hold.*
NARRATOR: Rip was surprised at the stranger's appearance. He was a short square-built old fellow, with thick bushy hair and a grizzled beard. His dress was of the antique Dutch fashion. He bore on his shoulder a stout keg. The stranger made signs for Rip to approach and help him with the load.
MUSIC: *Out.*
RIP (*No pause*): You need some help, and you have met up with the right fellow. Here, shift it to my shoulder. (*Grunting*) My, but this keg *is* heavy. What's in it? My name is— (*Suddenly aware of the fact*) But you know who I am, for you called me by name. "Rip Van Winkle," you cried. Your name is what? (*Pause*) You are not very talkative, are you? (*Cheerfully*) Well, on the other hand, I talk too much. By the way, this is my dog, Wolf. Wolf, say hello.
WOLF: *Growls and whines.*
RIP: That is no way to talk to a stranger. And now, sir, where do we go with this keg?
MUSIC: *Repeat preceding theme of mystery. Sneak and hold under.*
NARRATOR: But the stranger spoke not a word. Instead, he

beckoned Rip to follow him. They clambered up a narrow gully, apparently a dried-up river bed. As they ascended, Rip every now and then heard long rolling peals, like distant thunder. The sound seemed to issue out of a deep ravine that lay ahead. Passing through this ravine, they came to a hollow. It was like a small amphitheatre, surrounded by perpendicular precipices. The area seemed to have over it a twilight grayness. A silence hung heavy, one that inspired awe and checked familiarity. Still Rip's companion spoke not a word. On entering the amphitheatre, new objects of wonder presented themselves. On a level spot was a company of odd-looking personages playing at ninepins. They were dressed in quaint fashion. Their faces, too, were peculiar. One had a large head and small piggish eyes; the face of another seemed to consist entirely of nose. They all wore beards. Nothing interrupted the stillness, but the noise of the bowling balls.

MUSIC: *Out into:*

SOUND (*In strong*): *Thunder. Up and out.*

RIP (*Amazed*): Well, what do you know, Wolf. So that is the thunder we heard. Those bowling balls as they play ninepins. I have never seen them before, have you, Wolf?

WOLF: *Whines uneasily.*

RIP: Don't be uneasy. They don't talk, but neither do they appear unfriendly. You know, they look just like the people in that old Dutch painting Nicholas Van Vedder has hanging in his house.

SOUND: *Another peal of thunder.*

RIP (*Calling out*): Very well bowled, sir. Excellent! (*To* WOLF) Hmm! He might at least answer me. I was only being friendly. (*Surprised*) So! Look, one of them is coming toward us.

WOLF: *Barks wildly, and continues, fading off, until his voice is lost in the distance.*

Rip (*Calling out, against* Wolf's *barking*): Wolf, Wolf! Come back. Come back, I say. Wolf! (*Moaning*) Now why did old Wolf do that? Something is bothering him. (*Philosophically*) He won't go far, and if he does, he'll find his way back home.

Hudson: Good evening.

Rip: Good evening to you, sir.

Hudson: You may put down that keg.

Rip: Thank you. It *is* rather heavy. (*A bit nervously*) Your friends like to bowl. (*No answer*) I—I hope I am not bothering you.

Hudson: We have been expecting you, Rip Van Winkle.

Rip: First that other man called me by name, and now you. You know who I am. How?

Hudson: It does not matter.

Rip: You are strangers hereabouts.

Hudson: No, far from strangers.

Rip: I thought I knew everyone for miles around, but I do not know any of you.

Hudson: Naturally.

Rip: Why "naturally"?

Hudson: We came to these parts long before you were born.

Rip (*Puzzled*): Then you keep yourselves well hidden.

Hudson: We do.

Rip: What is your calling?

Hudson: We follow the sea.

Rip: Sailors?

Hudson: Yes.

Rip (*Trying to make conversation*): My dog, Wolf, he got frightened, I guess. He ran away, but he'll be back.

Hudson: He won't return.

Rip: No?

Hudson: No.

RIP: I live some distance from here—in a little village.
HUDSON: Yes, I know that.
RIP: But how?
HUDSON: It does not matter.
RIP: I find your remarks very puzzling. I wish you would explain them.
HUDSON: Later, perhaps. First we will drink from the keg.
MUSIC: *Light fantasy. Sneak and hold under.*
NARRATOR: As Rip watched, his companion, who seemed to be the leader, emptied the contents of the keg into large flagons. At a command from him, Rip served the peculiar assortment of men. They stared at him as they drank, and in such a manner, that his heart turned within him. His knees knocked together. But by degrees Rip's apprehension subsided. He even ventured to taste the beverage. He repeated this several times, until his head started to swim. After a while, the leader beckoned to Rip.
MUSIC: *Out.*
HUDSON: You wish to know more about me and these men?
RIP: Well, yes, I do.
HUDSON: Then I shall tell you. First, let me say that you are the first person in many years to see me and my crew.
RIP: Thank you.
HUDSON: A great many years ago I discovered this river.
RIP: What river?
HUDSON: *This* river, the one that stretches below us.
RIP: The Hudson!
HUDSON: The Hudson.
RIP: Then—you're . . . you're—
HUDSON: Yes, I am Hendrick Hudson.
RIP: You are joking.
HUDSON (*Warningly*): I do not joke.
RIP: And these men are your crew?

Hudson: The original crew that first sailed up the river with me.
Rip: Excuse my saying so, but you—all of you—you're dead.
Hudson: According to you, and people like you—yes.
Rip: Today, while I rambled, I saw the river, but not a sign of your boat, the—er—the—
Hudson: The "Half Moon." No, you failed to see it. We sail cloaked in a sheet of billowing fog. We sailed past this city—New Amsterdam, now known as New York—past it and up the river.
Rip: Then what Nicholas Van Vedder told me is true. He told me of the legend concerning you, but I did not really believe him.
Hudson: We keep a vigil here, once in every twenty years. I pause here and there, en route, to see what is being done with the territory I discovered.
Rip: Are you satisfied, Captain Hudson?
Hudson: In part, only in part.
Rip: You will be here much longer?
Hudson: No. We leave tonight on the tide.
Rip: And—
Hudson: We will not return for another twenty years.
Rip (*Sighing*): I never thought I would meet a company of ghosts.
Hudson: How do you know we are ghosts?
Rip: Well, Captain Hudson, what *are* you then?
Hudson: Guardians of this river, as I have told you.
Rip (*A bit sleepily*): Well, I don't know what to make of all this. Should leave . . . long way home. Wife . . . she . . . expects me. . . . (*Yawns*)
Hudson: You need be in no hurry, Rip Van Winkle.
Rip (*Getting sleepier*): My eyes . . . blurred . . . swimming. Tired. May as well rest . . . for . . . few minutes. (*A long, drawn-out moan.*)

HUDSON: Rest well, Rip, for you deserve it.
MUSIC: *A theme showing the passing of time. Forte and out into:*
SOUND: *Twittering of birds. Hold under.*
RIP (*Yawns deeply*): Where am I? (*Suddenly awake*) Oh! Surely I have not slept here all night. But I have. What excuse shall I make to Mrs. Van Winkle? Captain Hudson and his crew—where are they? Hmph! Disappeared! Oh, that flagon! That flagon! What was in it? (*Groans*) Well, I must get up. (*Groans*) My joints! Stiff! These mountain beds don't agree with me. My gun. Ah, here it is. (*Angrily*) But this can't be my gun, not this rusty old firelock. It's that crew of Hudson's, they've stolen my gun. And where's Wolf? (*He whistles twice, then calls.*) Wolf! Here, Wolf! (*He whistles again.*) Even my dog has left me. If only I can find Captain Hudson. (*Suddenly realizing it*) They've gone, every one of them. Last night the captain said they were sailing on the tide. A good thing, for it is their fault I stayed away all night. May as well face my wife's tongue.
SOUND: *Birds out.*
MUSIC: *Sneak and hold under.*
NARRATOR: The morning was passing away, and Rip was famished. So he shouldered the rusty firelock and turned his steps homeward. It was with considerable difficulty that he did so, for the terrain seemed to have changed. He found the gully up which he and his companion had ascended the preceding evening; but a mountain stream was now foaming down it. Eventually, however, he made his way to familiar ground. As he approached the village he met a number of people.
MUSIC: *Out.*
RIP: Good morning.
MAN: Morning.
WOMAN: Are you lost?

RIP: Lost! No, not at all. Why should I be?
MAN (*Fading a bit*): Strange appearing character.
WOMAN (*Fading*): Yes, and did you notice his beard?
RIP (*To himself*): Now, who are those strangers? And this talk of a beard— (*Suddenly*) They were talking about me. My beard *has* grown. It's almost a foot long. How could that happen overnight! I could swear that the village has grown larger. It seems to have more people and houses.
BIZ (*Fading in*): *A group of children laughing and calling out. Sustain under* RIP'S *speech.*
RIP: At last! Children! My friends. At least they won't be strangers. (*He calls out*) Good morning, boys and girls. Good morning to you.
BIZ: *Stops abruptly.*
BOY: What a funny looking old man.
RIP: Don't you remember me, your old friend, Rip Van Winkle?
GIRL: He frightens me.
GIRL 2: Me, too.
RIP: You are joking with me.
BOY 2: We never saw you before.
GIRL: Mr. Graybeard!
BOY: An old scarecrow!
GIRL 2: He frightens me. Let's run away.
GIRL: Yes, let's. Hurry!
BIZ (*Fading away*): *Children hooting and yelling at* RIP, *as they run off.*
RIP (*Hurt*): Now, that is a fine reception to give me. But as a matter of fact, I didn't really recognize them. Surely this is my native village, my home, which I left only yesterday. There are the Catskills, down there is the Hudson.
MUSIC: *Repeat previous theme. Sneak in and hold under.*
NARRATOR: It was with some difficulty that Rip found his own house. He found it had gone to decay—the roof fallen in, the windows shattered, the doors off the hinges. He entered the

house. It was empty, apparently abandoned. He hurried forth, and hastened to his old resort—the village inn. It, too, was gone. A large rickety building stood in its place. The sign read: "The Union Hotel, Jonathan Doolittle, proprietor." The great tree was gone. In its place reared a pole, and from it fluttered a flag, on which was an assemblage of stars and stripes. The sign no longer carried the ruddy countenance of King George the Third. Instead, it bore the face of a stranger. Underneath was painted: "General Washington." A crowd was gathered about the door. A bilious-looking fellow, his pockets stuffed with handbills, was haranguing vehemently.

MUSIC: *Out.*

POLITICIAN (*A rolling voice*): And in conclusion, I say that at this next election keep in mind that I am for citizens' rights and liberty. Remember that, remember Bunker Hill and Yorktown, the heroes of '76, and remember me when you cast your vote in this forthcoming election. Send me to Congress. Thank you.

BIZ: *Clapping and shouts. Ad libs.*

PUFFING MAN: You, old man, are you a Federal or a Democrat?

RIP (*Bewildered*): I don't know.

PUFFING MAN: Indeed! You must be one or the other.

NASAL VOICE: What brings you to this election rally with a gun on your shoulder, and a mob at your heels?

RIP: These people followed me.

NASAL VOICE: Are you trying to start a riot?

PUFFING MAN: I'll wager he is.

SHARP TONGUE (*A woman*): That's it, he's here to make trouble.

BIZ: *Angry ad libs from onlookers.*

RIP (*Protesting*): Gentlemen, kind folks, I am but a poor, quiet man, a native of the place, and a loyal subject of the king, God bless him!

BIZ: *Angry voices.*

NASAL VOICE: He's a Tory. A Tory!
SHARP TONGUE: A spy!
PUFFING MAN: Hustle him away. Drive him from this village.
POLITICIAN: Just a minute! I'll get to the bottom of this.
BIZ: *The voices die out.*
POLITICIAN: Now sir, just what do you want here?
RIP: I mean no harm. I'm just searching for some of my neighbors.
SHARP TONGUE: Neighbors! A likely story.
NASAL VOICE: If you have friends hereabouts, name them.
RIP: They used to gather at the old inn, which should be standing here.
POLITICIAN: Name them.
RIP: Well, there was Brom Dutcher.
VOICE: Brom Dutcher went off into the army. He never came back again.
RIP: Where's Van Bummel, the schoolmaster?
SHARP TONGUE: He went off to the wars, too; now he lives in the West—in the Ohio country.
RIP: And Nicholas Van Vedder?
PUFFING MAN: Nicholas Van Vedder! Why, he's dead and gone these eighteen years.
RIP: I do not understand all this strange talk. Doesn't anybody here know Rip Van Winkle?
RIP 2ND (*A lazy voice*): Yes, I'm Rip Van Winkle.
RIP: You! But you're only a young man.
RIP 2ND: Maybe, but I'm still Rip Van Winkle. Who are you?
RIP: I wish I knew. I'm not myself. I'm somebody else. You, you say you're me. I was myself last night, but I fell asleep on the mountain, and they've changed my gun, and everything's changed, and I'm changed, and I can't tell what's my name, or who I am.
NASAL VOICE: Poor chap!
PUFFING MAN: He seems harmless enough.

NASAL VOICE: I wonder.
POLITICIAN: Maybe we should take his gun away.
SHARP TONGUE: He's wild looking, if you should ask me.
RIP 3RD (*A very young boy*): Mama, I'm afraid.
JUDITH (*Now a woman in her middle twenties*): Hush, Rip, hush! The old man won't bother you.
RIP: Did you say the child's name is Rip?
JUDITH: It is.
RIP: What is your name?
JUDITH: Judith Gardenier.
RIP: And your father's name?
JUDITH: Rip Van Winkle was his name. It's twenty years since he went away from home, with his gun, and nobody has seen him since then. His dog came home without him. I was then but a little girl.
RIP: Where's your mother?
JUDITH: Oh, she died but a short time ago. She broke a blood vessel yelling at a New England peddler.
RIP: Yes, I can imagine. Young lady, Judith, don't you know me? I'm your father—young Rip Van Winkle once—old Rip Van Winkle now! Does nobody recognize me?
BIZ: *A few ad libs of surprise from crowd.*
OLD WOMAN: Let me in. Let me look at this man. (*Pause*) Sure enough! It is Rip Van Winkle. Welcome home, neighbor. Where have you been these twenty years?
MUSIC: *A theme of rejoicing, forte and fade under.*
NARRATOR: Rip's story was soon told, for the whole twenty years had been to him but a single night. The neighbors stared when they heard it. Some were seen to wink, while others put their tongues into their cheeks. Rip's daughter took him home to live with her. She had a snug, well-furnished house, and a fine husband. As for Rip's son, he was employed on the farm, but evinced an inherited disposition.
MUSIC: *Out.*

Rip: Son, your sister left word that she wants you to mend that broken chair.

Rip 2nd (*Uninterested*): Oh, that's past mending, I'm afraid. Besides, Father, I have something more important to do.

Rip: And what might that be?

Rip 2nd: I promised to take some of the village boys on a fishing trip. I'm the only one who knows just where the good streams are.

Rip: I wish I were younger. I'd join you. By the way, Rip, you're being married?

Rip 2nd: I'm contemplating it.

Rip: Does the young lady try to tell you what to do?

Rip 2nd: No.

Rip (*A sigh of relief*): See that she continues that way. Goodbye, son. Have a good trip.

Music: *Repeat preceding theme. Sneak and hold under.*

Narrator: Old Rip resumed his old habits. He soon found many of his old cronies, though all the worse for time and wear. Having nothing to do, he took his place once more on the bench at the inn door. Soon he was reverenced as a chronicler of the old days. It was some time before he could comprehend the strange events that had taken place during his twenty-year sleep. He learned that he now was a free citizen of the United States. There was, however, but one species of despotism which he despised, and that was—petticoat government. Happily, that was at an end. Of course, as chief story-teller of the village, his most familiar tale was his own.

Music: *Out.*

Rip: Well, there I was playing ninepins with Captain Hendrick Hudson and his crew. They had just sailed up the Hudson to look over things. They liked me and gave me something to drink that made me sleep for twenty years. (*Slight fade*) And Hudson, he took me aside and he said: "Rip Van Winkle, you are a . . .

Music: *Repeat theme. Forte and fade under.*
Narrator: Even to this day the people of that section never hear a thunderstorm but they say it is Hendrick Hudson and his crew playing ninepins. And it is a common wish of all henpecked husbands in the neighborhood, when life becomes difficult, that they might have a quieting draught of Rip Van Winkle's flagon.
Music: *Up full to finish.*

THE END

The Young Man with the Cream Tarts

by Robert Louis Stevenson

MUSIC: *Weird, brooding theme. Forte and fade under.*
JOHN: It is a weird, strange, almost incredible story I have to relate—a freak happening that but a handful of people know about. If you have no heart for a story of icy, bloodcurdling suspense, I advise against your listening—for fear is no trifling passion to be toyed with by the uninitiate!
MUSIC: *Up and out.*
JOHN: My name is John Geraldine. In 1870, during the reign of Victoria, I returned from five years' service in India. Due to poor health, I resigned my commission as captain in the Coldstream Guards. I had not long been out of service when an emissary of Prince Florizel of Bohemia offered me a colonelcy in the Prince's own regiment. I accepted, only to find life in the Court of Bohemia placid and quite uneventful. One day, almost a year following my entry into Prince Florizel's service, he sent for me. (*Fading*) When I reported to his quarters, he said to me . . .
PRINCE: Colonel Geraldine, have you ever been bored?
JOHN: Very often, Your Highness.
PRINCE: I'm happy to hear you say that, because I am bored, extremely bored.
JOHN: I wish I could suggest some remedy.
PRINCE: It's adventure I'm in search of—some unusual adventure.
JOHN: I'm afraid you'll not find it in Bohemia.
PRINCE: Why not London?

JOHN: London?
PRINCE: Yes . . . London.
JOHN: Why not?
PRINCE (*Briskly*): Have your luggage packed. We leave tomorrow . . . in search of the Great Adventure!
MUSIC: *Ominous. Up and under.*
JOHN: In London the Prince and I took up rooms in Wigmore Street, Cavendish Square. And then we searched relentlessly for adventure—combing London by day and night. But nowhere did we find it. Then one raw, cheerless evening in March, after having walked miles in the thick fog, in the neighborhood of Leicester Square, the Prince called a halt.
MUSIC: *Out.*
PRINCE: Well, Colonel, we seem dogged by bad luck.
JOHN (Wearily): Your Highness, if you don't mind the suggestion, I think we should call it an evening. It's quite late, and if you're half as damp as I am, and one-third as tired, you'll—
PRINCE (*Cutting in*): I know, I know. I also could do with some dry clothing and sleep. Fact is, though, I'm a bit hungry. Here's an oyster bar. What do you say to a spot of food?
JOHN (*Fading*): I don't suppose another hour will make any great difference.
SOUND (*Fade in background of restaurant*): *A few people ad libbing. Noise of dishes and glassware. Have it rise and fall during this scene.*
PRINCE (*Satisfied*): Ah! Not a bad snack. Fact is, this food is exactly what I needed.
JOHN: More than . . . adventure, Your Highness?
PRINCE (*Laughs*): You're a sharp one, Colonel. We go out in search of adventure and end up by eating.
JOHN: I've just about given up hope. If there is any adventure to be found in London, so far it has eluded us.
PRINCE: Perhaps tomorrow we'll discover one. Or we could

find one right here in this restaurant. Yes, even right here. (*He breaks off.*) What are you staring at?

JOHN: Look—over there. That young man that just came in. What the deuce is he carrying on that tray?

PRINCE: Can't make out from here.

JOHN: Whatever it is, he is offering it to the patrons.

PRINCE: Listen!

YOUNG MAN (*Slightly away*): Have a cream tart, sir? Very delicious. No charge, absolutely free.

PATRON: I say, steer off! Mind your own affairs.

YOUNG MAN (*Closer*): Very well! How about you, sir?

SECOND PATRON: Don't mind if I do.

YOUNG MAN: Very dainty . . . extremely satisfying. There you are, sir. (*Against the following dialogue between* PRINCE *and* JOHN, *he sings*) Cream tarts! Cream tarts! No charge! Entirely free! Have a cream tart. Delicious cream tarts. Cream tarts!

PRINCE: Why do you suppose he's handing out those cream tarts? Queer thing to be doing this time of night.

JOHN: He seems harmless enough.

YOUNG MAN (*Now on mike*): How about you gentlemen? Will either of you honor a stranger? I can vouch for them—having eaten over two dozen of them since five o'clock.

PRINCE: I will eat one if you will tell me the spirit in which it is given.

YOUNG MAN: The spirit, sir, is one of mockery.

PRINCE: And whom do you propose to mock?

YOUNG MAN: I am not here to expound my philosophy, but to distribute these cream tarts. Let me say that I heartily include myself in the ridicule of the transaction.

JOHN: Your unique method of passing an evening interests us.

PRINCE: If my friend and I eat your cakes, we shall expect you —in return—to join us later at supper.

THE YOUNG MAN WITH THE CREAM TARTS

YOUNG MAN (*Uncertain*): I still have these cream tarts to get rid of. That means more restaurants to be visited.

PRINCE: Why don't we go along—and after you've finished, supper and some conversation.

YOUNG MAN: Gentlemen, I am a man of foolish decisions! I accept! First—your cream tarts . . . and then we're off!

MUSIC: *Up and under for narration.*

JOHN: For the next hour the Prince and I followed the young man with the cream tarts . . . from one restaurant to another. After the last tart had disappeared, we went to a small French restaurant and asked for a private dining room.

MUSIC: *Gradually out.*

JOHN (*No pause*): After the coffee had been served and the cigars lighted, the young man made a nervous motion of rising.

YOUNG MAN: Sorry to be rude, but I should be leaving. I have another engagement.

PRINCE: You haven't fulfilled your bargain. You promised to talk with us.

YOUNG MAN (*Troubled*): Very well, but I can stay only a few minutes.

PRINCE: If you're adventure-bound, tell us about it. My friend, here, and I are also in search of it.

YOUNG MAN: My engagement is a secret one.

JOHN: All the better. If your secret is a silly one, you need have no delicacy with us—for we are two of the silliest men in England.

YOUNG MAN: But I don't know you.

PRINCE: And we don't know you. Tell us about yourself.

YOUNG MAN: There is every reason why I should not.

JOHN: All the more reason to tell it to a pair of fools like us.

YOUNG MAN: My name I shall keep to myself. From my parents I received a hare-brained sense of humor and a comfortable inheritance.

PRINCE: Evidently you still have the sense of humor.
YOUNG MAN: Yes, but the money is gone . . . wasted. I spent the last of it tonight on that silly gesture of the cream tarts, saving only forty pounds. I have no friends . . . my fiancée has broken off our engagement. I have no position . . . no skill. And that, in brief, is my story.
JOHN: You speak of having saved forty pounds. Why forty?
YOUNG MAN: I am reserving that for a particular reason.
PRINCE: How fortunate we have met. Perhaps it is fate.
YOUNG MAN (*Eagerly*): Are you two also ruined?
PRINCE: This supper was a final gesture.
YOUNG MAN: You're really ruined?
PRINCE: Yes. Ruined by acts of which neither should feel proud. Now nothing remains.
YOUNG MAN (*Softly*): There is always Death's private door.
JOHN (*Sharply*): What do you mean?
YOUNG MAN: I have my admission. (*Laughs bleakly*) Imagine! A man cannot even die without money.
JOHN: You're talking in riddles.
YOUNG MAN: Fortunately, there is a way of solving my particular riddle.
JOHN: Be more explicit.
YOUNG MAN: Up to the present there has been no organized method for a man to step from this troubled world into the next. For the escapist—no definite exit from life to death. (*He pauses.*)
PRINCE: You know the exit?
YOUNG MAN: Yes.
PRINCE: Then please help us find it, too.
YOUNG MAN: Can you raise eighty pounds between you?
PRINCE: Just about.
YOUNG MAN: Good! For forty pounds each is the entry money.
PRINCE: To what?

YOUNG MAN: The Suicide Club!
JOHN: Suicide Club?
PRINCE: What the deuce is that?
YOUNG MAN: For such as I, and all others who wish to die without posthumous scandal, the Suicide Club has been founded. As to its management, its history, its ramifications, I am myself uninformed.
PRINCE: And its constitution—what of it?
YOUNG MAN: What I know of it, I am under oath to say nothing.
PRINCE: And two men, such as us, who would welcome death, might be admitted?
YOUNG MAN: If you are serious, I will introduce you tonight to a meeting.
PRINCE: And death—?
YOUNG MAN (*Ominously*): You may expect it tonight. And if not tonight—at least sometime within the week, you will be easily relieved of your existences. Let us leave at once for . . . Death's private door.
MUSIC: *Ominous, weird—forte and then under.*
JOHN: Our cab left us in a section I did not recognize. The three of us passed through a dark court and to a door, through which we passed by means of a key the young man with the cream tarts carried. We stood in the darkness of a room . . . and while the young man fumbled with a table lamp, I could feel my heart pounding like surf against a wild shore.
MUSIC: *Out.*
JOHN (*No pause*): Then our host turned to us, his face leering almost hideously in the dim light.
YOUNG MAN: Here we are, gentlemen. Remember, it still is not too late to escape. Reflect before you take the next step. This is the crossroad.
PRINCE: We are not turning back.

YOUNG MAN: Last month, a newcomer fainted dead away—right where you are standing. It took all my persuasive powers to make him go through with it. (*Short laugh*) He died two days later, and in a most interesting manner.

JOHN: What are we to do next?

YOUNG MAN: Wait here. I will send in the President.

PRINCE: Yes, we want to meet him.

YOUNG MAN: A little warning. (*Ominously*) Be frank in your answers. The President is not a man to be trifled with.

SOUND: *Door squeaks open and closed.*

JOHN: Your Highness, we're mad to go through with this. On the other side of that door stands—

PRINCE (*Calmly*): What?

JOHN: Perhaps death.

PRINCE: And most certainly adventure—something we've been searching for.

JOHN: But the risks!

PRINCE: I not only realize them . . . but am enjoying every second.

JOHN: The consequences may be grave. I insist that we leave immediately.

PRINCE: Frankly, I doubt if we'd be able to leave.

JOHN: It's a chance we must take. Consider your position—heir to a throne. If anything should happen to you, there'd be a scandal. Come, let's clear out of this den.

PRINCE (*Amused*): If it is a den, perhaps they keep live devils on the premises . . . and that could be very amusing.

JOHN: I can't help but feel that something horrible is going to happen. The young man with the cream tarts, he's unbalanced.

PRINCE: No more so than you and I for coming here. Relax, Colonel, relax and enjoy yourself.

SOUND: *Door handle rattled.*

PRINCE (*Sotto voce*): Sshh! Someone's coming in.

THE YOUNG MAN WITH THE CREAM TARTS

SOUND: *Door squeaks open, then closed.*
PRESIDENT (*Coldly*): Good evening. I am told you wish to speak to me.
PRINCE: We desire to join the Suicide Club.
PRESIDENT (*Abruptly*): What is that?
PRINCE: I believe you are the person best-qualified to give us information on that point.
PRESIDENT: *I?* (*Curtly*) You are mistaken. This is a social club—for members only. I ask you to get out at once.
JOHN: This gentleman must know what he is talking about. Perhaps we should leave.
PRINCE: We have come here upon an invitation of a friend of yours, who doubtless has told you why we are here. Let me remind you, sir, that a man in my position has very little to lose.
PRESIDENT: Meaning exactly what?
PRINCE: Unless you admit me and my friend, you'll bitterly repent ever having let us in this far.
PRESIDENT: A threat?
PRINCE: Yes. (*Beat*) My friend and I are desperate.
PRESIDENT (*Curt laugh*): You are a man after my own heart—right to the point. (*Transition into coldness*) What are your qualifications for joining? Why do you think you should be admitted?
PRINCE: Because within the next two weeks a certain company will discover that I, as trustee for an estate, have spent all the money it contained.
PRESIDENT: On what?
PRINCE: The usual thing. A fast, easy life.
PRESIDENT: And now—?
PRINCE: Yes.
PRESIDENT: And *you*—why do you think you are tired of life?
JOHN: I . . . I—well, I . . . it's this way—

PRINCE (*Briskly*): My friend, the major, was cashiered for stealing regimental funds. (*Maliciously amused*) He also cheated at cards.
PRESIDENT (*Grunts*): Hmmphh! To look at him, one would not give him credit for that much strength of character.
JOHN (*Angrily*): Look here, you—
PRINCE: Mr. President, you must be a good judge of men. Cross-examine us as you will. But in the end, I know you will admit us—a pair of derelicts.
PRESIDENT: Perhaps I can strain the regulations. Mind you, I say, perhaps.
MUSIC: *A theme of foreboding. Sneak under and hold.*
JOHN: A half-hour later the Prince and I, under assumed names, had been admitted to the Suicide Club. Much as we disliked it, after paying our forty pounds, each of us swore to say nothing of what we might see take place. After this ceremony, we stepped into the next room.
MUSIC: *Out.*
SOUND (*Cast ad libs*): *Weave in and out of scene.*
JOHN (*After slight pause*): The room that the President led us into was small. There were present eight men, including ourselves. Despite the brisk conversations taking place, there was in the air a nervous tension which, at any moment, threatened to explode. The Prince and I looked around in silence.
PRINCE: Will you look at that apparition over by the window? Never saw such a hideous face.
JOHN: He's beckoning.
PRINCE (*Sardonically*): May as well greet our brother member. (*Pause*) Good evening. You wish to speak to us?
MALTHUS: Yes. You obviously are newcomers, and therefore wish information. You have come to the proper source. Come —through this door. We can talk in peace. (*Laughs*) Peace! You find peace only in death, they say.

THE YOUNG MAN WITH THE CREAM TARTS

SOUND: *Door squeaks open, then closed.*

MALTHUS: Welcome, gentlemen, welcome! I always like to see new faces here. So many of the old ones have a way of disappearing . . . almost too rapidly.

PRINCE: You must be an old member.

MALTHUS: It is two years since I first visited this charming club.

PRINCE: Two years! But I was under the impression that—

MALTHUS: My case is peculiar. I'm an honorary member—one who rarely visits. My bad health has procured for me this little immunity, for which I pay an advanced rate. Then, too, my luck is good.

JOHN: We're not too well acquainted with procedure. Perhaps you can enlighten us.

MALTHUS: Of course. Ordinary members, such as yourselves, return here every evening until fortune favors them.

PRINCE: And our friend, the President?

MALTHUS: Ah, I hope you have the chance to know him better. A droll fellow—the very soul of ingenuity—(*He bites into the words.*) and probably the most corrupt man in London. For three years he has pursued his artistic calling.

PRINCE: And why has he never been chosen?

MALTHUS: Because he never plays.

PRINCE: Plays what?

MALTHUS: It is done by cards. How, you shall soon see. No, our President never plays. He shuffles and deals for the club.

JOHN: Convenient for him.

MALTHUS: Necessary, you should add. After all, it takes a man of brains to organize and operate a club such as ours.

PRINCE: Look here, Mr. . . . er . . .

MALTHUS: Malthus is the name.

PRINCE: Mr. Malthus, aren't these people afraid to die?

MALTHUS: Of course—very afraid. Fear is the strongest passion of all. And so it is fear you must trifle with if you wish to taste the joys of living.

JOHN: Are you afraid?

MALTHUS: Envy me, sir, envy me, for I am a coward.

JOHN: After the person is selected, how is his end carried out?

MALTHUS (*Chuckles*): One of us is chosen Death's High Priest.

JOHN (*As though shuddering*): You don't mean we—they kill each other.

MALTHUS: Exactly, exactly. Very ingenious.

JOHN: Then I might be nominated to kill my own friend.

MALTHUS: Or he to kill you. (*Agreeably*) Now shall we join the others? I believe the game is about to begin. By the way, do you like cards?

MUSIC: *Spine-tingling theme. Sneak and hold under.*

JOHN: In the main room the members quietly took their places around a large green table presided over by the President. In his hand he held a pack of cards. I dropped into a chair . . . the Prince on my left. . . . Mr. Malthus on my right. The young man with the cream tarts sat directly across from me. His face twitched nervously.

MUSIC: *Out.*

JOHN (*Beat*): Another man wiped his brow with a large red handkerchief. A tension seemed to hover over the room.

MALTHUS (*Sotto voce*): Watch for the ace of spades, which is the sign of death.

JOHN: The ace of spades.

MALTHUS: And the ace of clubs which designates the executioner of the night.

JOHN: The ace of clubs.

SOUND: *Cards shuffled.*

PRESIDENT: Your attention, gentlemen. Remember to turn over your card as soon as it is dealt.

THE YOUNG MAN WITH THE CREAM TARTS 135

MUSIC: *Agitato, suspense. Sneak in and hold under.*

JOHN: The President started dealing. I was conscious of a deadly chill . . . a contraction about my heart . . . of sweat on my back. Mr. Malthus' first card was the nine of clubs. I uncovered mine—the three of hearts. The Prince drew the king of hearts. The young man with the cream tarts gazed at his card . . . fascinated.

MUSIC: *Out.*

PRESIDENT: Turn over your card. (*Pause*) Turn it over.

YOUNG MAN: I . . . I am the . . . the killer.

PRESIDENT (*Calmly*): You will leave the room.

YOUNG MAN: The killer.

PRESIDENT: I'll call you when I'm ready.

MUSIC: *Ominous theme. Forte and fade under.*

JOHN: The deal came around again. Each man turned over his piece of pasteboard . . . but still death's card had not shown up. The players' eyes bulged in excitement. Suddenly Mr. Malthus flipped over his card.

MALTHUS (*Gasps*): No . . . no . . . can't be . . . not so.

PRESIDENT (*Quietly*): The ace of spades.

MALTHUS: Please . . . beg of you . . . cannot . . . don't want to die. I'm afraid.

MUSIC: *Up briefly and under again.*

JOHN: We left Mr. Malthus seated at the table . . . his head in his hands . . . and made our way out into the gray, dank fog of early morning. Death was about to claim Mr. Malthus in one horrible form or another, and there was nothing the Prince or I could do about it.

MUSIC: *Surges up and out.*

JOHN (*Down*): The morning newspapers carried the story.

PRINCE (*Reading*): "This morning about three o'clock, Mr. Bartholomew Malthus of 16 Chepstow Place, Westbourne Grove, on his way home from a party, fell over the upper parapet in Trafalger Square, fracturing his skull and breaking a leg and an arm. Death was instantaneous. Mr. Malthus, accompanied by a friend, was engaged in looking for a cab at the time of the unfortunate occurrence. The victim had been in bad health for some time, and it is thought his fall may have been occasioned by a seizure."

JOHN: A seizure! If they only knew.

PRINCE (*Slowly*): I know. It's ghastly!

JOHN: There's only one thing for us to do, and that's go to the police.

PRINCE: We can't do that.

JOHN: We must. If we tell them, once and for all it will break up this Suicide Club.

PRINCE: And I repeat we can't do that. We swore an oath last night that we'd reveal nothing.

JOHN: But an oath extracted by such a man wouldn't hold.

PRINCE: And what would the police's attitude be toward us? They'd hold us as accessories.

JOHN: But we're innocent, and we can prove it.

PRINCE: In our own eyes, yes; but in the eyes of the police, no.

JOHN: Then we're to allow this madman of a President to go on destroying lives?

PRINCE: We are seeing this through. Tonight we take our places around the green table at the Suicide Club!

MUSIC: *Theme of restrained excitement. Up and under.*

JOHN: That evening a strange, hushed note of excitement hung heavily over the Suicide Club. There were but a few members present, all of them subdued.

MUSIC: *Gradually out.*

JOHN (*No pause*): The President, urbane as ever, walked from member to member. He was especially cordial to the Prince and me.

SOUND: *A few background ad libs from three or four men.*

THE YOUNG MAN WITH THE CREAM TARTS

PRESIDENT: So happy to see you gentlemen back. By the way, concerning this morning's job, what did you think?

PRINCE: Splendid! According to the newspaper chaps, Mr. Malthus died instantly.

PRESIDENT: Quite likely. Poor Malthus! I shall hardly know the club without him. Nice sort of chap.

PRINCE: He seemed affable, if a bit frightened.

PRESIDENT: Quite! (*Fading*) And now if you will excuse me, I have some bookkeeping to attend to.

JOHN (*Softly*): What a monster! If only I could—

PRINCE: Not so loud, Colonel. (*Calls out*) Good evening.

YOUNG MAN (*Fading in, depressed*): Good evening.

PRINCE: The young man with the cream tarts. And how are you?

YOUNG MAN: Not so chipper. (*Bitterly*) How I wish I had never brought you two to this infamous hole.

PRINCE: Come now. No need to feel sorry for us.

JOHN (*Slightly sarcastic*): No . . . we're quite delighted at being here.

YOUNG MAN: If you could have heard old Malthus plead with me for his life. If you could have heard his scream as he fell. (*Shuddering*) How I hope tonight that I draw the ace of spaces.

SOUND (*Slightly away*): *Gavel pounding on table.*

PRESIDENT (*Slightly away*): Attention, gentlemen . . . attention, please. Kindly take your places. Places, everyone.

MUSIC: *Sneak in. Grim, ominous theme. Hold under.*

JOHN: Once again we took our places around the big green table—the young man with the cream tarts, the Prince and myself. The President, smiling pleasantly, started dealing. The cards went around once . . . twice . . . and still no ace of spades or clubs. On the third round, the young man with the cream tarts uncovered his card. He half rose out of his chair.

Music: *Out.*
President: Well, we are waiting, sir.
Young Man (*A hollow tone*): Again! Again I've drawn it—the ace of clubs.
President: How fortunate you are.
Young Man: I can't go through with it again . . . murder another helpless soul.
President: No hysterics, please.
Young Man: But I—
President (*Sternly, but without raising his voice*): You understand me, I believe. (*Pleasantly*) Now shall we continue? One for you, sir . . . one for you . . . and you . . . and you. (*Pause*) Sir, your card. Turn it over. (*A beat*)
John (*Dully*): The . . . the . . .
President: The ace of spades.
Music: *Up ominously, as a brief time bridge. Hold and out.*
President: Allow me to say that I am pleased to have met you . . . and also pleased to have done you this trifling favor. At least you cannot complain of delay.
John: No . . . I suppose I can't.
President: On the second evening. What a rum stroke of luck.
John: What are my instructions?
President: Just before two o'clock you will proceed along the Strand in the direction of the city, until you meet the young man who drew the ace of clubs.
John: Then what?
President: Leave everything in his hands. He has his instructions. And now—I wish you a very pleasant stroll. (*A pause*)
Sound: *Big Ben booming in distance. Two strokes.*
Music: *Sneak in—ominous, showing the walk of death. Hold under.*
John: I walked as though in a dream . . . a horrible nightmare of distorted shadows . . . of faint night noises. . . . Not a

THE YOUNG MAN WITH THE CREAM TARTS 139

soul passed me. I relived my past life a hundred times. Jumbled questions racked my mind. Why was I here? Would Death seize me? And the Prince—where was he? Why had he deserted me? My whole body shook and dripped with perspiration. I shivered . . . and then stopped walking as a shadow approached me.

MUSIC: *Out.*
YOUNG MAN: I—it's you! You! Why did you come?
JOHN: I . . . I hardly know.
YOUNG MAN: But you really don't want to die . . . and I . . . I don't want to murder again. (*Wildly*) But I have to . . . don't I?
JOHN: Yes . . . I suppose you do.
YOUNG MAN: Yes . . . of course. And with this rope. Look —for your neck, just as he said . . . wrapped round and tightened until . . . until—
PRINCE (*Quietly*): Until nothing, my insane friend.
JOHN: Your Highness!
YOUNG MAN: You—What are you—?
PRINCE: Don't move. I know how to use this revolver.
YOUNG MAN: So you followed me?
PRINCE: Every step of the way.
YOUNG MAN: What are you going to do?
PRINCE: You'll know soon enough.
YOUNG MAN: I'm glad you're here—but you'll never—
JOHN: He's reaching for something. Stop him.
PRINCE: Drop it.
YOUNG MAN (*Mumbling*): Too . . . late.
JOHN: What did you put in your mouth?
YOUNG MAN (*Swallowing*): Something quick . . . very quick . . . and . . . and . . .
PRINCE: Poison!
YOUNG MAN (*Gasping*): Yes . . . best way . . . out . . . the

easiest way . . . (*Groaning*) Be gone in . . . minute . . . gone. . . .

MUSIC: *Cuts in over—up briefly and out.*

JOHN: But I'm still puzzled. I appreciate your saving my life, but I'd like to know a few details.

PRINCE: As the young man with the cream tarts stated, I followed him.

JOHN (*Quizzically*): By the way, early this afternoon, where did you disappear to? You were gone several hours.

PRINCE: Now you're spoiling my surprise.

JOHN: I have already had more surprises than I can digest.

PRINCE: This afternoon, I realized that the President of the Club should be punished . . . but I also realized I could not go to the police.

JOHN: And?

PRINCE: So I visited the Bohemian Embassy.

JOHN: Why?

PRINCE: To select the eight stout men now surrounding the Suicide Club. Here is what I intend to do. (*Fading a bit*) I want you to listen very carefully, for you will have to . . .

MUSIC: *Up and under.*

JOHN: Within the next half-hour we were back at the Suicide Club. The long mirror at one end of the room reflected a strange scene. Twenty members of the club sat around the long green table. The President was in his usual place . . . and Prince Florizel and myself sat across from him. The subjects of the Prince, called in from the Bohemian Embassy, stood in the background—watching closely for any sign of trouble. (*Music out*) Finally the Prince rose and spoke to the huddled, dejected group. . . .

PRINCE: My position is a most peculiar one. I cannot rely upon the law to deal with you. We stand outside the gates of ordinary justice. So from now on, *I* represent justice. As many of

THE YOUNG MAN WITH THE CREAM TARTS 141

you have been driven into this strait by lack of money, I shall help you find employment. I even have a solution for your honored President.

CAST: *Surprised ad libs.*

PRINCE: Mr. President, I have a diversion to propose. Colonel Geraldine, my aide, will explain it to you.

JOHN: Perhaps the President likes to travel—say on the Continent.

PRESIDENT: What are you driving at?

JOHN: I am planning a trip on the Continent . . . and I ask—or should I say I request that you accompany me.

PRESIDENT: Why?

JOHN: For one very good reason. . . . Travel has its dangers. Switzerland has many high crags and deep lakes. Hunting accidents in the Black Forest are not uncommon. It is so easy to be unseated from one's horse and trampled to death. Men have been known to fall in the path of a rushing train.

PRESIDENT: That won't happen to me.

JOHN: Perhaps you are right. But the power of perpetual suggestion can force action even upon the strongest character. Perhaps even upon you.

PRESIDENT: It's a living death.

JOHN: A subtle one which may strike at any hour . . . on any day. Tonight . . . tomorrow . . . next month . . . a year from today. Perhaps it will come quietly . . . perhaps violently.

PRESIDENT: You seem sure of yourself.

JOHN: I am—*very sure!* Because the decision rests with *you.* You are the one to name the day and the hour. You who have held the lives of others so cheaply should not hesitate to make your decision. And remember—the sooner you make it . . . the less mental torture you will suffer.

MUSIC: *Forte and then segue to narrative theme.*

JOHN: It happened three months later in a lonely section of Austria. The land was swampy and filled with quicksand. Suddenly, and without warning, the President of the Suicide Club made a dash down the slimy trail. I followed quickly. And there—at the edge of the quicksand, I found a few faint footprints . . . and a hat floating in the black muck. Was it an accident . . . or was it the power of suggestion? Who—knows?

MUSIC: *Up to curtain and out.*

THE END

The Spy

by James Fenimore Cooper

MUSIC: *A strong narrative theme. Forte and fade under.*
NARRATOR: It was near the close of the year 1780, when a solitary traveler rode through a valley in Westchester, a common ground for both British and American troops. Suddenly the man reined in his animal and stared ahead. In front of him lay a country house superior to that usually found in this rural area. In appearance the traveler looked to be fifty. He wore a powdered wig, and covering one eye was a black patch. Almost too casually he shifted his gaze toward the direction from which he had just come. And then he spurred his tired horse into a gallop. A few minutes later he was standing before the main door of the house.
MUSIC: *Out.*
SOUND: *Brisk rapping on door with riding crop. After a brief pause door opens.*
FRANCES: Good evening, sir.
HENRY (*Gruffly*): Good evening. I am a traveler seeking food and bed.
FRANCES: This is not an inn, sir. It's my father's residence.
HENRY: And your father is—
FRANCES: Mr. James Wharton of New York.
HENRY: Then I am not mistaken. Your father is the Tory.
FRANCES: We are neutral, sir.
HENRY: You have a brother—a captain in His Majesty's army.
FRANCES (*Falteringly*): Y-yes, sir.
HENRY: A scoundrel, so it is said.

WHARTON (*Away*): Frances, who is there?
FRANCES (*Calling back*): A traveler, Father.
WHARTON (*Fading in*): Then please bid him step in. The night air is cold, indeed.
HENRY: Good evening, sir.
WHARTON: Good evening.
HENRY: It is my understanding that your daughter here is betrothed to a Major Peyton Dunwoodie of the Virginia Horse, a rebel of the worst order.
FRANCES: He may be a rebel, as you put it, but he's also a brave man.
HENRY (*In his normal voice*): As brave as your dear brother, would you say?
FRANCES (*Stunned*): Henry!
WHARTON: My dear son.
HENRY: Father . . . Frances.
MUSIC: *A short dramatic bridge. Forte and out.*
WHARTON: But, Henry, this was an awful risk you took—slipping through the American lines in disguise.
HENRY: Perhaps you're right, Father, but remember I haven't seen either of you in a year.
FRANCES: But if you're caught, you'll be held as a spy.
HENRY: There is nothing here to spy on.
WHARTON: Remember what happened to Major Andre? The Rebels are constantly passing through here.
HENRY: Have they bothered you?
WHARTON: No, for I have kept, as far as they know, a strict neutrality.
FRANCES: And then Peyton has done everything to see that we are not molested.
HENRY: I knew you could count on Dunwoodie.
WHARTON: If it weren't for him, we'd be in a sorry fix. If it were known that I am a Tory, everything we own would be confiscated by the Rebels.

THE SPY

HENRY: And you're to keep up that pretense, Father, even if it means you're turning against me.
WHARTON: Dunwoodie knows different.
FRANCES: But he'll say nothing.
WHARTON (*Wearily*): I'll offer up a prayer when this revolution ends.
HENRY: And if it doesn't end the way you think it will, you'd better make plans to sail to England.
FRANCES: You think, then, there's a chance that England will lose?
HENRY: Washington is offering more resistance than we had bargained for. If America receives the aid of France, it will make our winning that much more difficult.
CAESAR (*Fading in*): Excuse me, Mr. Wharton, but there's a man to see you.
FRANCES (*Alarmed*): Henry, go up the back stairs.
HENRY: Who is he, Caesar?
CAESAR: Harvey Birch, the peddler. He's got some tobaccy for you, Mr. Wharton.
WHARTON: I'll see him presently.
HENRY: It's all right. Have him come in, Caesar.
FRANCES: But he'll recognize you.
HENRY: Harvey Birch can be trusted.
BIRCH (*Fading in*): Good evening, Mr. Wharton . . . Miss Frances.
WHARTON: Good evening, Birch.
FRANCES: Evening.
BIRCH: Your disguise is quite convincing, Captain Wharton.
HENRY: Thank you, Harvey.
WHARTON: You won't give him away?
BIRCH: Since I supplied the disguise, I hardly think so.
FRANCES: What do you mean—you supplied the disguise?
BIRCH: Just what I said, Miss Frances.
HENRY: Harvey Birch has been engaged by General Clinton

to supply him with information concerning the Rebel troop movements.

BIRCH: And from the way Major Dunwoodie and his troops keep after me, I seem to have struck a hard bargain. Washington has now raised the price on my head to fifty guineas.

WHARTON: Then how do you dare penetrate the American lines?

BIRCH: There are ways, Mr. Wharton.

WHARTON: You must be greedy for money.

BIRCH (*Coolly*): I am. I also want to see the Rebels beaten. Captain, do you still have the pass I gave you?

HENRY: I do.

BIRCH: Were you forced to use it on the way here?

HENRY: Yes, once. When I passed through the American pickets at White Plains.

BIRCH: Then you very well may do so again when you leave tonight.

FRANCES: But he's just arrived.

BIRCH: You had better cut short your visit. A troop of Virginia Horse under Captain Lawton is only a few miles away. Lawton serves under Major Dunwoodie.

HENRY: I'll stay here until morning.

BIRCH: And I advise you to leave immediately with me.

HENRY: I brought myself in, and I can take myself back, Harvey. Our bargain called for you to supply me with a disguise and a pass, and you were to let me know when the coast was clear. Evidently you were mistaken about the last.

BIRCH: I was, and that's why I'm here to warn you. If you're caught in that disguise and carrying that pass— (*He pauses significantly.*)

HENRY: I'm staying.

BIRCH: I've warned you. Here's your tobacco, Mr. Wharton. That'll be ten shillings—hard money.

Sound: *Clink of money on table.*
Wharton: There you are, and thank you.
Henry: Never too late to make a profit.
Birch: That's right. Good night. And a last word—watch out for Captain Lawton. The devil can't deceive him. I've tried, and succeeded only once.
Music: *An ominous bridge. Forte and fade under.*
Narrator: Two members of the Wharton family retired that night with troubled minds. As for Henry, he slept quietly. The next morning at breakfast, Caesar entered the room hurriedly.
Music: *Out.*
Caesar: Run, Mr. Henry, run! Here comes the rebel horse. Look out the window.
Wharton: Quick! Out the back way.
Frances: Too late. They're circling the grounds.
Henry (*Calmly*): Help me on with my disguise, Father. The wig . . . and now . . . the eye patch . . . and this cloak. If they ask you who I am, tell them just a stranger whom you gave lodging to for the night.
Caesar: Shall I let them in, Mr. Wharton?
Wharton: You have no choice.
Caesar (*Fading*): I'll tell them you're at breakfast, and can't be disturbed.
Wharton: Poor old Caesar! He's so fond of you, Henry.
Henry: You're more worried than I am. Come, let's finish our breakfast.
Sound: *Clatter of dishes. In distance* Lawton *can be heard ad libbing.*
Frances: I'm too nervous to eat anything.
Henry: If you value my life, eat.
Lawton (*Fading in*): Good morning.
Wharton: Good morning, sir.

LAWTON: You have no cause for alarm. I have only a few questions to ask you.
WHARTON (*Stumbling*): By all means.
LAWTON: A peddler named Harvey Birch lives nearby, I understand.
WHARTON: He does.
LAWTON: Have you seen him?
WHARTON: We used to, sir.
FRANCES: He was here last night.
LAWTON: Indeed!
WHARTON: He brought me some tobacco, which I bought.
LAWTON: And he brought nothing more?
WHARTON: Not a thing.
LAWTON: Too bad I missed him, for I want nothing more than to break Mr. Birch of his unsocial habits. I have a nice drawing room waiting for him—the guard house.
WHARTON: What has he done?
LAWTON: Birch is a spy in the pay of the British, and a very active one. If I catch him, he'll dangle from the limbs of one of his namesakes. Has anyone else been here?
WHARTON: Only this gentleman, sir.
FRANCES: He's a stranger to whom we gave lodging.
LAWTON: I'm sorry to see the gentleman has a head cold.
HENRY (*In a gruff voice*): I have no cold.
LAWTON: Since you've covered your own hair with that dusty wig, I thought you were protecting it from the cold. Might I examine it?
HENRY (*Pointedly*): You are.
LAWTON: Ah! Your hair indeed is black. And this eye patch— (*As though ripping it off*) Once it's removed, you look completely changed. Quite a handsome young man, indeed. Allow me to introduce myself. I'm Captain John Lawton of the Virginia Horse.

HENRY: And I am Captain Henry Wharton of His Majesty's 60th regiment of foot.
LAWTON (*Slowly*): Captain Wharton, I pity you.
WHARTON: He is not a spy.
FRANCES: He's done no harm. He came only to see us.
LAWTON: Captain Wharton, were you ignorant that our pickets have been below you for several days?
HENRY: I didn't know it until I reached them, and then it was too late to retreat. I had to pass through them. I came here to see my father and sister, thinking that your parties were around Peekskill.
FRANCES: Please let him go.
LAWTON: That I cannot.
FRANCES: But he's not a spy, believe me.
LAWTON: I'm not the commander of the party, Miss Wharton. Major Dunwoodie will have to decide what is to be done with your brother.
WHARTON: Major Peyton Dunwoodie?
LAWTON: Yes.
FRANCES: Then we're safe.
LAWTON: I hope so. He should be here any minute. Captain Wharton, I'm forced to place you under guard.
MUSIC: *A short bridge of suspense. Forte and out.*
DUNWOODIE: What you ask of me is impossible, Frances. This is no game we play at; it's war. Your brother is a prisoner, and as such I can't let him go. I can't forfeit my honor.
FRANCES: Yet you swear you love me . . . that you want to marry me.
DUNWOODIE: And I swear it again, but you can't use that to make me turn Henry loose. When I know the circumstances, perhaps I can accept his parole, and later arrange for his exchange. I have some influence with Washington.
FRANCES: Have you seen Henry?

Dunwoodie: No. I came directly to you. I'll go to him now. I'll do everything possible. Believe me, Frances.

Frances: If anything happens to Henry, it would mean the end of everything between us, Peyton, for I couldn't marry a man who had been instrumental in causing his death.

Dunwoodie: I didn't capture your brother. All I can repeat is that I'll do everything to save him.

Music: *An ominous bridge. Forte and out.*

Henry: There's nothing more to tell you, Peyton. I used this disguise to enable me to visit my father and sister, without incurring the danger of becoming a prisoner of war.

Dunwoodie: And you passed through our lines in it?

Henry: I did.

Dunwoodie: How?

Henry: By using this pass. Here. (*Beat*) As it bears the signature of Washington, I assume it's forged.

Dunwoodie: Where did you get this paper?

Henry: That's a question I believe you have no right to ask.

Dunwoodie: I'm merely trying to aid you. This signature is no forgery. It's Washington's signature. The rest of the paper is in another hand. I'm going to have to bring you to our headquarters at the Highlands . . . and I cannot accept your parole.

Henry: It's just as well, for I didn't intend to give you my word.

Dunwoodie: We leave in the morning.

Music: *A theme of impending doom. Forte and fade under.*

Narrator: Major Dunwoodie left his friend, Henry Wharton, under heavy guard and went out into the cool October night air.

Music: *Out, and into:*

Sound: *Bull frogs "chug-a-lugging" away in distance. Sustain under.*

Narrator (*No pause*): He had proceeded but a few steps when Captain Lawton glided into view.

THE SPY

LAWTON (*Softly*): Psst! Major.
DUNWOODIE: What is it? Oh, you, Captain Lawton.
LAWTON: Keep your voice down, sir.
DUNWOODIE (*In the same sotto voce*): What's wrong?
LAWTON: To your right, sir. See—a shadow.
DUNWOODIE: Probably one of our guards.
LAWTON: It's not. Unless I'm very wrong, it's a person we want.
DUNWOODIE: He's coming this way.
LAWTON: Draw back into the shadows.
DUNWOODIE: When he comes by, grab him.
LAWTON: Ready. Here he is. (*Loudly*) I have him.
DUNWOODIE: I have his arm.
SOUND: *A struggle.*
LAWTON: No you don't. Let's take a look at you. (*Beat*) I thought so—Mr. Harvey Birch.
BIRCH: I am. This makes the second time you've captured me, Captain Lawton.
LAWTON: The first time you got away. But not this time.
DUNWOODIE: You're a traitor, Birch, and I have the right to order your execution this night.
BIRCH: You should allow me to prepare myself.
DUNWOODIE: You're too dangerous to the liberties of America to be allowed to live. Time and again you've gained information, which you've sold to the British. Tomorrow I'm going to hang you.
BIRCH: Would Washington act so hastily?
DUNWOODIE: Yes, in your case, I believe he would.
BIRCH: I demand that my case be brought before him.
LAWTON (*Surprised*): And why would the commander-in-chief give your case special attention?
DUNWOODIE: What have you got in your hand?
BIRCH: Something you'll not see. I know the conditions of my service.
DUNWOODIE: If that paper is important, let me have it.

BIRCH: No—it dies with me. (*Sound of swallowing*)
LAWTON: He's swallowing it.
DUNWOODIE: Stop him.
BIRCH (*Gulping*): No—it's too late. It's gone.
DUNWOODIE: Whatever it was does not matter. Tomorrow you swing. Take him to the guard, Captain.
LAWTON: Yes, sir. (*Suddenly*) Stop! He's taken my pistol.
BIRCH: Stand back, both of you. And now your pistol also, Major Dunwoodie. Thank you.
LAWTON: I don't know how he did it.
BIRCH: A peddler develops a quick hand, Captain Lawton. And don't come near me, or call the guard. All I want is a few seconds. I'm sparing you, both of you.
DUNWOODIE: Why?
BIRCH: I can't explain.
DUNWOODIE: Who is your accomplice?
BIRCH: A great man.
LAWTON: That's all you can tell us?
BIRCH (*Pointedly*): That's all I *will* tell you. And now—good night. (*Fading*) I'll leave your pistols at the edge of the meadow.
LAWTON: We'll catch you sooner or later, Birch.
BIRCH (*Away*): For your sake, and for others like you, I trust you don't. (*Fading away*) Good evening, gentlemen.
LAWTON: Shall I call out the guard, Major?
DUNWOODIE: No. Let him get away. He spared our lives.
LAWTON: Why?
DUNWOODIE: I can't explain it. He's a strange sort of man. Too bad he isn't on our side.
LAWTON: He'll turn up again, and when we least expect him.
DUNWOODIE: I almost hope he doesn't. Tomorrow we'll move Captain Wharton out of his reach.
MUSIC: *Sombre theme. Forte and fade under.*

THE SPY

NARRATOR: The next morning, under a strong guard, Henry Wharton was taken to Washington's headquarters at the Highlands, preparatory to standing trial. Several days later, by order of Washington, Mr. Wharton and Frances were removed to the same place. And trailing them was Harvey Birch, the spy!

MUSIC: *Forte and fade under.*

NARRATOR: Three days later the trial of Captain Henry Wharton began. Colonel Singleton, president of the board of three officers, spoke to the prisoner.

MUSIC: *Out.*

SINGLETON: It is an accusation against you, that, as an officer of the enemy, you passed the pickets in disguise . . . and you therefore have subjected yourself to the punishment of a spy.

HENRY: It is true that I passed your pickets in disguise.

SINGLETON: The prisoner can retract that declaration, if he pleases. His confession, if taken, goes fully to prove the charge.

HENRY (*Proudly*): I retract nothing.

MUSIC: *A grim theme. Forte and fade under.*

NARRATOR: After the court had heard the damaging testimony of the prisoner, Captain Lawton and Major Dunwoodie took the stand. They were followed by Caesar, the servant, and Mr. Wharton. It now seemed possible that Henry Wharton might escape the charge of spying, and be committed as a prisoner of war. And then Frances Wharton was called in.

MUSIC: *Out.*

SINGLETON: Miss Wharton, did either you or your father receive word from your brother that he would pay you a visit?

FRANCES: No. We knew nothing of it until he arrived.

SINGLETON: Was this his first visit?

FRANCES: No. It was his fourth over a long period.

SINGLETON: During his first three visits, was he in disguise?

FRANCES: No, he wore his uniform. At the time the English forces were in the area.
SINGLETON: During this last visit did he at any time leave the house?
FRANCES: No.
SINGLETON: Aside from you and your father and possibly the servants, did he converse with anyone else?
FRANCES: With no one—no one, excepting a neighbor.
SINGLETON: Who is this neighbor?
FRANCES: The peddler—Harvey Birch.
BIZ: *Low surprised ad libs from spectators.*
SOUND: *Gavel struck on wood, sharply.*
HENRY (*Interrupting*): May I remind the court that Harvey Birch is a known sympathizer to the English cause. Also, he has already been condemned to death by your tribunal, if caught. Birch merely supplied me with my disguise and the pass I used.
SINGLETON (*Solemnly*): Captain Wharton, a more dangerous man than Harvey Birch is not ranked among the minor members of our foe. He is a spy—artful, elusive, scheming. He has been a constant thorn in our side. Your connection with him is unfortunate.
SOUND: *Rap of gavel on wood.*
MUSIC: *Dramatic. Forte and fade.*
NARRATOR: The court adjourned. Fifteen minutes later it again assembled. Henry Wharton rose and faced the board. The witnesses leaned forward eagerly as Colonel Singleton read from a piece of paper.
SINGLETON: "Captain Henry Wharton, of His Majesty's 60th regiment of foot, has been detected in passing the lines of the American army, and in disguise. Thereby, according to the laws of war, he is liable to death. This court recommends him to be executed by hanging, before nine o'clock tomorrow morning."

SOUND: *Gavel struck twice.*
MUSIC: *Forte and fade under.*
NARRATOR: No sooner had the court adjourned, than Major Peyton Dunwoodie had jumped into the saddle and pelted for Washington's headquarters. Meanwhile, Henry Wharton, in company with his father and sister, awaited word.
MUSIC: *Out.*
WHARTON (*Wearily*): He's been gone over two hours.
FRANCES: I have every faith in Peyton. I feel certain he can get Washington to set aside the sentence.
HENRY: I wouldn't count on it.
FRANCES: Even Colonel Singleton is speaking in your behalf; and now, since he presided over the board, he should carry extra weight.
HENRY: No matter what the decision may be, I want you to keep your promise to Peyton to marry him.
FRANCES: How can I think of marriage at a moment like this?
HENRY: You love Peyton. Don't let anything stand in the way.
FRANCES: I promise.
HENRY: And you're to take Father with you.
WHARTON: You mustn't give up hope so easily.
HENRY: I'm prepared for any eventuality, Father.
DUNWOODIE (*From outside*): Open up, sentry.
SENTRY: Yes, sir.
FRANCES: It's Peyton.
SOUND: *Bolt slid back. Door open.*
HENRY: What's the final verdict?
DUNWOODIE: Here—read.
HENRY (*Reads*): "The sentence is approved. George Washington."
MUSIC: *Grim. Forte and fade.*
NARRATOR: At the request of Henry Wharton, Major Dunwoodie sent Caesar off to a nearby village to bring a minister. Meanwhile, Henry, weary of pacing his small and heavily-

guarded room, fell into a half-slumber. The afternoon had worn itself into autumn grayness by the time Caesar returned, a weird-appearing man at his heels. The stranger's countenance was sharp and unbending. His hair, a mixture of gray and black, was long and lank, and a pair of thick spectacles covered his eyes. His clothing, from head to toe, was of rusty black. This was the appearance of the man whom Caesar presented to Captain Lawton, in command of the guard detail.

MUSIC: *Out.*

LAWTON: And where did you find this . . . individual, Caesar?

CAESAR: In Fishkill, Captain.

LAWTON: And you, sir, you are a minister?

BIRCH (*A sepulchral tone*): I am.

LAWTON: Not a very prepossessing one, I might say.

BIRCH (*Thunders*): Judge not, lest ye be judged. Pursue, if ye must thy war-like ways, but do not take it upon thyself to criticize one engaged in the work of the Lord.

LAWTON: I'm not deaf, sir.

BIRCH: Nor am I blind to thy evil ways.

LAWTON (*Nettled*): You're here to aid Captain Wharton.

BIRCH: I am here to lend him comfort.

LAWTON: Very well. (*Suddenly*) Hold on! I've seen you some place.

BIRCH: Your ways, your haunts, your companions are not mine.

LAWTON: But I can't place you.

BIRCH: Allow me to be led to the prisoner, so that I may cut short this distasteful conversation.

LAWTON: Caesar, give this pass to the sentry. It will admit the reverend.

CAESAR: I'd like to be with the captain, too, sir.

LAWTON: The pass will admit you, also.

CAESAR: Thank you, Captain Lawton.

LAWTON: On your way.

Birch (*In a ringing voice*): Beware lest thy weakness driveth thee headlong unto the bosom of destruction. The ways of Providence are not to be judged by men. Many are called, but few are chosen.

Lawton (*Impatiently*): Be off with you.

Birch: It is easier to talk of humility than to feel it. Remember my words, vile worm. (*Fading*) And if you heed not what I say, I call upon your head the wrath that will make of you a publican and a Pharisee. . . . (*A pause, then*):

Sound: *Bolt drawn. Door open.*

Sentry: Here you are. I'll leave the door open.

Birch: Sentry, know thy duty, but do not overstep thy bounds.

Sentry: I have my orders.

Birch: Can not this servitor and I have privacy in spending a few moments unobserved with this man whose soul will soon depart from his body?

Caesar: Mr. Sentry, this man is all right.

Sentry (*Growls*): Oh, I suppose it's all right. I'll close the door, then. Let me know when you're done with him.

Sound: *Door closed.*

Caesar: Mr. Henry, sir, I bring the minister to you.

Henry (*Fading in*): He makes enough noise, I must say.

Birch (*In his normal voice*): But it answers the purpose.

Henry (*Amazed*): Who are you?

Birch (*Calmly*): Under this disguise, I'm your friend Harvey Birch.

Henry: Good heavens—Harvey!

Birch (*Lowering his voice*): Not so loud! Caesar, stand by the door and listen.

Caesar: Yes, Mr. Birch.

Birch: My neck is practically in a noose this very second, but I couldn't stand by and see you hanged—not when you are innocent.

HENRY: But this disguise . . . your getting passed in here—how did you manage?

BIRCH: I met Caesar as he was going to Fishkill to get the minister. Between us we worked out this plan. If it works, you're saved; if not, we'll both swing in the morning.

HENRY: You'd better clear out, for you'll never smuggle me past the guard.

BIRCH: Unless you leave with me—and within the hour—your chance is lost. After darkness tonight, your guard is being doubled, and you're to be allowed to see no one. And that order comes from higher in command than your friend, Dunwoodie.

HENRY (*As though shrugging*): I may as well say "yes," for I've nothing to lose.

BIRCH (*In a low voice*): Here, put this on.

HENRY: What is it?

BIRCH: A black mask. Caesar's changing places with you.

HENRY: That's not fair to him.

BIRCH: They'll not bother him. Your friend, Dunwoodie, will get him off. Here—slip it on. (*Beat*) There!

HENRY: I'll never get through wearing this.

BIRCH: It's already starting to get dark.

CAESAR (*Whimsically*): You know, Mr. Henry, I don't think you look like me.

BIRCH: And now this wig. So! Now you, Caesar, slip on this black wig. No, no, straighten it out. And now the pair of you change clothes, right down to your shoes. And hurry.

CAESAR: I'm getting the best of this bargain.

BIRCH: Don't waste time in talk. Hurry, I tell you. Every second counts.

HENRY (*Grunting*): I still say we won't get away with this.

BIRCH: Now slip on his coat, Captain. There we have it. And there's only one man in the American army who could detect you.

HENRY: And who is he?
BIRCH: The man who made you prisoner—Captain Lawton. Now, you, Caesar, you sit here in the shadow, and don't speak a word to anyone. If you do, you'll betray us. Understand!
CAESAR: I'll keep quiet as long as possible.
BIRCH: Then we're off.
CAESAR: Good luck to you, Captain Henry.
HENRY: God bless you, Caesar.
BIRCH: Follow me, Henry, and don't talk, or look back, or give any sign of anything wrong. And walk slowly. Don't run unless I tell you to do so.
HENRY: I understand.
BIRCH (*Raising his voice*): Open up, guard. I am done.
MUSIC: *Ominous. Sneak in and hold under.*
NARRATOR: The door swung open. Harvey Birch and Henry Wharton stepped into the corridor, the sentry shutting and bolting the door after them. When the pair stepped out into the autumn shadows, they encountered a dozen dragoons loitering about. Followed by Henry, Birch moved past them. Out of the corner of his eye, the peddler could see Major Dunwoodie and Captain Lawton in conversation. Birch and Henry had nearly cleared the dragoons, when one of them blocked their path.
MUSIC: *Out.*
DRAGOON: You, psalm singer! Have you done your duty!
BIRCH (*In his assumed voice*): Aye, wastrel, I have indeed, and I leave behind a young man ready to meet his fate, his mind now at rest.
DRAGOON: Then you have time to give us a psalm.
BIRCH: Be not blasphemous!
BIZ: *Other dragoons ad lib:* "Yes, sing for us." "A bright tune."
BIRCH (*Thunders*): Silence! Blasphemers! At least have respect for me. (*In low voice*) Henry, stroll away from me . . . and wait.

HENRY (*Sotto*): I understand.
BIRCH (*To the others*): I shall call your attention, my brethren, to that portion of Scripture which you will find in the—
LAWTON (*Fading in*): What's taking place here?
DRAGOON: We were just having sport with the psalm singer, Captain Lawton.
BIRCH: Aye, and disrespectful they are.
LAWTON: Clear away you men.
BIZ: *Voices saying: "Yes, sir." "Sorry, sir." A few ad libs as they fade away.*
LAWTON: You, are you done with Captain Wharton?
BIRCH: I am.
LAWTON: Then off with you. (*Suddenly*) Hold on!
BIRCH: Yes?
LAWTON: Why is Caesar accompanying you? (*Calls out*) Caesar!
BIRCH (*Quickly*): Caesar, as you call him, is accompanying me so that he may get my copy of "Thoughts on Eternity," which he will deliver to Captain Wharton, so that he may compose his mind during these last hours.
LAWTON: Very well. You know, I've seen you before somewhere.
BIRCH: I doubt that, sir. What is your name, sir?
LAWTON: Captain John Lawton.
BIRCH (*Promptly*): I've never heard of you before, let alone seen you. And now I wish you a good evening.
MUSIC: *Repeat the previous ominous theme. Sneak in and hold under.*
NARRATOR: With dignity Harvey Birch strolled toward the waiting Henry Wharton, and together they set off, Captain Lawton staring after them. Every step was a torturous mile to the escaping pair. Any second they expected a cry and a volley of shot. Still they kept on.

Music: *Out.*

Birch: Don't look back whatever you do. And keep slightly in back of me as though you were the servant you're supposed to be.

Henry: Where are we headed?

Birch: To that woods directly ahead. Once we gain it, they'll never catch us.

Henry: I'm hoping I have the strength to reach it.

Birch: They've captured me four times, and each time I've gotten away. This will make the fifth.

Henry: I wonder then why you follow your calling.

Birch: Because I serve a great man.

Biz (*This can be faintly heard in the background*): *Excited ad libbing.*

Henry: They've discovered my escape.

Birch (*Philosophically*): I'd hoped for more time.

Henry: Look—they're taking to their horses.

Sound (*Far-to-near perspective*): *Rifle shot.*

Birch: On the run. Come on!

Henry: How much farther?

Birch (*Panting a bit with the exertion*): A few more yards.

Henry: Here they come.

Birch: Run faster.

Henry (*Panting*): These shoes are slowing me down.

Birch: Here—in here . . . these bushes.

Sound: *Crashing noise of bushes as they are trampled. Up briefly and out.*

Birch: We're safe, now.

Sound: *Troop of cavalry fading in from distance, at gallop.*

Henry: They'll find us.

Birch: A chance we'll have to take. Keep down.

Sound: *Horses fade in rapidly and then out into the distance.*

Henry: We're safe. Thank heaven.

BIRCH: You're not safe until you reach New York and the British lines. (*Fading*) We have a long walk ahead of us, but I know the path. Follow me. (*A pause, then*):

HENRY (*Fading in*): Look—ahead of us—our outposts. You need come no farther, Harvey, unless you wish. I can make my way from here in.

BIRCH: Then I'll take my leave.

HENRY: Will I see you again?

BIRCH: I can't say.

HENRY: This war can't last forever.

BIRCH: It may end sooner than we expect. So long as the Americans stand, they are too good for the best troops in the royal army.

HENRY (*Sternly*): You talk as though you wished Washington's army success.

BIRCH: I wish success to the good cause only.

HENRY: You're a brave man, Harvey Birch.

BIRCH (*Simply*): If my small bit helps, I'm well rewarded. Good-bye.

MUSIC: *A powerful theme. Forte and fade under.*

NARRATOR: The lessening shadow of the war shifted to the south. The end of the long war was in sight. And when many of the American troops were shifted to the southern theatre, with them went Major Peyton Dunwoodie and his bride, Frances. Accompanying them were Mr. Wharton and Caesar. (*Beat*) Just before the American Army moved to Yorktown, General Washington admitted to his presence a strange visitor.

MUSIC: *Out.*

WASHINGTON: It has been many months since we've met.

BIRCH: Almost a year, Your Excellency.

WASHINGTON: Harvey Birch, the time has come when our connections must cease. Henceforth and forever we must be strangers.

BIRCH: I'm sorry to learn that, sir.
WASHINGTON: It's necessary. Since I assumed command of the Army, it has become my duty to know many men, who, like yourself, have been my silent arms in procuring intelligence. I have trusted you above all others. On your fidelity depended the fortunes of many men. You held their lives in your hand.
BIRCH: Thank you, General.
WASHINGTON: And while you posed as a spy of the enemy, never have you given the British any information other than that I instructed you to give. Many times you risked your life. And if you had been caught, there was nothing I could have done to save you.
BIRCH: That was our bargain, General.
WASHINGTON: It is now my duty to pay you for these services. I wish it could be a large sum, but ours is a poor country.
BIRCH: I'll not touch a penny of it, sir.
WASHINGTON: But you're getting older. What will you subsist on?
BIRCH: My hands.
WASHINGTON: Understand, you must go to your grave with a reputation of having been an enemy of America. That veil cannot be lifted for years—perhaps never.
BIRCH: I'm content.
WASHINGTON: Once I gave you a paper. Do you still have it?
BIRCH: No, General. I was forced to swallow it.
WASHINGTON: I believe I understand. Would you like a similar one?
BIRCH: I would treasure it.
WASHINGTON: You shall have it, my very faithful friend.
MUSIC: *Pay-off pattern. Forte and fade under.*
NARRATOR: Years later, during the War of 1812, there occurred an important action in the west—the Battle of Lundy's Lane. During it, an old man, an unknown American volunteer, fell

in action; a man who had fought bravely. Under a flag of truce, the exchanging of the wounded and dead fell upon the shoulders of General Sir Henry Wharton, the same man whose life Harvey Birch had saved during the Revolution. His American counterpart was General John Lawton, the Virginian cavalryman, who, years before, had captured Henry Wharton. In inspecting the dead, Sir Henry and General Lawton paused by the body of the American volunteer.

MUSIC: *Out.*

LAWTON: Poor fellow! He fought valiantly for us today, Sir Henry. (*Pause*) His face is familiar.

HENRY (*Pointedly*): You always were very keen at remembering faces, General Lawton.

LAWTON: Look—he's wearing a small tin box around his neck.

HENRY: May as well open it.

LAWTON: There's a piece of paper inside, Sir Henry. (*A pause*)

HENRY: What does it say?

LAWTON (*Dazed*): If only I had known at the time. Here, Sir Henry, you read it.

HENRY (*Reads*): "Circumstances of political importance, which involve the lives and fortunes of many, have hitherto kept secret what this paper reveals. Harvey Birch has for years been a faithful and unrequited servant of his country. Though man does not, may God reward him for his unselfish conduct. . . . Signed . . . George Washington."

MUSIC: *Curtain. Forte. Hold and out.*

THE END

The Great Stone Face

by Nathaniel Hawthorne

NARRATOR: One afternoon a mother and her little boy sat at the door of their cottage, talking about the Great Stone Face. They had but to lift their eyes, and there it was plainly to be seen, with the sunshine brightening all its features.

MUSIC: *A narrative theme, majestic in tone. Sneak in and hold under.*

NARRATOR: Embosomed amongst a family of stone mountains, there was a valley so spacious that it contained many thousand inhabitants. All the people had a kind of familiarity with the Great Stone Face, which was a work of Nature formed on the side of a mountain by some immense rocks. It seemed as if an enormous giant had sculptured his own likeness on the precipice. There was the broad forehead, the nose, and the vast lips, which, if they could have spoken, would have rolled thunderous accents from one end of the valley to the other. Truly, the Great Stone Face seemed alive! Its features were noble, and the expression grand and sweet, as if it were the glow of a vast, warm heart, that embraced all mankind. According to the people, the valley owed much of its fertility to this benign expression that was continually beaming over it.

MUSIC: *Out.*

NARRATOR: And so it was that a mother and her little boy sat at their cottage door, talking about the Great Stone Face.

ERNEST (*As a young boy*): Mother, I wish the Great Stone Face could speak. Its face is so kind, I'm sure its voice would be the same. If I were to see a man with such a face, I'm certain I should love him.

MOTHER: If an old prophecy should come to pass, we may see a man with exactly such a face as that.

ERNEST (*Eagerly*): What prophecy? Tell me.

MOTHER: It is a story older even than the original Indian settlers. It is said that some day a child will be born hereabouts, who will be destined to become the noblest person of his time, and whose face will bear an exact resemblance to the Great Stone Face.

ERNEST: And has this man ever appeared among us?

MOTHER: No. He has not yet appeared.

ERNEST: I hope that I shall live to see him.

MOTHER: Perhaps you may, Ernest, perhaps you may.

MUSIC: *Repeat the opening narrative theme. Forte and fade under.*

NARRATOR: And Ernest never forgot the story that his mother told him. It was always in his mind, whenever he looked upon the Great Stone Face. He grew up in the valley, assisting his mother. Ernest had no teacher, but in his mind the Great Stone Face became one to him. When the day's work was over, he would gaze at it, addressing it.

ERNEST: I like talking to you, Great Stone Face, even though you cannot really answer me. I hope to grow up to be a good man—not a great one. If I can do good and help others, then I shall be happy. Even now, each day I try to accomplish one good deed. I hope you are pleased with me. I believe you must be, for you're smiling at me.

NARRATOR: About this time a rumor spread throughout the valley.

MUSIC: *Out.*

1ST VILLAGER: The letter arrived today. It says that he is returning to our valley.

2ND VILLAGER: It is said he is rich.

3RD VILLAGER: As Croesus! His fleet of ships covers the world, bringing him furs from the Arctic, spices and tea from the Far East, and pearls and diamonds from Africa.

2ND VILLAGER: Even the ocean yields tribute to him—oil from the whales.

1ST VILLAGER: Like Midas in the fable, it is said that whatever he touches changes into yellow gold. They say it would take him a hundred years to count his vast wealth.

3RD VILLAGER: And now he dreams of his native valley. Here amongst us he is to end his days.

4TH VILLAGER: What is his name?

1ST VILLAGER: His name? Why, his name is—

3RD VILLAGER: Goldweight, Goldpenny.

2ND VILLAGER: Something to do with gold.

1ST VILLAGER: His name is Gathergold. Mr. Gathergold.

MUSIC: *A narrative theme. Sneak and hold under.*

NARRATOR: Still another rumor spread. It reached the ears of young Ernest, who rushed to his mother.

ERNEST (*Excitedly*): The people say that Mr. Gathergold looks just like the Great Stone Face.

MOTHER: But they have never seen Mr. Gathergold.

ERNEST: The people say he is kind and generous.

NARRATOR: The people were more ready to believe that Mr. Gathergold was the image of the Great Stone Face when they learned he was to erect a great marble home on the site of the humble farmhouse where he was born. And soon this edifice rose, a building so beautiful and dazzling that they stared in wonderment. It was all glass and marble, gold and silver. Of course the simple villagers were not allowed to see its interior, but it was whispered around that—

1ST VILLAGER: There is no iron or brass in the house, just gold and silver.

2ND VILLAGER: His bed is studded with diamonds and other precious gems.

MUSIC: *Up and out.*

NARRATOR: The great day arrived. Mr. Gathergold was to arrive, ready to occupy his shining marble castle. The crowd gathered by the side of the road, young Ernest among them. As he waited, he looked up at his silent friend.

ERNEST: Just think, Great Stone Face, soon I will see this great man, who resembles you. I'll know him instantly.

BIZ: *Voices crying out: Here he comes. Here comes Mr. Gathergold. Look at his four horses and his carriage.*

NARRATOR: A splendid carriage dashed round the turn of the road. From within it appeared the face of Mr. Gathergold. His face was as yellow as his gold. He had a low forehead, small, sharp eyes and very thin, hard lips.

BIZ: *The People: The very image of the Great Stone Face! Sure enough, the old prophecy is true. Here at last is the great man.*

NARRATOR: And, what perplexed Ernest, they seemed actually to believe that here was the likeness which they spoke of. An old beggar woman called out.

BEGGAR: Alms, Mr. Gathergold, alms.

NARRATOR: And Mr. Gathergold's claw-like fingers dropped a few coins into the dust—copper coins. Nevertheless, the onlookers cried.

BIZ: *People: Look! Now we know he is the very image of the Great Stone Face. Yes, now there is no doubt.*

NARRATOR: In the background, Ernest turned sadly from the wrinkled shrewdness of Mr. Gathergold's visage, and gazed up the valley.

ERNEST: Great Stone Face, tell me they are wrong. Tell me that this man is not the one I am waiting for.

NARRATOR: And the kindly face seemed to smile back at Ernest, and the stone lips seemed to say: He will come! Fear not, Ernest, some day the right man will come!

MUSIC: *A majestic theme. Sneak under and hold.*
NARRATOR: The years went on, and Ernest grew into a young man. He attracted but little attention from the other inhabitants, for they saw nothing remarkable in his way of life. They did not know that the Great Stone Face had become a teacher to him—a symbol of wisdom and kindness and sympathy. (*Beat*) As for Mr. Gathergold, his great wealth had deserted him before his death. And the people of the valley no longer spoke of him in reverent tones.
MUSIC: *Out.*
1ST VILLAGER: They say he has not a copper left—the old skinflint.
2ND VILLAGER: I quite fail to see how people could have thought he looked anything like the Great Stone Face.
3RD VILLAGER: There never was any resemblance. Never!
1ST VILLAGER: How easily some people are impressed. Take me, I never thought there was anything noble about old Gathergold.
2ND VILLAGER (*Fading*): Nor I.
3RD VILLAGER (*Fading deeper*): Nor I.
NARRATOR: It so happened that a native-born son of the valley had become a great general. On the battlefield, he was known under the nickname of Old Blood-and-Thunder. This war-weary veteran signified his intention of returning to the valley, there to find peace. When this news reached the valley, there was considerable excitement. It was the village schoolmaster who first made the discovery. Ernest was present when this learned man said.
SCHOOLMASTER: How stupid we have been! How very stupid of us!
1ST VILLAGER: Stupid?
2ND VILLAGER: How?
3RD VILLAGER: Why?

SCHOOLMASTER: We all remember Old Blood-and-Thunder—that is, most of us do. Why, he grew up in this valley.
ERNEST: But he left here when he was a very young man.
SCHOOLMASTER: Quite true, Ernest. But his noble, great features have not changed.
1ST VILLAGER: You mean—?
SCHOOLMASTER: I mean that Old Blood-and-Thunder looks exactly like the Great Stone Face.
1ST VILLAGER: Why, I believe you are right.
2ND VILLAGER: True, there is a great resemblance.
3RD VILLAGER: Then he is the man of prophecy.
SCHOOLMASTER: Of course he is.
ERNEST (*Protests*): But, good neighbors, you cannot truthfully say this until you have seen the great general.
SCHOOLMASTER (*A gentle reproving tone*): Now, now, Ernest, how can you say we are wrong? Look, we are four men of the same mind. I'm certain the other people of the valley will agree with us.
ERNEST: Perhaps you are right. I am but a simple man of the soil.
SCHOOLMASTER: Of course I am right. Now we must prepare a great welcome for our eminent friend. There must be a banquet . . . speeches.
MUSIC: *Martial theme. Forte and fade under.*
NARRATOR: On the day of the great festival, Ernest, with all the other people of the valley, left their work, and proceeded to the spot where the banquet was to take place. The tables were arranged in a cleared space in the woods. Eastward and directly in back of the main table there was a fine view of the Great Stone Face. Ernest tried unsuccessfully to make his way toward the main table, but the crowd was too dense. So unobtrusively he remained in the background. To console himself, he turned towards the Great Stone Face, which, like

a faithful friend, smiled at him. Meanwhile, he listened to the remarks of various individuals who were comparing the general with the face on the mountainside.

MUSIC: *Out.*

1ST VILLAGER: It is the same face, to a hair.

2ND VILLAGER: Wonderfully like, that's a fact.

3RD VILLAGER: I call it Old Blood-and-Thunder himself, in a looking glass.

1ST VILLAGER: And why not? He's the greatest man of the age.

NARRATOR: And then all three of the villagers joined together.

THREE VILLAGERS: To the general. Hooray, hooray, hooray!

NARRATOR: And the great crowd assembled lent its voice.

BIZ: *Shout from a tremendous crowd. (Note: Use recorded crowd noise.)*

NARRATOR: The general rose to thank the people. Ernest saw him. There stood the great general, almost in the shadow of the Great Stone Face. Unlike any of the others, what Ernest saw was a war-worn countenance, full of energy and iron will. But completely lacking was the gentle wisdom, the deep, tender sympathy always present in the Great Stone Face.

MUSIC: *Sneak in and hold under.*

NARRATOR: And as Ernest looked, his face fell. He said to himself.

ERNEST: This is not the man of prophecy. The world must wait longer.

NARRATOR: As he walked away, Ernest gazed at the Great Stone Face. It seemed to be smiling down at him, and from its stone lips seemed to come words directed solely at Ernest. "Fear not, Ernest, fear not. He will come. You must be patient."

MUSIC: *Forte briefly and then down into background.*

NARRATOR: More years sped swiftly and tranquilly away. Ernest still dwelt in his native valley, and now was a man of middle age. He still labored for his daily bread, and was the same simple-hearted man that he had always been. Then one Spring evening he lifted his face skyward and spoke quietly. It was a simple prayer from his heart.

ERNEST: I have spent many hours on worldly things. I have not made the most of the time that has been mine. I have not helped my neighbor. Perhaps it is not too late for me to do good. I shall try.

NARRATOR: And so Ernest became a preacher, an unordained man of God. And now the silent, good deeds which he had always performed, also flowed forth in speech. Every spare moment, more than he rightfully could afford, was spent tramping the valley, pausing here and there at a farm.

MUSIC: *Out.*

FARMER: Good morning, Ernest. You're an early traveler.

ERNEST: I have walked all night.

FARMER: But why?

ERNEST: Yesterday afternoon a friend told me you needed help in getting in your hay. That is why I have come.

FARMER: And you walked all night to get here?

ERNEST: We must work swiftly. The rain is threatening.

FARMER: You are a good friend. If only I could pay you, but I am poor.

ERNEST: I ask no money; only your friendship.

FARMER: That I gladly offer, as does everyone else in the valley. You are rich in friends, Ernest.

ERNEST: Then I am thankful and feel well repaid. And now I ask but one favor.

FARMER: Name it.

ERNEST: I would like shelter for the night.

FARMER: Of course.

ERNEST: Tomorrow is the Sabbath. I ask that tomorrow morning you gather your family and the neighbors by your brook.

I would like to read from the Scriptures and then speak a few words to them.

FARMER: We always welcome your sermons, Ernest. You never preach . . . just advise in a kind sort of way.

MUSIC: *Sneak in and hold under.*

NARRATOR: And so Ernest, traveling the length and breadth of the valley, aided his neighbors. He uttered truths that molded the lives of those that heard him. His listeners never suspected that Ernest was more than an ordinary man; least of all did Ernest himself suspect it. But, inevitably as the murmur of a rivulet, came thoughts out of his mouth that no other human lips had spoken.

MUSIC: *Up to finish.*

NARRATOR: When the valley people's mind had had time to cool, they were ready enough to acknowledge their mistake.

1ST VILLAGER: The people were in error.

2ND VILLAGER: Yes, they were.

3RD VILLAGER: Why, Old Blood-and-Thunder no more resembles the Great Stone Face than . . . well, than our friend Ernest does.

NARRATOR: Not long after this, Ernest stopped at an inn kept by one of his many friends. He waved a newspaper in the air and thrust it upon Ernest.

LANDLORD: Here—read this. Read it and rejoice!

NARRATOR: The story ran on for many paragraphs. In effect it said: Here is an eminent statesman, the greatest politician of our times, the most eloquent speaker our country has ever known. His wondrous voice is known throughout the civilized world. He is the people's choice, this stalwart man, whose face exactly resembles that phenomenon of his native valley—the Great Stone Face. Small wonder he has been dubbed Old Stony Phiz.

LANDLORD: Old Stony Phiz! The name suits him. Look,

Ernest, here is a picture of him. Don't you agree that he looks exactly like the Great Stone Face?

ERNEST (*Grudgingly*): Well, yes—

LANDLORD: Ah! I thought you'd agree.

ERNEST: But it might be the artist's skill more than anything else.

LANDLORD: How can you say such a thing, Ernest? The two are as alike as two peas in a pod. And just think, Old Stony Phiz is a native of this valley, and he's going to run for President. And what's more, he'll be elected.

ERNEST: Why?

LANDLORD (*Floundering*): Because—because—why, because he's a great orator and a—a—(*Sharply*) You mustn't ask such a question, Ernest. Remember, he was born here and—

ERNEST: He has never been back since he left.

LANDLORD: Of course not. Old Stony Phiz is an important man; and now that he's going to run for President, we must honor him.

NARRATOR: And so the people of the valley wrote a letter to Old Stony Phiz. One of his campaign managers read it and then showed it to the great man.

STONY PHIZ: Hmmm! Hmmmm! A very nice letter.

MANAGER: They want you to pay them a visit.

STONY PHIZ: I'm too busy. This campaigning takes a great deal out of me.

MANAGER: You might be making a mistake.

STONY PHIZ: Me make a mistake? I never make a mistake.

MANAGER: You were born there. Your nickname comes from that freak bit of stone up there.

STONY PHIZ: The Great Stone Face.

MANAGER: Yes. By the way, do you actually look like the Great Stone Face?

STONY PHIZ: Why, er—(*Promptly*) Why, certainly I do.

MANAGER: When your tour takes you into that area, you easily could swing by your old home.

STONY PHIZ: Well—it *is* an idea.

MANAGER: The newspapers will like it: "Presidential candidate visits old home town friends." Besides, it will give fresh impetus to the belief in your resemblance to the Great Stone Face.

STONY PHIZ: Very well! Write and tell them to prepare to welcome me.

MUSIC: *Brass band playing lively and patriotic air. Forte and fade under.*

NARRATOR: The big day arrived. The valley folks turned out to greet their hero, Old Stony Phiz. Among these was Ernest. Despite two previous disappointments, hopefully and buoyantly he set out to behold the likeness of the Great Stone Face. There was music, a band which made the echoes of the mountains ring and reverberate. Even the far-off mountain precipice itself seemed to be swelling the echoing chorus, as if saying: "The man of prophecy is coming." The enthusiasm of the people was so contagious that even Ernest shouted as loudly as the loudest.

ERNEST: Hurrah for Old Stony Phiz!

1ST VILLAGER: Here he is, now.

2ND VILLAGER: Look at Old Stony Phiz.

3RD VILLAGER: And look at the Great Stone Face.

1ST VILLAGER: See if they aren't alike as twin brothers.

MUSIC: *Fades out under following narration.*

NARRATOR: Ernest stared eagerly at the approaching carriage. At first glance its bowing and smiling occupant did seem to resemble the old familiar face upon the mountainside. It was a strong face with boldly-hewn features. But the stateliness, the expression of divine sympathy, that illuminated the Great Stone Face were lacking in the statesman's face. Something had been originally left out, or had departed. It was evident to Ernest that Old Stony Phiz's life was as empty as his eyes; no high purpose had endowed them with reality. The man at Ernest's elbow poked him and screamed.

1st Villager: Look! Is he not the very picture of your Old Man of the Mountain?

Ernest: No! I see little or no likeness.

1st Villager: Then so much the worse for the Great Stone Face. (*He yells*) Hurrah for Old Stony Phiz.

Narrator: But Ernest turned away, melancholy and despondent. He turned his gaze up toward his silent friend and spoke to him.

Ernest: Three times now I have been bitterly disappointed. Today I beheld the man who might have fulfilled the prophecy, and has not willed to do so. Oh, tell me, will the right man ever be found?

Narrator: And the stone lips seemed to reply: Be patient. I have waited longer than you, and am not yet weary. Fear not. The man will come.

Music: *A peaceful theme. Sneak in and hold under.*

Narrator: The years hurried onward. And now they began to scatter white hairs over the head of Ernest. They made reverent wrinkles across his forehead, and furrows in his cheeks. He was an aged man. But not in vain had he grown old. His wrinkles and furrows were sage inscriptions that Time had etched. And Ernest had ceased to be obscure. Even though he had not sought it, fame came to him in the valley from the outside world. Learned men came from far to converse with him.

Music: *Out.*

Narrator (*No pause*): Two such men visited him late one Spring, when the whole valley was bathed in the scent of the wild flowers and the green woods. One was a sage, the other a philanthropist. Ernest received them with gentle sincerity.

SAGE: I am supposed to be a sage and scholar, but compared to your knowledge and philosophy, my own lacks depth and stature.

ERNEST: You are a famous man, much more knowing than I.

SAGE: Most of my knowledge comes from books. But yours—where does it come from?

ERNEST: From Mankind and Nature and God.

PHILANTHROPIST: All I have to do good with is my money. I should like to aid you, Ernest.

ERNEST: How?

PHILANTHROPIST: By settling upon you a sum large enough for you not to worry, large enough for you not to have to work with your hands.

ERNEST: I wish to continue to worry about how I can aid my fellow man, and I wish to continue working with my hands. From laborious work, I draw strength and comfort. I am afraid I must reject your kind offer.

PHILANTHROPIST: I didn't expect your refusal.

ERNEST: And I didn't expect your offer. I'm afraid if I accepted it, I might change.

NARRATOR: His guests took their leave and made their way through the graying shadows of the late afternoon. Once they paused to look up at the Great Stone Face.

PHILANTHROPIST: Why are you staring so intently? If you ever return, you will find the Old Man of the Mountain still up there.

SAGE: Look closely. (*Pause*) Tell me if anything strikes you as odd.

PHILANTHROPIST: Why—you know, I—

SAGE: Go on.

PHILANTHROPIST: I know I've seen the very likeness of that image in a human face.

SAGE: And so have I.

PHILANTHROPIST: But I don't remember where.

SAGE: It's probably just an illusion. Come, we had better hurry. It's getting dark.

MUSIC: *A peaceful, quiet theme. Sneak and hold under.*

NARRATOR: During these years a new American poet reached prominence. He likewise was a native of the valley, but had spent most of his life amid the din of the cities. Often, however, did the mountains of his childhood lift their snowy peaks into the clear atmosphere of his poetry. Neither was the Great Stone Face forgotten, for the poet had celebrated it in a famous ode. This poet also wrote of his human brethren—men and women, touched with the common dust of life, who daily crossed his path. The songs of this poet found their way to Ernest.

MUSIC: *Out.*

NARRATOR (*No pause*): And as he read stanzas that caused the soul to thrill within him, Ernest lifted his eyes to the vast countenance beaming on him so benignantly.

ERNEST: My dear friend, tell me: Isn't this poet worthy to resemble you?

NARRATOR: The Face seemed to smile, but answered not a word. (*A transition*) One summer morning a man alighted from the train, which stopped close by to where Ernest lived. The stranger did not stop at the hotel, which had formerly been the residence of Mr. Gathergold. Instead he asked directions to Ernest's cottage. The latter looked up as the Stranger approached him.

POET: Good day, sir. Can you give a traveler a night's lodging?

ERNEST: Very willingly. You seem very weary, my friend. Have you traveled far?

POET: Quite some distance. I have come to see you.

ERNEST: I am honored. Please sit down.

THE GREAT STONE FACE

NARRATOR: For the next few hours Ernest and the Stranger talked. The Stranger had talked with the wittiest and wisest, but never before with a man like Ernest. He was fascinated by the valley-dweller's thoughts and feelings, which gushed up with such natural freedom. And Ernest was moved by the living images which the poet flung out of his mind, and which peopled the air by the cottage door with shapes of beauty. As Ernest listened, he imagined the Great Stone Face was listening too.

ERNEST: Who are you, my strangely gifted guest?

POET: In your hand you hold a book of poems. You were reading them when I first spoke to you.

ERNEST: They are the finest poems I have ever read.

POET: You know me, then, for I wrote them.

ERNEST (*Slowly*): You . . . wrote these . . . great poems! (*Pause*)

POET: Why do you look so sad?

ERNEST: Because all my life I have awaited the fulfilment of a prophecy; and when I read these poems, I hoped that it might be fulfilled in you.

POET: I understand. You had hoped to find in me the likeness of the Great Stone Face.

ERNEST: Yes. That is what I had hoped.

POET: And you are as disappointed with me as you were with Mr. Gathergold and Old Blood-and-Thunder and Old Stony Phiz. So you must add my name to that illustrious trio, and record another failure of your hopes. I am not worthy to be typified by that majestic image looking down at us.

ERNEST: And why? These poems—are they not thoughts divine?

POET: They are more of an echo. My life has not corresponded with my thought. My poems are but grand dreams.

ERNEST: And why have you so dreamt?

POET: Because I have lived among poor and mean realities. Sometimes I lack faith in the grandeur and beauty which my own words proclaim. I am not worthy of real greatness. That is why you cannot discover in me the image of your Great Stone Face.

MUSIC: *An ethereal theme. Sneak and hold under.*

NARRATOR: At the hour of sunset, as had long been his custom, Ernest went to speak to an assemblage of his neighbors. The Poet followed him to a small natural amphitheatre. Slightly elevated was a small niche, spacious enough to admit a single human figure. Into this natural pulpit, Ernest ascended. His audience sat on the sweep of green grass below him. Ernest started to speak.

MUSIC: *Out.*

ERNEST (*Projecting*): My good friends, I am going to use as my subject . . . humility. Humility is something all of us (*Fading gradually*) should recognize, particularly in ourselves. It is a virtue which none of us can afford to overlook. It is a . . .

MUSIC: *Sneak in same theme and hold under.*

NARRATOR: As the poet listened, he realized that Ernest's words had power, because they accorded with his thoughts; and his thoughts had reality and depth, because they harmonized with the life which he had always lived. The poet, as he listened, knew that the being and character of Ernest were a nobler strain of poetry than he had ever written. The poet's eyes wandered to the Great Stone Face. In the golden light of the setting sun, the Great Stone Face wore hoary mists around it, like the white hairs around the brow of Ernest. Both wore a look of grand beneficence that seemed to embrace the world. At that moment the poet threw his arms aloft and shouted.

POET: Behold! Behold! Ernest is himself the very likeness of the Great Stone Face.

Biz: *Ad lib of a few surprised voices.*
Narrator: Then all the people looked, and saw what the poet said was true. The old prophecy was fulfilled.
Music: *Up to finish.*

THE END

The Laurence Boy

*From "Little Women"
by Louisa May Alcott*

MUSIC: *A quiet, reminiscent theme. Establish and fade under.*
ALCOTT: This is a chapter from one of my favorite books. It was written many years ago, and, so many say, has withstood the test of Time. I know quite a bit about it, for I wrote this story. My name is Louisa May Alcott, and the book is "Little Women."
MUSIC: *Forte and then under.*
ALCOTT: This chapter starts on a winter's afternoon, right after Christmas. Jo March, sprawled out on the sofa, is engrossed in a book. Over by the sunny window seat Meg is busy with some sewing. Her eyes lift from her work and she stares out at the road heavy with snow.
MUSIC: *Out.*
MEG: Jo.
JO: Yes?
MEG: He's coming down the road.
JO: Who?
MEG: Why, the Laurence boy.
JO (*Unconcerned*): Well?
MEG: He's walking with his tutor. Come and take a look at him.
JO: You look at him, Meg. I'm reading.
MEG: Have you ever met him?
JO: No.
MEG: Neither have I. I think I'd like meeting him, though. Wouldn't you?

THE LAURENCE BOY

Jo: Mmmm! Maybe!

Meg: He's very nice looking.

Jo: Never had a chance to see him.

Meg: Small wonder . . . the way his grandfather keeps him away from everyone. Making him study so hard. Marmee says the Laurence boy is very nice, though he never speaks to anyone.

Jo: He's probably a snob.

Meg: Probably just bashful. (*Pause*) I wonder how much longer he'll be staying with his grandfather?

Jo: Why don't you ask him?

Meg: Now, Jo, don't be so unladylike.

Jo: You're the one who's being unladylike, staring out the window at that Laurence boy. You wouldn't catch me doing it. Not that I really think it's unladylike. It's just that I'm not interested in seeing him.

Meg: Then why are you staring over my shoulder?

Music: *Light theme. Up and under.*

Alcott: The next day Mrs. March returns from having delivered the two younger girls, Beth and Amy, to their aunt's, where they are to spend a few days.

Music: *Out.*

Alcott (*No pause*): As Mrs. March enters, she calls out.

Marmee: Meg . . . Jo! Girls!

Meg (*Coming in*): Marmee! Oh, I'm so glad you're back.

Marmee: I was only gone overnight.

Meg: We missed you.

Marmee: Was everything all right? Did you help Hannah with the dusting?

Meg: Indeed we did. What's that note you're holding?

Marmee: It's for you.

Meg: For me?

Marmee: And Jo.

Jo (*Fading in*): And who's using my name? (*As though embracing her*) Marmee, I'm glad you're back. My, but you look fine.
MARMEE: Getting away for overnight was a welcome change. This note is for you and Meg. It was waiting at the post office.
Jo: It's very elegant appearing. Let me open it.
SOUND: *Rustle of paper*.
MEG (*Eagerly*): Well?
Jo (*She reads*): "Mrs. Gardiner would be happy to see Miss Margaret and Miss Josephine March at a little dance on New Year's Eve."
MEG: A dance!
Jo: Christopher Columbus!
MEG: Marmee, may we go? May we?
MARMEE: I think it would be very nice if you went.
MEG: I've never been to a New Year's dance, never! Now what shall we wear?
Jo: What's the use of asking that, when you know we shall wear our poplins.
MEG (*Disappointed*): Oh!
Jo: We haven't anything else.
MEG: If I only had a silk.
MARMEE: You may have one when you're eighteen.
MEG: Two years is an awful long time to wait, Marmee.
Jo: I'll have to wait three years. (*Shrugging*) Oh, well!
MARMEE: I'll go and take a look at your dresses right now. (*Fading*) Don't worry. I'm certain you'll both look very well.
Jo: I'm sure our poplins will look like silk, and they're nice enough for us. (*Suddenly*) Oh, dear!
MEG: What's wrong?
Jo: Meg, your dress is as good as new. But mine—I forgot the burn and tear in it. Whatever shall I do?

MEG: You can mend the tear.

Jo: But the burn shows badly, and I won't be able to take it out.

MEG: I have it! You must sit still all you can, and keep your back out of sight. The front is all right.

Jo: I suppose I can do that.

MEG: I shall have a new ribbon for my hair. My new slippers are lovely and my gloves will do, though they aren't as nice as I'd like.

Jo: My gloves are stained with lemonade, and I can't get any new ones, so I shall have to go without.

MEG: You *must* have gloves, or I won't go.

Jo: Don't be stubborn.

MEG: Gloves are more important than anything else. You can't dance without them.

Jo: Or without shoes, for that matter.

MEG: Stop joking! If you don't wear gloves, I should be so mortified.

Jo: Then I'll stay still. I don't care much for company dancing. It's no fun to go sailing around. I like to fly about and cut capers.

MEG: You can't ask Mother for new ones. They're so expensive and you're so careless.

Jo: I know. Marmee said, when I spoilt the others, that she couldn't get me any more this winter.

MEG (*Anxiously*): Can't you make them do?

Jo: I can hold them crumpled up in my hand, so no one will know how stained they are.

MEG (*Tentatively*): Well—!

Jo: No! I'll tell you how we can manage—each of us will wear one good one and carry a bad one. Don't you see?

MEG: Your hands are bigger than mine, and you'll stretch my gloves dreadfully.

Jo: Then I'll go without. I don't care what people say.

MEG: Very well. You may wear one of my gloves, only don't stain it. And, Jo, do behave nicely.

JO: I promise.

MEG: Don't put your hands behind you, or stare, or say Christopher Columbus, will you?

JO: Don't worry about me. I'lll be as prim as I can, and won't get into any scrapes—if I can help it.

MEG: Good! Now I'll write a note of acceptance to Mrs. Gardiner.

JO: I hope she'll have something good to eat.

MEG: Now, Jo, there you go again.

JO: There's certainly nothing inelegant about getting hungry, is there? Christopher Columbus!

MUSIC: *Up briskly and under*.

ALCOTT: On New Year's Eve the March house is indeed a very busy place. Hannah, the woman of all work, has been washing and ironing most of the day. There has been an early supper. For the past hour, there has been a great deal of running up and down stairs and much laughing and talking. Meg, wanting a few curls around her face, has sought Jo's aid. Right now Jo is pinching her sister's papered locks with a pair of hot tongs.

MUSIC: *Out*.

MEG (*Sniffing*): Ought they to smoke like that?

JO: It's just the dampness drying.

MEG: What a queer smell! It's like burnt feathers.

JO: Hold still while I take off the papers and you'll see a cloud of little ringlets. (*Pause*) Now, look in the mirror.

MEG (*Pause*): Oh, oh! What have you done? Look at my hair. It's . . . it's all burnt and frizzled.

JO: I'm sorry.

MEG: I can't go looking like this.

MARMEE (*Fading in*): What's the matter with my little women?

MEG: Marmee, look at my hair.
JO: Just my luck! You shouldn't have asked me to do it.
MEG: You always spoil everything, Jo.
JO: The tongs were too hot.
MARMEE: Don't be so upset, Meg. It isn't really spoilt. Here, we'll just frizzle it a bit, and tie your ribbon so the ends come on your forehead a bit. It will look like the latest mode.
MEG: Serves me right for trying to be so fine. I wish I'd let my hair alone.
MARMEE: It will soon grow out again. (*Pause*) There! Now look at yourself.
MEG: It doesn't look so bad, does it?
MARMEE: You both look very nice.
JO: Except for the patch on the back of my dress.
MARMEE: If you're careful, it won't show. Meg, aren't those shoes too tight for you?
MEG: Not a bit. They fit perfectly.
MARMEE: They look pretty snug. Now put on your capes. And have you both got nice pocket handkerchiefs?
JO: Yes, spandy clean. Meg has cologne on hers. Marmee, I do believe you'd ask that if we were all running away from an earthquake.
MARMEE: A lady is always known by her neat boots, gloves and handkerchief. Have a good time, and leave at midnight, when I send Hannah after you. And, Jo—
JO: Yes, Marmee, I know. I'll be on my very best behavior.
MUSIC: *Gay theme. Up and under.*
ALCOTT: And out the door and down the path and along the road go Meg and Jo, their eyes as sparkling as the stars overhead in the moon-filled winter's sky. Every room in the Gardiner house is lighted. Inside, the girls stand waiting for their hostess to greet them. As they do, Meg gives some last-second advice to Jo.

Music: *Out into:*
Biz: *Ad lib of voices of young people.*
Meg: Now don't forget to stand with your back to people. Straighten your sash. Now smile.
Jo: I know I shall forget. If you see me doing anything wrong, just remind me by a wink, will you?
Meg: No, winking isn't lady-like. I'll lift my eyebrows if anything is wrong, and nod if you are all right.
Jo: I'll keep watching you.
Meg: Now hold your shoulders straight and take short steps and don't shake hands if you are introduced to anyone.
Jo: I always shake hands.
Meg: It isn't the thing to do.
Jo: How *do* you learn all the proper ways? I never can. (*She hums aloud.*)
Meg: Jo, stop humming and stop that prancing. (*Low voice*) Here comes Mrs. Gardiner.
Mrs. Gardiner: Good evening, girls.
Meg *and* Jo: Good evening, Mrs. Gardiner.
Mrs. Gardiner: I'm glad you're here. Do have a good time.
Meg: Oh, we shall, Mrs. Gardiner.
Jo: Christopher Columbus! Er, I mean—yes, of course.
Mrs. Gardiner: I'm sure you know most of the others. If there is anyone you wish to meet, ask me or my Sally.
Meg: Don't worry about us, Mrs. Gardiner.
Mrs. Gardiner: I shall see you later. (*Fading*) Be sure to enjoy yourselves.
Music (*As though coming from another room*): *Piano and violin playing a lively nineteenth century dance. Hold under.*
Jo: Isn't that music gay?
Meg: Won't it be awful if no one asks me to dance?
Jo: Won't it be awful if someone asks me to dance? (*Pause*) Here comes someone now.

THE LAURENCE BOY

Boy 1: Good evening. I'm John Forbes. I'm from Boston.
Meg: I'm Meg March and this is my sister, Jo.
Boy 1: How do you do?
Jo: Fine. (*As though pumping his hand*) How are you? Glad to meet you.
Boy 1: Say, you have quite a grip, you know.
Meg (*Horrified*): Jo, I told you—
Jo: Hope you don't mind my shaking hands?
Boy 1: Er, no. Miss Meg, would you do me the honor of dancing with me?
Meg: I'd be delighted.
Boy 1: Perhaps I can find a partner for you, Miss Jo.
Jo: Don't bother. I'll watch this one out.
Boy 1: Will you excuse us?
Jo: Gladly! I mean—certainly.
Meg (*Fading*): Don't forget what I told you, Jo.
Jo (*To herself*): It would have been awful if he'd asked me to dance. If I stay here out of harm's way, perhaps no one will bother me. (*Pause*) That red-headed boy . . . coming this way. Oh, Christopher Columbus!
Boy 2: Good evening.
Jo: Good evening.
Boy 2: Would you do me the honor of—
Jo: Oh, no, I can't.
Boy 2: All I—
Jo: Thank you so much, but I can't. My sister, the girl over there in the silver dress, she's lifting her eyebrows at me.
Boy 2: But I don't understand. (*Fading a bit*) Why are you backing away from me?
Jo: I always back away, especially at parties.
Boy 2 (*Fading*): You're a funny girl.
Jo (*Breathlessly*): Yes, I know—very funny. Excuse me. (*A sigh of relief*) Whew! That was close. I've got to get out of

sight before someone else asks me. Here—this little curtained nook. I can hide in here and watch. (*Beat*) Ah!

LAURIE: Excuse me, but you're stepping on my foot.

Jo (*Startled*): Excuse *me*. I didn't know anyone was in here.

LAURIE (*Laughs*): Don't mind me. Stay, if you like.

Jo: But shan't I disturb you?

LAURIE: Not a bit. I only came here because I don't know many people. I felt rather strange.

Jo: So do I. Don't go away, please, unless you'd rather.

LAURIE: I think I've had the pleasure of seeing you before.

Jo: You have? Where?

LAURIE: You live near me. Next door.

Jo: Of course. You're the Laurence boy.

LAURIE: Yes.

Jo: We did have such a nice time over your Christmas present—the ice cream and candy and flowers.

LAURIE: Grandpa sent it, or rather brought it over.

Jo: But I'll wager you put it into his head. Come now—own up!

LAURIE: You could be right and you could be wrong, Miss March.

Jo (*Teasing him*): I thought so, Mr. Laurence; but I'm not Miss March. I'm only Jo. Plain Jo!

LAURIE: I'm not Mr. Laurence. I'm only Laurie.

Jo: Laurie Laurence—what an odd name!

LAURIE: My first name is Theodore, but I don't like it, for the fellows call me Dora. So I made them call me Laurie instead.

Jo: I hate my name too—so sentimental! I wish every one would say Jo, instead of Josephine. How did you make the boys stop calling you Dora?

LAURIE: I thrashed them.

Jo: Well, I can't thrash Aunt March—it was her idea to name me Josephine—so I suppose I shall have to bear it.

LAURIE: Don't you dance, Miss Jo?

Jo: Just Jo.
Laurie: Don't you dance, Jo?
Jo: I like it well enough if there is plenty of room, and every one is lively. In a place like this I'm sure to upset something or tread on people's toes or do something dreadful, so I keep out of mischief and let Meg sail about.
Laurie: Meg is your sister?
Jo: The oldest. The others are Beth and Amy.
Laurie: I've seen them.
Biz: *Dance music stops. There is applause from the dancers, as though coming from next room. The party-goers' voices continue to ad lib and laugh in the background.*
Jo: Don't you dance?
Laurie: Sometimes.
Jo (*Questioningly*): Oh?
Laurie: You see I've been abroad a good many years, and haven't been in company enough yet to know how you do things here.
Jo: Abroad! Oh, tell me about it. I love to hear people describe their travels. Have you been to England and Scotland and France and Italy and—and—? Tell me about it.
Laurie (*Laughs*): Hold on! I hardly know where to begin.
Jo: England?
Laurie: Yes, I've been there—London and Kent and Hampshire and all the way across to Cornwall, which is very picturesque and rocky.
Jo: And Scotland?
Laurie: By train all the way to Glasgow, and then to Edinburgh. Last summer some of my class went on a walking trip through Switzerland with one of the teachers.
Jo: And you went, too?
Laurie: Oh, yes.
Jo: Where did you go to school?

LAURIE: Vevay. The boys there hardly ever wear hats.
Jo: I should think they'd catch cold.
LAURIE: No, for it's much warmer there than here. There is a fine lake at Vevay, and we used to go rowing on it. I like to row.
Jo: So do I.
LAURIE (*Protests*): But girls don't row.
Jo: Oh, but I do; that's because I'm a tomboy, I guess.
LAURIE (*Laughs*): You're a funny girl.
Jo: How I'd like to go to Europe! Did you go to Paris?
LAURIE: We spent last winter there.
Jo: Can you talk French?
LAURIE: We were not allowed to speak anything else at Vevay.
Jo: Do say something. I can read it, but can't pronounce. Something simple, now.
LAURIE: Qui est cette jeune demoiselle avec les jolies pantoufles?
Jo: How nicely you do it. Let me see—you said, "Who is the young lady in the pretty slippers," didn't you?
LAURIE: Oui, mademoiselle.
Jo: It's my sister Margaret, and you knew it was. Do you think Meg's pretty?
LAURIE: Yes. She makes me think of the Swiss girls, she looks so fresh and quiet, and dances so well.
Jo: I must remember to tell her that. She'll feel highly complimented.
LAURIE: Oh, please don't. It would embarrass me.
Jo: I'm certain she'd like you, too.
LAURIE: Now I am embarrassed.
Jo: I suppose you are going to college soon? From my room I can see you studying away.
LAURIE: Not for a year or two. Not before I'm seventeen anyway.

THE LAURENCE BOY

Jo: Aren't you but fifteen?

Laurie: Sixteen next month.

Jo: How I wish I were going to college! You don't look as if you liked it.

Laurie: I hate the idea. Studying and having a good time.

Jo: Don't you like having a good time?

Laurie: Oh, certainly, but not in the ordinary way.

Jo: Then what do you like?

Laurie: To live in Italy, and to enjoy myself in my own way. Italy is my idea of paradise—sunny, warm, and very peaceful.

Music: *Piano and violin start again, playing a lively polka. Continue under scene.*

Jo: I shouldn't hold you here. That's a splendid polka. Why don't you go and try it?

Laurie: If you will come, too.

Jo: I can't.

Laurie: Oh? And why not?

Jo: I told Meg I wouldn't because—(*She laughs.*)

Laurie: Because what?

Jo: Promise you won't tell?

Laurie: Never!

Jo: Well, I have a bad trick of standing before the fire, and so I burn my frocks, and I scorched this one; and, though it's nicely mended, it shows. Meg told me to keep still, so no one would see it. You may laugh, if you want to; it is funny, I know.

Laurie (*Gently*): Never mind that. I'll tell you how we can manage: there's a long hall out there, and we can dance grandly.

Jo: Suppose someone sees us?

Laurie: No one will. Please come!

Jo: Very well! I will.

Music: *Up briskly for a few seconds. Then out.*

Biz: *Applause and ad libs from others.*

Laurie (*Breathlessly*): There! That was a fine dance!

Jo: It is the first time I have ever done the polka. (*Laughs*) And no one even saw my burnt dress.

Laurie: Here—suppose we sit on the stairs. (*Pause*) I hope we dance again some time.

Jo: So do I! (*Pause*) Now, what shall we talk about? Tell me more about Italy.

Meg (*Away—calling*): Jo! Oh, Jo!

Jo: Meg is calling me. Will you excuse me?

Laurie: Of course. (*Fading*) Come back, though, please. I'll wait here.

Jo: What is it, Meg?

Meg: Come in this room.

Jo: What's wrong?

Meg: I've sprained my ankle. My heel turned and gave me a bad wrench. I can hardly stand and I don't know how I'm ever going to get home.

Jo: I knew you'd hurt your feet with those silly shoes. I'm sorry, but I don't see what you can do, except get a carriage or stay here all night.

Meg: I can't stay here. The house is full of guests.

Jo: I'll get a carriage.

Meg: You can't without it costing ever so much, and it's such a long way to the stable, and no one to send.

Jo: I'll go.

Meg: It's too far.

Jo: Perhaps I can get Laurie to do it.

Meg: Don't ask anyone.

Jo: But, Meg, what will you do?

Meg: I'll sit here, for I can't dance any more. As soon as supper is over, start looking for Hannah.

Jo: But she won't be here until midnight. People are going out to supper now. I'll stay with you.

THE LAURENCE BOY

MEG: No, Jo, run along and bring me some coffee. I'm so tired, I can't stir.
JO: I'll be right back.
BIZ: *Background voices in louder.*
SOUND: *Dishes and silverware.*
JO: May I have some coffee, please?
WAITER: Yes, Miss.
JO: Just a little sugar and cream.
WAITER: Here you are, Miss.
JO: Thank you.
SOUND: *Cup upsetting in saucer.*
JO: Oh, what a blunderbuss I am. Upsetting my cup.
LAURIE: Can I help you?
JO: Laurie, look how clumsy I am. I was carrying this coffee to Meg, and someone shook me. I've stained my skirt and Meg's glove. Oh, dear!
LAURIE: Too bad. I was looking for someone to give this coffee and ice cream to. May I take it to your sister?
JO: Oh, thank you!
LAURIE: Where is she?
JO: Follow me. I'd carry the cup and plate, only I know I'd upset them. I'm so clumsy.
LAURIE: Let me worry about them.
JO: That's very nice of you, I'm sure. Meg, here's your coffee. And this is Laurie; Laurie, this is my sister, Meg.
LAURIE: How do you do?
MEG: Not so well, thank you.
LAURIE: How about you, Jo? (*He calls out*) Oh, waiter!
WAITER (*Fading in*): Yes, sir.
LAURIE: I'll take that coffee and ice cream you have on the tray.
WAITER: Yes, sir.
SOUND: *Rattle of dishes.*
LAURIE: And another for myself.
SOUND: *Dishes.*

LAURIE: There! Food and drink for the hungry. This is pleasant—just the three of us sitting around.
JO: Of course there are probably fifty other people here.
MEG: At least.
LAURIE: But we are the only ones that count. Well, aren't we?
BIZ: *All three laugh.*
MUSIC: *Light theme. Up and under.*
ALCOTT: The three young people sit there for the next half-hour, talking. Even particular Meg thinks to herself that Laurie is a nice boy, and not at all snobbish. When he excuses himself, Meg rises.
MUSIC: *Out.*
BIZ: *Background of others ad libbing under.*
MEG: We've got to leave, Jo. My ankle is paining me something dreadful. I can scarcely walk.
JO: Lean on me.
MEG: I wish we could find Mrs. Gardiner to say good-night.
JO: I wish you'd let me go to the stable and hire a carriage. You can't walk all the way home.
MEG (*Firmly*): I'll have to, that's all. We can't afford to hire a carriage. It costs too much money, and that's something we don't have.
LAURIE (*Fading in*): And then public carriages are never as nice as private ones. (*Laughing*) I couldn't help but overhear you.
JO: You're leaving, Laurie?
LAURIE: Yes, my uncle's carriage is outside waiting. I'd like to see you home.
JO: It's so early. You can't mean to go yet.
MEG: That isn't right to take you away.
LAURIE: I always go home early—I do, truly. Please let me take you home. It's on my way, you know. (*Fading*) And Meg can't walk that far on such a weak ankle.

THE LAURENCE BOY

Biz: *The background voices fade out. A pause, then:*
Sound: *Horse's hoofs on dirt road. Hold under.*
Jo: I must say this is capital! A ride home in a fine carriage. I feel like a titled lady.
Laurie: Perhaps some day you will be that, Jo.
Meg: Not Jo. She's too harum-scarum.
Jo: Laurie, you know we—my sisters and I—always thought you a snob, but now we know differently.
Meg: You're too blunt. Excuse her, Laurie.
Laurie: There is nothing to excuse. On my part, I always thought you girls sort of distant. I often wanted to meet you, but I wasn't certain you'd feel that way, too, so I was afraid to speak.
Sound: *Hoofs up and to a halt.*
Jo: Home already.
Meg: Thank you, Laurie.
Laurie: It was a pleasure. Here, let me help you.
Sound: *Slight squeaking noise as door of carriage opens.*
Laurie: Step down. (*Pause*) Well, good night.
Jo: We hope to see you soon.
Laurie: I only live next door.
Meg: That's very close, you know. Good night.
Jo: Night.
Laurie (*Fading a bit*): I've had a fine time. And be on the watch for my invitation.
Sound (*From off in distance*): *Church clock striking 12 times.* (*Over sound.*)
Jo: Meg, it's midnight.
Meg: The New Year.
Jo (*Calling out*): Oh, Laurie.
Laurie (*Away*): Yes, Jo.
Jo: Happy New Year.
Meg: And many of them.

LAURIE: Let's hope it will be the first of many happy ones for all of us.
JO: It will be, Laurie, I'm sure. We'll be the best of friends from now on . . . and for many, many years to come.
ALCOTT: And Jo is right, for all the March girls, as the years unfold, are going to accept Laurie as a close friend. And if you read my story, "Little Women," you'll discover how Laurie became more than just a friend to one of the four March girls. It's a romance which indirectly received its start on this same New Year's Eve, many years ago.
MUSIC: *Up and out.*

THE END

The Juggler of Our Lady

by Anatole France

MUSIC: *A theme that starts quietly. Sneak and hold under.*

NARRATOR: In the days of King Louis there lived in France a poor juggler by the name of Barnabas, a native of Compiègne, who wandered from city to city performing tricks of skill and prowess. . . .

MUSIC: *Segue to gay carnival theme. Hold under.*

NARRATOR: . . . On fair days he would lay down in the public square a worn and aged carpet. Then after having attracted a group of children and idlers, he would assume the strangest postures, and balance a pewter plate on his nose. At first the crowd regarded him with indifference.

BOY 1: Oh, he's just another juggler.

GIRL 1: And not a very clever one.

MAN 1: Come, let us depart.

NARRATOR: But when, with his hands and head on the ground, Barnabas threw into the air and caught with his feet six glittering copper balls, he elicited a murmur of admiration from his audience.

GIRL 1: Oh, how clever.

BOY 1: I've never before seen such a feat.

GIRL 2: That must take much practice.

MAN 1: Oh, yes, indeed it must.

BOY 2: What is his name?

MAN 2: He is named Barnabas.

GIRL 1: Perform some more, Barnabas.

NARRATOR: And when, as a finale, Barnabas assumed the form

of a wheel and in that position juggled twelve knives, he elicited a delighted murmur from his audience.

BOY 1: How wonderful.

GIRL 1: How clever!

BOY 2: And he is not young.

GIRL 2: He must be the cleverest juggler in all France.

MAN 1: In all the world.

MAN 2: Reward him. Throw him some coins.

GIRL 2: Here, Barnabas.

GIRL 1: Here are some coins.

BOY 2: Catch, Barnabas.

MUSIC: *Up and segue to sad theme. Hold under.*

NARRATOR: But Barnabas had a hard time making a living. Earning his bread by the sweat of his brow, he bore more than his share of miseries. Besides, he was unable to work as much as he would have liked. In order to exhibit his wonderful talents, he required the warmth of the sun and the heat of the day. In winter time he was no more than a tree stripped of its leaves, in fact, half-dead. The frozen earth was too hard for the juggler. And so during the bad season he suffered from hunger and cold. But, since he had a simple heart, he suffered in silence. He never thought about the origin of wealth or about inequality. He firmly believed that if this world were evil, the next could not but be good. He lived the life of an honest man. He was indeed a good man, fearing God, and devout in his adoration of the Holy Virgin. When he went into a church he never failed to kneel before the image of the Mother of God. And he would look up at her kind and patient face and thus address her:

BARNABAS: My Lady, watch over my life until it shall please God that I die, and when I am dead, see that I have the joys of Paradise.

MUSIC: *Out.*

NARRATOR: One day, after a day of heavy rain, he trudged along a road, his juggling balls under his arm and his knives wrapped up in his old carpet. He was seeking some barn where he might go supperless to bed, when he saw a monk going in his direction. They fell into conversation.

PRIOR: Friend, how does it happen that you are dressed all in green? Are you perchance going to play the part of a fool in some play?

BARNABAS: No indeed, Father. My name is Barnabas, and my business is that of juggling. (*Sighs*) It would be the finest calling in the world if I could eat every day.

PRIOR: Friend Barnabas, be careful what you say.

BARNABAS: Have I said something wrong Father?

PRIOR: Remember, Barnabas, there is no finer calling than the monastic. The priest celebrates the praise of God and the saints. The life of a monk is a perpetual hymn to the Lord.

BARNABAS: Father, I spoke like an ignorant man. My estate cannot be compared to yours, and though there is some merit to balancing a stick on the end of your nose, it is in no wise comparable to your merit. I wish I might, like you, sing the Office every day, especially the Office of the Very Holy Virgin, to whom I am especially and piously devoted. In order to enter the monastic life, I would willingly give up the art by which I am known in more than six hundred cities and villages.

PRIOR: Friend Barnabas, in you I see a well-disposed man, an earnest man. Come with me and I will see that you enter the monastery of which I am the Prior.

MUSIC: *A religious theme. Forte and fade under.*

NARRATOR: Thus did Barnabas become a monk. In the monastery he found great peace, a quiet sanctuary. He performed but simple tasks, for Barnabas had only one real skill, that of juggling. And Barnabas found that the monks celebrated most magnificently the cult of the Holy Virgin, each of them bringing to her service all the knowledge and skill which God had given him.

MUSIC: *Segue to religious Christmas pattern. Hold under.*

NARRATOR: That year many weeks before Christmas, the monks commenced their offerings to Mary, the Mother of God. The Prior, for his part, started writing a special prayer, setting forth the virtues of the Holy Virgin. As it was written, Brother Maurice began copying it with a cunning hand on pages of parchment. And Brother Alexandre prepared to decorate it with delicate miniatures representing the life of the Queen of Heaven. Brother Marbode was cutting an image of stone—an image of the Holy Virgin watching over the Christ Child, and when finished, this was to be placed inside the altar rail. Brother Jacques was writing a hymn, while Brother François was preparing to set the words to music. Three other brothers were busying themselves with the building of a crib and manger and figures of the Holy Mother and the Christ Child, complete with the Three Wise Men. Indeed, with one lone exception, there was not a monk in the entire monastery who did not have some Christmas offering to make to the Mother of God. And that lone exception was, of course, Barnabas. The Prior, noting his saddened air, spoke to him.

MUSIC: *Out.*

PRIOR: Why are you sad, Brother Barnabas, during this greatest of all seasons?

BARNABAS: Alas, Father, I see all this activity about me—the other brothers all with their tributes to the Holy Mother. And I have nothing to offer. I am but very poorly educated and I have no skill save my juggling.

PRIOR: You have your faith, Barnabas, and that is most important.

BARNABAS: Yes, good Father, I have that, and that is all, that is all.

PRIOR: Perhaps if you offer up to the Holy Mother a special prayer, you may be answered.

NARRATOR: Barnabas went to the chapel and, kneeling before the statue of the Holy Virgin, he said:

BARNABAS: Alas! I am so unhappy, just as I told the Prior. I am unhappy because I cannot, like my brothers, give worthy praise to you, O Holy Mother of God, to whom I have consecrated all the love in my heart. I am such a stupid fellow, without art. I can write no prayer to you, like the good Prior. And if I could write it, I would be unable to copy it in so fine a hand, like Brother Maurice is doing, nor could I decorate it with rich miniatures, like Brother Alexandre. Brother Marbode is cutting out of stone an image of you watching over the Christ Child. Brother Jacques is writing in your honor a special Christmas hymn, while Brother François is setting those beautiful words to equally beautiful music. Every Brother is doing something to honor your sacred memory, and I, stupid Barnabas, have nothing to offer.

NARRATOR: Thus did Barnabas lament and abandon himself to his misery. One evening in the refectory, he heard a monk tell a story.

MONK: It took place here many years ago. The Brother's name was Jean. He could not, poor man, recite anything but the "Ave Maria."

MONK 2: Only the "Ave Maria"!

MONK 3: Indeed, he must have been a sorry sight.

MONK: Yes, he was scorned for his ignorance, was Brother Jean, but after his death a remarkable event took place.

MONK 2: An "event"!

MONK 3: Tell us, Brother, what happened?

MONK: After he died there sprang from his mouth five roses.

MONK 3: Five roses!

MONK: Five roses, in honor of the five letters in the name Maria. Thus was his holiness made manifest.

MUSIC: *Christmas hymn. Sneak and hold under.*

NARRATOR: In listening to this story, Barnabas was conscious once more of the Holy Virgin's beneficence. But he was not consoled by the example of the happy miracle, for his heart was full of zeal and he wanted to celebrate the glory of his Lady in Heaven on Christmas. He sought for a way in which to do this, but in vain, and each day brought him greater sorrow. He even volunteered to sing with the choir that was to accompany the Mass on Christmas morning.

MUSIC: *Out.*

NARRATOR: The choirmaster listened to Barnabas. Afterwards he drew him aside.

CHOIRMASTER: I am sorry, Brother Barnabas, but I cannot have you in the choir.

BARNABAS: I do not sing very well?

CHOIRMASTER: You do not sing well, Brother Barnabas. Your voice is . . . is—well, you have no voice at all.

NARRATOR: Despite the newly-fallen snow that blanketed the monastery grounds, Barnabas walked back and forth, his head bowed. He was so lost in sadness, he did not at first hear the voice of the Prior.

PRIOR: Again you are grieving, Brother Barnabas. Why?

BARNABAS: Good Prior, my sadness lingers on me, because I have no gift for the Holy Mother. Tomorrow is Christmas and, when the others make their offerings, I shall have nothing to give. I shall be but a sorry sight.

PRIOR: Have faith, Barnabas, have faith. (*Fading*) She is all-knowing. Have faith and she will reward you.

MUSIC: *A sacred Christmas hymn. Sneak and hold under.*

NARRATOR: The next morning ushered in a sacred Christmas at the monastery. At Mass the monks knelt in prayer, while the Prior celebrated the holy ceremony. During it, Barnabas kept his head bowed, for he wished to shut out the sight of the fine gifts made by the other monks and offered up as a part of the service. But he could not shut out the fine prayer, in the form of a sermon, which the Prior had written, and which he read from Brother Maurice's finely-copied parchment, decorated by Brother Alexandre. He likewise could not shut out the voices of the choir when it sang Brother Jacques' Christmas hymn set to music by Brother François; nor could he shut out his own glaring lack of contribution to the Holy Virgin.

MUSIC: *Out*.

NARRATOR: That noon when the monks sat down to their Christmas dinner of soup and goose and pudding, Barnabas was absent. He had no appetite. His eyes lacked lustre, his head was bent, his steps dragged as he walked around the grounds of the walled-in garden. He said to himself:

BARNABAS: I am such a meagre, little man . . . an uneducated and most untalented man. I am unworthy to wear the cloth of the Church. Christmas Day is almost passed and I, alone among these talented men, have failed to contribute anything to the great feast of Our Lord. Mary, Mother of God, pray for me, a humble man with no talent. (*Fading*) Pray for me, O dearest Mary, Mother of God, forgive me.

NARRATOR: The afternoon of Christmas melted into evening. Vespers and the benediction passed. At last the monks went to their simple cells where sleep descended upon them. And with them went a sorrowful Barnabas. For several hours he lay awake, unable to fall off to sleep. Finally he sat up. There was hope in his eyes. He reached out, groping at the corner of his tiny cell. Then he quietly opened his door and stole down the darkened corridor. Several minutes later, Brother Alexandre, he who had painted the fine miniatures on the parchment containing the Prior's special sermon to the Holy Mother, looked in at the semi-darkened chapel. What he saw made him start. He opened his mouth as though to speak, to call out, to protest, but no words came forth. He made a motion of entering the chapel, but something seemed to hold him back. Fascinated, he watched, and then he whirled around. He practically ran from the chapel, his white robe flapping around his bare ankles, his sandals slapping against the stone floor. Out of breath, he paused at the door leading to the Prior's cell. Without calling out or knocking, without waiting for permission, he entered. Shaking the startled and sleepy Prior by the shoulder, he almost yelled.

ALEXANDRE: Prior . . . Father . . . rise . . . rise and follow me.

PRIOR: Brother Alexandre, why do you enter in such a fashion? What is wrong?

ALEXANDRE: A great sin is being committed . . . a sacrilege.

PRIOR: Sin . . . sacrilege—whatever do you mean?

ALEXANDRE: I cannot bear to tell you. You must see for yourself. This is a matter that only you can pass upon.

PRIOR: It cannot be that serious.

ALEXANDRE: But it is, Prior, it is. Please follow me.

NARRATOR: The Prior, led by Brother Alexandre, hurried to the chapel. Outside, they paused.

CHOIR: *A capella, celestial effect of humming "Ave Maria." Sneak in and hold under scene.*

NARRATOR: Through the open door of the chapel, the Prior and Brother Alexandre saw a remarkable sight. They saw Barnabas before the image of the Holy Virgin, his head on the floor and his feet in the air. He was juggling six copper balls and twelve knives. In honor of the Holy Virgin he was performing the tricks which had in former days brought him the greatest fame. This was Barnabas' humble offering to Her, the only gift he could make, one that was born out of his great devotion and steadfast faith. Brother Alexandre, horrified at what he thought to be a great sacrilege, made a motion to rush toward the ex-juggler. But the Prior raised his hand.

PRIOR (*Sotto voce*): Be charitable, Brother Alexandre.

ALEXANDRE (*Protesting*): But this is wrong. He will be punished.

PRIOR: It may be as you say, but be gentle. Tell Brother Barnabas he must stop juggling.

ALEXANDRE: He has lost his wits.

PRIOR: He is a simple man, a good man. Now go to him.

NARRATOR: But scarcely had the Prior stopped talking, when a wonderful thing took place. The two men saw the Virgin slowly descend from the altar. With a fold of her blue mantle, she wiped away the sweat that streamed over the juggler's forehead. Then the Prior, bowing his head down to the marble floor, uttered reverently:

PRIOR: Blessed are the pure in heart, for they shall see God.

CHOIR: *Segue into a chorus of "Ave Maria." Up to finish.*

THE END

The Legend of Sleepy Hollow

by Washington Irving

MUSIC: *An easy, bucolic theme. Sneak in and hold under.*

NARRATOR: In the bosom of one of those spacious coves which indent the eastern shore of the Hudson there lies a small market port known as Tarrytown. Not far away is a small valley. From the listless repose of this place, this sequestered glen has long been known as Sleepy Hollow. Its lads, descendents of the original Dutch settlers, are called the Sleepy Hollow Boys. A drowsy, dreamy influence seems to hang over the land, and to pervade the very atmosphere. Some say the place is bewitched and that the inhabitants walk in a continual reverie. The dominant spirit haunting this enchanted region, and commander-in-chief of all the apparitions of the air, is a ghostly figure on horseback, minus a head. It is said to be the ghost of a Hessian trooper, whose head had been carried away by a cannon ball during the Revolution. And ever and anon, this Headless Horseman of Sleepy Hollow is seen by the country folk, hurrying through the night, as if on the wings of the wind.

MUSIC: *Out.*

NARRATOR: The only tavern in the region was that operated by Yost Van Houten, and called "The Peter Stuyvesant." Late one sunny spring afternoon there gathered outside this backwoods retreat of good cheer Mine Host and Balthus Van Tassel, the most prosperous farmer in the neighborhood.

MUSIC: *A comic theme. Sneak and hold under.*

NARRATOR: Suddenly Yost Van Houten's mouth sprang open

like a steel trap. His mouth opened, but no words came forth. With a quivering finger he pointed. Balthus Van Tassel's gaze followed it. Striding up the hill was a very tall, but exceedingly lank man. He had narrow shoulders, long arms and legs, and feet that might have served as shovels. His whole figure hung together most loosely. His head was small, and flat at the top, with huge ears, large glassy eyes. He had a long nose that looked like a weathercock, perched on his spindle neck to tell which way the wind blew. Indeed he might be mistaken for some scarecrow escaped from a cornfield. Over his shoulder he carried a stick, at the end of which hung a small and rounded cloth, evidently containing his possessions. He advanced to the two inhabitants and made a bow.

MUSIC: *Out.*

ICHABOD: Good afternoon, gentlemen.

YOST: Good day, sir.

BALTHUS: A warm day.

ICHABOD: Can you tell me where I am?

YOST: Sleepy Hollow.

ICHABOD (*Sighing*): May I sit? Indeed, I'm most tired. Since this morning, I have walked close to thirty miles.

YOST: Where is your home?

ICHABOD: Mostly where I make it. I am a native of Connecticut.

BALTHUS: Dod is far avay, ja?

ICHABOD: Indeed, yes. I should introduce myself. I am Ichabod Crane, schoolmaster, singing teacher, storyteller, and man of letters, a graduate of Yale University.

BALTHUS (*Impressed*): A schoolmaster.

ICHABOD (*Unenthusiastically*): Unfortunately. (*Adding quickly*) But a very fine one.

YOST: I am Yost Van Houten, owner of this tavern, and this is Balthus Van Tassel, a farmer.

ICHABOD: Your servant, gentlemen.

Yost: Perhaps you would like some food.
Ichabod (*Brightening up*): Ah!
Yost: And a cool mug of cider?
Ichabod: *Ah!*
Yost: At a very reasonable cost.
Ichabod (*Downcast*): Oh!
Balthus: Ve need a schoolmaster for our children, Yost. Maybe dis gentleman vould like the position.
Yost: This is true, Balthus.
Ichabod: Oh, you could do much worse than to hire me.
Yost: Then the position is yours. Twenty dollars for the season and room and board.
Ichabod: I usually receive twenty-five dollars for the season.
Balthus: De last teacher, ve only paid fifteen dollars.
Ichabod (*Hastily*): I accept your offer. And now, as an advance, I would like some food. Thank you!
Music: *A light theme. Forte and fade under.*
Narrator: And that is how Sleepy Hollow gained its new schoolmaster, Ichabod Crane of Connecticut. He was a conscientious man and strove to drill knowledge into his pupils' heads. Although a just man in school, outside he was a companion to his pupils, particularly to those who had pretty sisters. Ichabod had two weaknesses. One was for a young and pretty girl, for he fancied himself as a charming and accomplished and very dashing figure, a most eligible bachelor. And his other weakness was food. And so if the pupil in question failed to have a pretty sister, he very possibly had a mother noted for her fine cooking. In reality, Ichabod was searching for a young and pretty wife, who could cook and who had means. But so far, romance had failed to beckon; indeed, it had not even gently nudged him. He had not been long in Sleepy Hollow before there presented itself what seemed to be an ideal opportunity. It all started in his schoolroom.
Music: *Out.*

THE LEGEND OF SLEEPY HOLLOW

PETER (*A young boy of 12*): The answer to the problem is three dollars and fifty cents.
ICHABOD: It is not! The answer is . . . is—er. . . .
PETER: Well?
ICHABOD: The answer is seven dollars and thirty-nine cents. That is how much the farmer paid for the cow.
PETER: I was figuring at last year's prices.
ICHABOD: Peter Van Tassel, don't try to be humorous with me. My scholars are far from brilliant. In fact, they are somewhat dense. But you . . . you are outstanding for your utter stupidity. You even abuse the privilege.
PETER: Why?
ICHABOD: I keep you after school in an effort to drive some learning into your head, and what do you gain from my instruction?
PETER: Nothing.
ICHABOD (*Warningly*): I ought to—
KATRINA (*Slightly away*): Good afternoon. May I enter?
ICHABOD (*Graciously*): Indeed, you may, my dear young lady. I was just finishing with this . . . this—
PETER: That's my sister Katrina.
ICHABOD: This splendid young brother of yours. . . .
KATRINA: Is he giving you trouble?
ICHABOD: Oh, not at all. He's one of my better pupils.
PETER: But you just said—
ICHABOD (*Cutting in*): Aren't you, Peter?
KATRINA: Peter is probably meant for farming, instead of school.
ICHABOD: Your brother is most ambitious.
PETER: Not in school, I'm not.
ICHABOD: I wasn't aware that Peter had such a charming sister.
KATRINA: Thank you, Mr. Crane.
ICHABOD: I am still new, and haven't managed to visit the homes of all my pupils.
KATRINA: We should be delighted to have you call, Mr. Crane.

ICHABOD: Thank you. Do you sing?
PETER: She has a voice like a crow.
KATRINA (*Warningly*): Peter!
ICHABOD: Perhaps you have heard that I am going to instruct the young ladies and gentlemen of Sleepy Hollow in psalmody. (*The Yankee asserting itself*) A full evening of useful instruction for the meagre fee of ten cents per pupil. I would enjoy having you, Miss Van Tassel.
KATRINA: Perhaps I'll join. Come, Peter, you're needed to help with the chores. Good day, Mr. Crane.
ICHABOD (*Archly*): Good-bye, Katrina.
PETER: Mr. Crane, I still say that cow cost the farmer only three dollars and fifty cents.
MUSIC: *Light, frivolous pattern. Forte and fade under.*
NARRATOR: And that was how romance entered the humdrum life of Ichabod. But Katrina Van Tassel, an extremely pretty and vivacious girl, did not succumb. She was polite and attentive to Ichabod, and that was all. But Ichabod, having a soft and foolish heart, redoubled his efforts. Katrina had numerous admirers, and chief among these was the formidable Brom Van Brunt, nicknamed Brom Bones because of his Herculean frame and great feats of strength, as well as his horsemanship. He was always ready for either a fight or a frolic, and had a waggish sense of humor. Truly, lanky Ichabod had great temerity in electing himself a rival of Brom Bones. Katrina joined the singing class, as did Brom.
MUSIC: *Out into:*
BIZ: *Mixed small chorus singing last stanza of an early American ballad. Example: "The Lass of Richmond Hill." It is a rather discordant, out-of-tune effect.*
ICHABOD (*As song ends*): Very commendable, but we need practice. And you must be careful of your diction. I shall now give you an example of how it should be sung.

SOUND: *Pitch pipe.*
ICHABOD: Do! (*He clears throat.*) Now listen. (*He sings the same stanza in a quavering voice that is off-key.*)
BROM: *As* ICHABOD *ends, he wails like a dog.*
BIZ: *Chorus titters.*
KATRINA (*Angrily*): Brom Bones, stop that. You should be ashamed of yourself, acting the fool.
BROM: I was just trying to sing like Mr. Crane.
KATRINA: You were not. We pay our money to learn something, and not to have you spoil our evening.
ICHABOD: Er, that is all for tonight. Class dismissed.
BIZ: *Young people saying: "Good night, Mr. Crane." "We'll be here next week." "Good night."*
ICHABOD (*Against voices*): Yes, next Tuesday night, the same time. (*As an aside*) Oh, Katrina.
KATRINA: Yes, Mr. Crane.
ICHABOD: Now, now, what have I said?
KATRINA (*Correcting herself*): Ichabod. I'm sorry that Brom was rude. I'm sure he meant nothing by it.
ICHABOD: Please don't allow the matter to bother you. I wonder—that is, will you allow me to see you home?
KATRINA (*Hesitantly*): I would, but I had planned to—
BROM (*Brusquely*): Come, Katrina, it's getting late.
ICHABOD (*Stiffly*): I have already asked Katrina's permission to accompany her home.
BROM (*Laughing*): You're well named. Crane. That's just what you look like. A crane! Come, Katrina.
KATRINA: Brom, you aren't a gentleman.
BROM (*Promptly*): I know it. Never said I was one.
KATRINA: I'm not going with you.
BROM (*Amazed*): No!
KATRINA: No!
BROM: Why not?

KATRINA: Are you ready, Ichabod?

ICHABOD (*Eagerly*): All ready! Oh, indeed yes.

BROM: This is your fault, Crane. You psalm-singing hypocrite, I've a mind to wrap you up and toss you into the river.

ICHABOD (*Frightened*): Now, now, there is a lady present.

BROM: In fact, maybe I'll do it right now.

ICHABOD: Remember my position in this community. I'm a schoolmaster.

KATRINA: You'll do no such thing, Brom. And until you learn better manners, you're not to speak to me. Understand? (*Aside*) Come, Ichabod.

ICHABOD: Of course. (*Aside*) And, Brom, remember—everything comes to him who waits.

BROM: I'll remember that. Never fear.

MUSIC: *A romantic theme. Forte and fade under.*

NARRATOR: For Ichabod to have openly taken to the field against Brom Bones would have been madness. Brom, so everyone said, was in a bad humor. But Ichabod was not to be thwarted. Therefore, he made his advances in a quiet and gently insinuating manner. Under cover of his character as a singing master, he made frequent visits to the Van Tassel farmhouse.

MUSIC: *Out into:*

ICHABOD: *Singing the last stanza of an early American love ballad. His voice, as usual, is cracked and nasal. As he ends:*

KATRINA: That was lovely, Ichabod.

ICHABOD: Thank you, Katrina. I sang it just for you.

BALTHUS (*Away. Calling out*): Katrina. Katrina, vat is wrong?

KATRINA (*Calling back*): Nothing, Father.

BALTHUS: I thought maybe dod new heifer was sick.

KATRINA (*Brightly*): Oh, no, Father. That was Mr. Crane singing.

BALTHUS: Oh, den dod is all right.

KATRINA (*To* ICHABOD): Father isn't very musical, Ichabod.

ICHABOD: Well, we all can't be talented, you know. Katrina,

there is something I wish to ask you. I'm not a wealthy man, but I'm ambitious. I'm also educated.
KATRINA: Everyone knows that.
ICHABOD: I know I have a future. But gazing ahead, I can see a hole.
KATRINA: In what?
ICHABOD: There is something missing.
KATRINA: Perhaps you'll find it.
ICHABOD: Oh, I have found it, Katrina, I have, indeed, found it. Katrina, what I want to ask you is—that is, will you, will you—
KATRINA: Let me interrupt you, Ichabod. I have something to ask you, something that can't wait. Will you help me?
ICHABOD (*Eagerly*): Yes, Katrina, anything.
KATRINA: I hope it isn't too late.
ICHABOD: I haven't promised myself to anyone else.
KATRINA: Good! Ichabod, come and help me carry in the milk. It's getting close to five.
MUSIC: *A comic theme. Up briefly and out into:*
SOUND: *Sawing wood. Hold for a few seconds. Then:*
PETER (*Away*): Hello, Mr. Crane. It's me—Peter.
SOUND: *Out.*
ICHABOD (*Breathing heavily*): Peter Van Tassel. You've come to pay me a visit.
PETER: (*Fading in*): No, not exactly.
ICHABOD: You caught me in the act of getting a bit of exercise.
PETER: Old Hans Van Ripper told me you're sawing to help pay off your debt to him. It's because of that money you borrowed from him to buy Katrina that book for her birthday. I read those poems. All about moonlight and love and things like that.
ICHABOD (*Stiffly*): Peter, unless you can behave like a gentleman, you may leave.
PETER: If I do, you won't get the message.

ICHABOD: Message, message! From your sister?

PETER: Well, not exactly. It's from my father and mother, too. We're having a quilting party tonight, and you're invited.

ICHABOD: How very thoughtful of your sister.

PETER: Everyone's going to be there. You like to eat, so I told Katrina you'd be there.

ICHABOD: Indeed, I will, Peter: indeed, yes.

PETER: Brom Bones'll be there.

ICHABOD: I have nothing in common with him.

PETER: I just gave him his invitation.

ICHABOD (*Stiffly*): Brom Bones is an uncouth bumpkin, a lazy good for nothing.

PETER: Shall I tell him what you said?

ICHABOD: No, no. Better not, Peter.

PETER: He's pretty mad at you.

ICHABOD: He has no reason to harbor such a feeling, for I do not even consider him a serious rival.

PETER (*Admiringly*): Mr. Crane, you certainly know how to make a big speech.

ICHABOD: Peter, I usually have but very little to say.

PETER (*Agreeing*): Oh, we all know that, Mr. Crane.

ICHABOD: Very little, indeed.

PETER: But you keep repeating it over and over. (*Fading*) Well, 'bye, Mr. Crane. I'll tell Katrina you'll be there tonight.

ICHABOD (*Musing to himself*): Ah, romance! Sweet, pretty Katrina. Ahhhh!

VAN RIPPER (*Fading in*): Say, dere, Mr. Crane, a few minutes ago you vass sawing vood. Ja! Now you do nothing, and dere iss still much vood. Ja.

ICHABOD: Hans, Mr. Van Ripper, I have a great favor to ask.

VAN RIPPER: I haff no money to lend.

ICHABOD: Don't be crass, Mr. Van Ripper, not at a moment such as this.

VAN RIPPER: Vat iss it you vant?
ICHABOD: I am going to the Van Tassel's quilting party this evening.
VAN RIPPER: So am I.
ICHABOD: It is such a long walk.
VAN RIPPER: Five miles.
ICHABOD: I thought perhaps you might loan me your mare.
VAN RIPPER: I am riding the mare.
ICHABOD (*Disappointed*): Oh.
VAN RIPPER: I might let you ride Gunpowder.
ICHABOD: Gunpowder! Me ride to a social gathering on Gunpowder?
VAN RIPPER: Better than valking. Remember, five miles each vay iss ten miles.
ICHABOD (*Resigned*): Thank you, Mr. Van Ripper. I accept your offer.
MUSIC: *A light theme. Forte and fade under.*
NARRATOR: Ichabod spent the rest of the afternoon preparing for the party at Van Tassel's. Then he mounted his gallant steed and set out. Gunpowder was a broken-down plough-horse that had outlived everything but his temper. He was gaunt and shagged and had a head like a hammer. One eye had lost its pupil and was glaring and spectral, but the other had the gleam of a devil in it. And Ichabod was a suitable figure for such a steed. He looked like a bouncing grasshopper. All in all, the combination of Ichabod and Gunpowder was an apparition as is seldom to be met in broad daylight. It was towards evening that Ichabod arrived at the Van Tassel's. From a small hill he surveyed the rich, rolling lands of Katrina's father. It was autumn and Van Tassel's property was fairly bursting with harvest treasures. Ichabod swelled with expectancy.
MUSIC: *Out.*

ICHABOD (*Musing*): Acre upon acre, and some day it well may be mine. Mrs. Katrina Crane. Mrs. Ichabod Crane. What a pleasant sound it has, like a rich melody. I have waited long enough. Tonight she shall say "yes." I'll wait no longer. Understand, Gunpowder, tonight I shall ask her.

BIZ: *Gunpowder whinnies contemptuously. A pause, then, fading in: Ad lib of many people chattering away. Hold under.*

BALTHUS: Ah, good evening, Mr. Crane. Velcome, velcome.

ICHABOD: Thank you for inviting me, Mr. Van Tassel.

BALTHUS: Everyone iss here. There is much good things to eat. Fall to. Help yourself. Eat up.

ICHABOD: Thank you.

BALTHUS: Enjoy yourself.

ICHABOD: Is Katrina—she, er—

BALTHUS: Yes, she iss here. Sitting over there mit Brom Bones. Your rival, ja. Better be careful of him. He iss a mighty fellow. (*Fading*) Now enjoy yourself, Mr. Crane. Eat up.

BIZ: *Background voices fade out as:*

NARRATOR: Ichabod took one look at the formidable Brom Bones, who, wearing a scowl, was deep in conversation with the fair Katrina. Deciding to bide his time, he attacked the food. He ate and ate, his spirits rose and rose. As they did, the thought again came to him that one day he indeed might be lord of all this scene of luxury and splendor. Then he would turn his back on keeping school, then he would face Brom Bones without flinching.

VIOLIN: *Being tuned up.*

NARRATOR: This was the signal for Ichabod to put his best foot forward. He approached the blooming Katrina and her sour-faced admirer.

BIZ: *Ad lib voices of guests in background.*

ICHABOD: Katrina, my dear Katrina, how lovely you look, but then you always look lovely.

KATRINA: Welcome, Ichabod. I've been waiting for you to recognize me.
ICHABOD: Good evening, Brom.
BROM: What's good about it?
ICHABOD: Everything. Katrina, this is a fine affair.
KATRINA: And I'm glad you're here, Ichabod.
VIOLIN: *Plays a bouncing country dance tune. Hold under.*
ICHABOD: You'll do me the honor, Katrina?
KATRINA (*Hesitantly*): Why, y-yes, I guess so. Brom doesn't dance.
ICHABOD: Oh, you don't. What a pity! But then we can't all have social graces, can we, Brom?
BROM (*Angrily*): Listen, you—
ICHABOD (*Graciously*): My arm, Katrina. Come!
VIOLIN: *Up briefly and under again.*
NARRATOR: Ichabod prided himself upon his dancing as much as upon his vocal powers. Not a limb, not a fibre about him was idle. To have seen his loosely hung frame in full motion, and clattering about the room, you would have thought Saint Vitus himself was figuring before you. He was the admiration of all. Katrina smiled up into his eyes, while Brom Bones jealously sat brooding in the corner.
VIOLIN: *Up full to end. Then:*
BIZ: *Applause from guests.*
ICHABOD: Thank you, Katrina. That was superb.
KATRINA: I enjoyed it, too.
ICHABOD: You'll dance with me again?
KATRINA: Later.
PETER: Mr. Crane. Mr. Crane.
ICHABOD: Yes, Peter?
PETER: My father and some of the men are in the next room. They're telling stories, and they want you there.
ICHABOD: Well, I—I want to talk with your sister.

KATRINA: Later, Ichabod. I should stay with the other guests. *(Fading)* Please excuse me now.

BIZ: *Background voices of guests out. A pause, then:*

YOST *(Fading in)*: And I remember my father telling me about Old Martling during the Battle of White Plains. A cannon ball came whizzing straight at his head, and Old Martling parried it with his sword. It whizzed round the blade and bounced to the ground.

BALTHUS: Ja, I haff heard dod story, too.

BIZ: *A few male guests saying: "A true story, it is." "I have seen the sword. It is bent." "Remarkable story."*

YOST: You, Schoolmaster Crane, perhaps you raise your eyebrows at these stories.

ICHABOD: Not at all, Yost. To the contrary, I do believe them. Indeed, I have made a close study of the supernatural—ghosts and devils and the like.

BIZ: *Voices: "Is that so?" "Mr. Crane knows about them, too." "He is a learned man."*

ICHABOD: Have any of you read Cotton Mather's "History of New England Witchcraft"? *(Pause)* Well, you should, for it speaks of black-robed witches that ride astride bolts of lightning, and about faceless gnomes that dance on banks of fog.

BROM *(Contemptuous)*: Hah! Stuff! I don't let things like that bother me.

ICHABOD: Nevertheless it's true.

BALTHUS: You shouldn't say Mr. Crane doesn't know vat he iss talking about, Brom Bones. He is a schoolmaster.

BROM: I didn't say I didn't believe in ghosts.

VAN RIPPER: I haff seen a ghost.

BALTHUS: You, Hans Van Ripper, you haff seen a ghost!

VAN RIPPER: The Headless Horseman of Sleepy Hollow.

BIZ: *A few gasps of surprise from the men.*

Yost: Tell us about it.

Van Ripper: He makes his headquarters down by the graveyard near the big brook. I vass coming home, und it vass late. He came out of the fog, carrying hiss head under hiss arm. Und he made me get up behind him. Ve galloped up und down hill. Und ven ve crossed the bridge, he threw me off, und den he disappeared in a clap of thunder.

Ichabod: That's a ghastly story.

Yost: But true, I'm certain, for one night the Headless Horseman galloped up and down the roof of my inn, and I saw him disappear in a sheet of fire.

Ichabod: It makes me shudder.

Balthus: Ja, the Headless Horseman is our most famous ghost in these parts.

Brom: You are talking about the Headless Horseman, but none of you has ever had the experience I once had.

Yost: Tell us, Brom.

Brom: It was very late at night. I was riding alone when all of a sudden I came face to face with him.

Balthus: You were frightened?

Brom: Of course not. He tried to make me climb up beside him, but instead I offered to race him. We did, and I was beating him all hollow when he got mad. When we reached the bridge, I looked behind and saw him vanish into the air. He was a bad sport.

Balthus: Dod iss quite a story.

Brom: A true one.

Ichabod (*Shuddering*): Good Heavens! I hope I never have the misfortune to meet up with him. I wouldn't know what to do.

Brom (*Warningly*): It's said that the Headless Horseman doesn't intend any harm to the natives hereabouts. It's strangers he doesn't like.

ICHABOD: But he wouldn't think of me as a stranger. After all, I live here.
BROM: You're still a stranger to him.
MUSIC: *An ominous bridge. Up and out.*
KATRINA: It's getting late, Ichabod. All the other guests have gone home.
ICHABOD: Including Mr. Brom Bones.
KATRINA: I'm afraid he doesn't like you.
ICHABOD: But of course you never were really interested in him. Katrina, I must talk to you.
KATRINA: Some other time. I'm quite tired.
PETER (*Fading in*): Say, I've learned a new problem. I'll ask you to try it, Mr. Crane.
ICHABOD: Some other day, Peter. I'm busy.
PETER: But you keep telling me I should learn to do my sums, and I've done so. This is a fine problem. Listen.
KATRINA: It will please him, Ichabod.
PETER: I'll tell you how old you are Mr. Crane, and how much you have in your pocket.
ICHABOD: Really?
PETER: Ready? Take your age and multiply by two.
ICHABOD: Yes.
PETER: Add five.
ICHABOD: Go on.
PETER: Multiply by fifty.
ICHABOD: By fifty. (*Pause*) Go on.
PETER: Subtract three-hundred and sixty-five.
ICHABOD: Mmmm! (*Pause*) Yes, I have it.
PETER: Add the loose change in your pocket. Well, go ahead.
ICHABOD: I have.
PETER: Your answer is what?
ICHABOD: What? Why, it's four-zero-zero-five. Is that correct?
PETER: If you say so. Know what? The first two figures in your answer is your age—forty.

ICHABOD (*Sputters*): Now, look here—
PETER: And the last two the change in your pocket—five cents.
ICHABOD: I am not forty. I'm—
PETER: But you figured it out, and you say you're never wrong. Well, good night, Mr. Crane. You're a good figurer.
ICHABOD (*Still fuming*): Why, I never . . . ridiculous. Katrina, you don't believe I'm that old.
KATRINA: Why should I mind how old you are? It makes no difference, believe me.
ICHABOD: You wonderful girl! Katrina, this is the greatest moment of your life. I have to tell you, for it's been gnawing at me inside all night long.
KATRINA: Indigestion?
ICHABOD: And now I can speak?
KATRINA: Of course.
ICHABOD: You don't mind?
KATRINA: Not in the least.
ICHABOD: How shall I begin? Oh, I've so carefully rehearsed all this, and now I'm speechless.
KATRINA: For the first time, probably.
ICHABOD: Katrina, I kneel before you.
KATRINA: You're liable to get housemaid's knee.
ICHABOD: I do so wish to bring happiness into your life.
KATRINA: You do?
ICHABOD: At first I thought it was Brom Bones, but tonight I know differently. Katrina, I love you. I want you to be my wife.
KATRINA: No.
ICHABOD (*Amazed*): What?
KATRINA (*Firmly*): No!
ICHABOD: I don't understand.
KATRINA: I know you don't.
ICHABOD: But I love you.
KATRINA: But I don't love you.

ICHABOD: I don't understand why not.
KATRINA: Of course you don't, for you're a ridiculous man.
ICHABOD: You don't mean that.
KATRINA: I most certainly do.
ICHABOD: And you don't love me?
KATRINA: Not in the least.
ICHABOD: But—I don't understand your attitude.
KATRINA: I was merely flirting. I was playing a trick on you, just to make someone else jealous.
ICHABOD: I don't believe you. You'll change your mind. I'll wait until you do.
KATRINA: Then you'll grow old waiting. (*Fading*) Good night, Ichabod.
ICHABOD (*Groaning*): Oh! Oh! Oh!
MUSIC: *A doleful theme. Forte and fade under.*
NARRATOR: And when Ichabod went to the stable to saddle Gunpowder for the homeward journey, that ancient animal greeted him with—
BIZ: *Gunpowder whinnies shrilly, a real horse laugh.*
MUSIC: *A doleful theme. Forte and under.*
NARRATOR: Heavy-hearted and crest-fallen, Ichabod rode homeward. The late hour was as dismal as himself. No sign of life disturbed him. All the stories of ghosts and goblins he had heard came crowding upon him. The night grew darker and darker. The stars disappeared behind the driving clouds. Ichabod had never felt so lonely and dismal. He was approaching the place where the Headless Horseman of Sleepy Hollow was said to make his headquarters. His heart began to thump. Nervously, he kicked the irritable and sleepy Gunpowder into a faster pace.
MUSIC: *Out into:*
SOUND: *Horse trotting on dirt road. Sustain under.*
ICHABOD: Come on, Gunpowder, you ugly brute. Hmphh! Made

a fool of by a young girl. She was laughing at me all the while. Now she's going to marry that lout, Brom Bones. How could she prefer him to me! Well, she's a foolish, light-headed girl, and she's not worthy of me. I can't understand it. (*Clucking*) Get along, Gunpowder. (*Suddenly*) What's that? By the side of the road.

SOUND: *Hoofs out.*

ICHABOD (*Frightened*): W-who's that? Who are you? A horseman! (*Realization*) A horseman! Good evening? (*Pause*) Where's your head? You're carrying it under your arm. You're the Headless Horseman of Sleepy Hollow. How are you? I've heard so much about you. Glad to see you, sir. I'm . . . I'm Ichabod Crane . . . schoolmaster. Been to a social affair. Just going home. Rather late. I'd like to stay and talk, but I should be getting along. So you'll excuse me, I'm sure. Come on, Gunpowder! Giddap!

SOUND: *Hoofs into clumsy gallop. Sustain under.*

ICHABOD (*Terrified*): Oh, he's following me. Right behind me . . . ohhh! Faster, Gunpowder, faster!

SOUND: *Hoofs out into:*

MUSIC: *A theme of pursuit. Forte and under.*

NARRATOR: And off dashed the decrepit Gunpowder, with the Headless Horseman in close pursuit. Even Gunpowder seemed to realize the situation was grave. As Ichabod approached a hollow, the girths of his saddle gave way. Seconds later the saddle—Hans Van Ripper's best saddle—slipped to the ground and was trampled underfoot. But this was no time for petty fears, Ichabod thought. He was approaching the bridge, the place where the ghostly and headless pursuer was, according to legend, supposed to disappear. Ichabod took heart. Safety at last. Another convulsive kick in the ribs, and Gunpowder sprang upon the bridge. He gained the other side. Ichabod looked behind to see if his pursuer had vanished.

According to rule he should. He saw the goblin rising in his saddle, and in the act of hurling his head at him. Ichabod endeavored to dodge, but too late. It encountered his cranium with a tremendous crash. Ichabod was tumbled into the dust. And Gunpowder, the Headless Horseman and his black steed passed him like a whirlwind.

MUSIC: *Up and out.*

NARRATOR: The next day, when Ichabod failed to put in an appearance, Yost Van Houten, the innkeeper, and Hans Van Ripper, from whom Ichabod had borrowed the horse, went searching for the missing schoolmaster. They paused by the fatal bridge.

YOST: The hoofs seem to stop here by the bridge. Then another set goes on up through the field. Strange!

VAN RIPPER: Maybe he vass drowned.

YOST: The water isn't deep enough. What are you staring at?

VAN RIPPER: Look—a hat. (*Pause*) Ja, it iss his. I recognize it.

YOST: Here are some footprints. Just a few, and then they disappear.

VAN RIPPER: You know vat I think. I think that Ichabod Crane vass spirited away from dis earth.

BROM (*Away*): Hello, there. Hello.

VAN RIPPER: It's Brom Bones. (*Calling out*) Hello, Brom.

BROM (*Fading in*): Well, did you find anything? Any sign of him?

VAN RIPPER: Nary a sign.

BROM: I don't understand it.

YOST: Do you suppose he—? Oh, no, it couldn't be.

BROM: What are you trying to say, Yost?

YOST: I wonder if he could have run across the Headless Horseman.

VAN RIPPER: He might have, at that.

YOST: Here is something else. Look—here.
VAN RIPPER: A broken pumpkin.
YOST: Might have fallen out of a passing wagon.
VAN RIPPER: What do you make of de pumpkin, Brom?
BROM: It looks as though it might have been thrown with a lot of force at some very hard object, like a man's head.
YOST: I guess that is the end of Mr. Ichabod Crane.
MUSIC: *A peaceful theme. Forte and fade.*
NARRATOR: The story persisted that Ichabod had been carried away by the Headless Horseman of Sleepy Hollow. As he was a bachelor, and in nobody's debt, the villagers gave him no further thought. Shortly after this incident, Brom Bones conducted the blooming Katrina to the altar. Even if Ichabod had left a forwarding address, it is doubtful if he would have been invited to the wedding. It is even more doubtful that he would have attended.
MUSIC: *Up full and out.*

THE END

My Double and How He Undid Me

by Edward Everett Hale

MUSIC: *Narrative theme: Light yet whimsically sad—sneak in and hold under.*
INGHAM: It is with a great deal of reluctance that I trouble you with a tale better left untold. Indeed, I would not trouble you at all, but for the importunities of my wife. She feels that a duty to society is unfilled till I have told why I had a double, and how he undid me. *What a story!*
MUSIC: *A few brisk comic chords—and then segue to leisurely background theme and hold under.*
INGHAM: My name is Fred Ingham. I'm married . . . and my wife's name is Polly. The small New England town we *did* live in was ideal, but for one point. You see, I'm a writer. Consequently, never a day went by but this happened—
WOMAN 1: Dear Mr. Ingham, won't you speak to the Ladies' Aid Society?
WOMAN 2: We'd love having you for tea.
MAN 1: You must come to the Community Club meeting.
MAN 2: To say nothing of the Boosters' Club.
GIRL (*Shrill voice*): Gee! May I have your autograph?
CHORUS: . . . "Mr. Ingham, won't you join our club . . . and do this . . . and that . . ."
WOMAN 1: Et cetera.
MAN 1: Et cetera.
WOMAN 2: Et cetera.
MUSIC: *Segue to comic chords—up and out.*
INGHAM: You see! (*Pause*) It got to the point where I never

had a chance to do any writing. Something just had to be done. At last came—opportunity!

SOUND: *Brisk knocking on door.*

INGHAM: And I, poor fool, answered. (*Briskly*) It happened this way: Polly and I were vacationing at a beach resort. One day, while strolling, we came to a shack. (*Slight fade*) We approached the place to ask for a drink of water.

SOUND (*Fade it in over latter part of* INGHAM'S *last line*): *Bell-buoy off in distance.*

POLLY: There's a couple sitting on the stoop. Ambitious looking, aren't they?

INGHAM: Probably a clam digger and his wife.

POLLY: Hope they won't mind our bothering them. I'm terribly thirsty. Fred! Fred, what's wrong. You're as white as a sheet. Are you ill?

INGHAM: Polly . . . look . . . look!

POLLY: G-good Heaven! I can't believe it. It's . . . it's uncanny. Your double!

INGHAM: Same color hair . . . identical features . . . even to a scar over the left eye. Polly, he's my twin. (*Determined*) I've got to speak to him.

POLLY: He's seen us. Now he's coming toward us.

DENNIS (*Fade in*): Good afternoon to yez. What would yez be wantin'? (*Yells*) Bridget, come here. 'Tis meself I'm starin' at. Thot's what I get for indulgin' meself too much.

MUSIC (*Brief comic bridge*): *Up and out.*

INGHAM (*Fading in*): But don't you see, Mr. and Mrs. Shea, it would be a wonderful opportunity for both of you. I know you'd like our town. We have a comfortable home . . . and we'd pay you well.

POLLY: You could do the cooking and help me with the housework, Mrs. Shea.

BRIDGET: Just call me Bridget—plain Bridget Shea. To tell the truth of the matter now, your offer appeals to me. I'm sick to death of livin' in this shack.

POLLY: I'm pleased to hear that, Bridget. We have a nice room waiting for you and your husband.

INGHAM: One important point in question, Polly. We haven't had an opinion from Mr. Shea.

BRIDGET (*Sharply*): Dinny, Mr. Ingham's spakin' to yez. Answer him.

DENNIS: Quiet, woman. I'll do me own talkin'. Mr. Ingham, to till yez the truth, I sorta like it here. After all it's a place to call ye own.

BRIDGET: Huh! Lissen to him, will yez: "a place of ye own." Ye mane it's nothin' but a bunch of boards we live in.

DENNIS: Quiet, ye noisy old chatterbox.

INGHAM: Perhaps you don't fully understand my offer and the reason for it.

BRIDGET: Faith, and you have to spake to him like you would a small gossoon.

DENNIS: Yez have in mind fer me to take ye place at public functions and the loike. Me, dressed in your clothes, would be ye.

INGHAM: Exactly.

DENNIS (*Pointedly*): Why?

BRIDGET: Now, ain't he the curious one. If questions was money, Dinny Shea'd be a rich man.

POLLY: You may as well tell him the rest, Fred.

INGHAM: Well, first of all, Dennie, I'm a writer. Consequently (*Slight fade*) I am constantly bothered by people who want me to belong to clubs and other similar organizations. . . .

MUSIC (*Short "time" bridge*): *Cuts in, drowning out* INGHAM *—hold briefly and out.*

DENNIS (*Slight fade-in*): But O'im tellin' ye, Mr. Ingham, now that yez and ye Missus have lugged Bridget and me all the ways up here, O'im not at all sure of the idea.

INGHAM: Nonsense! My own mother couldn't tell us apart. We'll have our first lesson. The first thing is to get rid of the manner in which you speak.

DENNIS (*Belligerently*): And what's wrong wit' the way I spake?

INGHAM: Nothing. But if you're to be *me,* instead of *you,* then the brogue—in public, at least—must go.

DENNIS: Will now, thot's a rasonable requist.

INGHAM: Remember, this will put you in active contact with many fine people.

DENNIS (*Unconvinced*): Will thot be puttin' any money in me pocket?

INGHAM: At these social gatherings, you'll eat a lot of fine meals.

DENNIS (*Brightening*): Now ye talkin' sinse. Would I mayhaps be gettin' a little nip on the soide now and again?

INGHAM (*Sternly*): Yes . . . but you'll refuse.

DENNIS (*Disappointed*): Oh!

INGHAM: Now for our lesson in diction. Now any time you're out and someone greets you, you'll say—

DENNIS (*Brightly*): The top of the day to yez.

INGHAM: No, no, Dennis. In answer to a casual salutation, you're to say: Very well, thank you. And you?

DENNIS (*With a brogue*): Very will, thank yez. And yez?

INGHAM: Now suppose someone comes to you and tells you how much he likes your—I mean *my* newest story, you're to say: I am very glad you liked it.

DENNIS: I'm viry glad yez loiked it.

INGHAM: Say you're at a public gathering and someone calls upon you to say a few words. You're to rise and say: There has been so much said, and, on the whole, so well said, I will not occupy the time.

DENNIS: They's been so much said, and, on the whole, so will said, thot I will not occupy the toime. Thot's if O'im asked to spake, yez say?

INGHAM: That's right. Now for the last speech. If you are asked what you think of what has been said by some one else in the room, you say this: I agree, in general, with my friend on the other side of the room.

DENNIS: I agree, in giniril, wit' me friend on the other soide of the room.

INGHAM: Remember—you're to memorize those four speeches and make use of them when the occasion demands it.

DENNIS (*Cocky*): Shure! Have no fears. Before yez know it, O'ill have yez runnin' fer Lord-Mayor of the town!

MUSIC (*Bridge*): *Some light conception of traditional Gaelic tune—up and out.*

DENNIS (*Just a faint suspicion of brogue*): There has been so much said, and, on the whole, so well said, that I will not occupy the time.

SOUND: *Two people clapping hands.*

INGHAM: Bravo! Bravo! Dennis. Well done.

POLLY: We're proud of you.

DENNIS (*Lapses into brogue*): Shure, 'tis nothin'. We Irish are the actors of the wurld.

POLLY: In such a short time you've certainly accomplished a great deal. But, Dennis, there is one thing you must watch. Be careful of your diphthongs.

DENNIS: Of course, ma'am. (*Double take*) What the divil is thot?

POLLY: We'll save that till the next lesson.

DENNIS: They's wan point thot's not been settled. What is goin' to happen whin O'im out playin' ye and you're also out bein' yeself?

POLLY: Oh, Fred, that's one we hadn't figured on.

INGHAM: That's all settled. When you're out, Dennis, I'll be home writing away to my heart's content, far from the madding crowd.

MY DOUBLE AND HOW HE UNDID ME 233

DENNIS: And still another point: When O'im not bein' ye, just where am I to kape meself?

INGHAM: When you're here at home, you're to keep out of sight.

DENNIS: On sich occasions, I suggest I rist me mind by sleepin'.

INGHAM: A shrewd thought. Now, still another point. Next week you are making your bow in public. I—or rather *you* are going to attend the meeting of the Centreville Ladies' Poetry Association.

DENNIS: Me debew in public. I shall smother thim wit' me personality.

POLLY: And you must be careful what you say to the ladies.

DENNIS: Have no fears, ma'am. Me ancestors was bards in the old sod.

SOUND: *Door bell rings—repeated.*

POLLY: Probably a salesman.

INGHAM: Well, don't let him in here.

DENNIS: 'Tis an idea. Let me try out me new part of bein' Mr. Ingham. Here—let me have your glasses. There.

SOUND: *Bell.*

INGHAM: Be careful, Dennis.

DENNIS: Thot I will.

SOUND: *Man's steps on wood. Door open.*

SALESMAN: Good morning, sir. I believe I have the honor of addressing the man of the house.

DENNIS (*Dignified. No brogue*): Yes.

SALESMAN: I represent the Acme Map Company of Boston.

DENNIS: Yes.

SALESMAN (*Glibly*): I am the bearer of a special offer which my company has authorized me to make to all members of this lovely town. We are giving away, at no cost, one beautifully colored three by five feet map of this grand and glorious State. In order to obtain this cartographical gem in three colors it is—

DENNIS (*Firmly*): No.
SALESMAN (*Laughs good naturedly*): Now, now, must we be obstinate?
DENNIS: No.
SALESMAN (*Archly*): Sales resistance, I see. Tut, tut!
DENNIS (*Into brogue*): Look—do yez observe *this?*
SALESMAN (*Horrified*): Your . . . fist!
DENNIS (*Grimly*): Yis—me fist. And if ye don't lave at once, O'im goin't paste yez one in thot mush of yours.
SALESMAN (*Fading*): Goodness . . . the man is insulting . . . threatening me with violence. Help!
POLLY (*Off*): Dennis.
DENNIS: Yis, mum?
POLLY: How did you do?
DENNIS: Shure and yez would have been proud. I was the viry issince of tact and good taste.
MUSIC (*Comic bridge*): *Forte and then fade under for:*
BRIDGET (*Admiringly*): Faith and yez look foine, Dinny . . . all dressed up in Mr. Ingham's blue suit. Ye'll be careful this afternoon, now, Dinny.
DENNIS (*Lording it*): Have no fears.
BRIDGET: And don't hog ye food.
DENNIS: Show some respect. Ye talkin' to the second Parnell.
BRIDGET: Drissed up loike thot, ye the image of me Uncle Shaemus from Sligo.
DENNIS: Except thot O'ive a forehead. Will, it's off I am to the Cintirville Ladies' Poetry Association.
MUSIC: *Up briefly and out into:*
FATUOUS LADY (*Fading in*): And dear, dear club members, in closing this meeting of the Centreville Poetry Association, may I say that we, all of us, have enjoyed to the utmost degree this chummy little literary get-together. Indeed we are most fortunate to have thriving here in our town such a cultural organ-

MY DOUBLE AND HOW HE UNDID ME

ization. Remember, it is only through the earnest efforts of clubs, such as ours, that love of poetry and culture can successfully be carried to those poor unfortunates who are starving for knowledge and love of beauty. Too, it is our task to carry the torch. Thank you, dear fellow club members.

SOUND: *Live applause.*

FATUOUS LADY: And I am quite sure that our distinguished guest, Mr. Frederick Ingham, who so kindly consented to be here, agrees with our purpose. Do you not, Mr. Ingham?

DENNIS: Very well, thank you. And you?

SOUND: *Surprised ad lib chatter of women—off mike.*

FATUOUS LADY: Perchance, Mr. Ingham, you did not gain the full significance of my remark?

DENNIS: I am very glad you liked it.

WOMAN (*Off mike. She giggles*): Mr. Ingham, you say the wittiest things. So brilliant!

DENNIS: I agree, in general, with my friend on the other side of the room.

MUSIC: *Bridge—up and out.*

SOUND: *Typewriter.*

POLLY (*Off*): Fred. Fred, dear. (*Pause, then fading in*) Fred, I want to talk to you. (*Sound out.*)

INGHAM: Yes, Polly.

POLLY: The morning mail.

INGHAM: Anything important?

POLLY: Couple of bills . . . and the newspaper. Read page two, second column. Here. . . .

INGHAM: My picture!

POLLY: Read what it says about you.

INGHAM: "Guest . . . Thursday afternoon French Club . . . Frederick Ingham . . . noted writer." But, darling, you shouldn't have sent Dennis there. They speak only in French.

POLLY: Read on.

INGHAM: "When addressed in French, Mr. Ingham briefly yet brilliantly replied in English." Evidently my double is doing right by me.

POLLY: And here's an invitation from Judge Stearns and his wife. We're invited to a dinner and reception at his home next week. The Governor will be present.

INGHAM: Fine! You and Dennis go. It's time you two made your joint debut in polite society.

POLLY: Dennis and Polly . . . songs and funny sayings.

MUSIC: *A few light chords—up and out into:*

SOUND: *Fade in at background of social gathering, intersperse live ad libs.*

DENNIS: Ye know, Mrs. Ingham, this is the foist time O'ive ivir worn a monkey suit. This blamed collar's sawin' me neck in two.

POLLY: You're doing famously, Dennis. But for goodness sakes, don't lapse into your brogue. And remember—use only the four speeches you've memorized.

DENNIS: Now will yez take a look at that woman comin' toward us. Look at the face on her. The red bazoo! She looks loike a battleship under full sail.

POLLY: That is our hostess . . . Mrs. Stearns.

DENNIS: O'id say from the soize of her, she should be out in the fields pullin' a plow.

POLLY (*Sotto voce*): Sshhh! Here she comes. Good evening, Mrs. Stearns. (*Sotto*) Dennis, bow . . . bow.

MRS. STEARNS (*Gushes*): Good evening, Mr. and Mrs. Ingham. How delightful to have you with us. How are you?

DENNIS: Very well, thank you. And you?

MRS. STEARNS: And your last story. Oh! Magnificent! So full of life! Such verve! Replete with description. But that is right, for the short story should be commensurate with human activity. On the other hand, it must not abstractly panegyrize

its subject to the utter disregard of his human frailty. Do you not agree, Mr. Ingham?
DENNIS: There has been so much said, and, on the whole, so well said, that I will not occupy the time.
MRS. STEARNS (*Archly*): Ah! Flatterer. Now I'm off.
DENNIS: I agree in general—
MRS. STEARNS: After dinner, the Judge and Governor wish to see you alone in the library, Mr. Ingham. (*Fading*) Well, toodle-lo!
DENNIS: Mrs. Ingham.
POLLY: Yes, Dennis?
DENNIS: Phat in the divil was thot stuffed bag of oats talkin' about?
MUSIC (*Short comic bridge*): *Washes in over sound.*
GOVERNOR (*Fading in*): And those are my views on the subject . . . one which every citizen should heed. What do you say, Judge Stearns?
STEARNS: I fully agree with you, Governor.
GOVERNOR: And you, Mr. Ingham, have you formed an opinion?
DENNIS: I . . . I—(*He rattles it out*) There has been so much said, and, on the whole, so well said, that I will not occupy the time.
GOVERNOR: A shrewd observation. Obviously you are a man who carefully chooses his every word.
DENNIS (*Emphatically*): Yes! I agree, in general, with my friend on the other side of the room.
STEARNS: You see, Governor, Fred Ingham is noted for his brief, yet shrewd statements. Not only is he a writer of note, but one of the brainiest men in the entire State. In fact, men like Fred Ingham are a rarity. (GOVERNOR *and* JUDGE STEARNS *laugh.*)
GOVERNOR: To get down to cases, Ingham. The chief reason Judge Stearns and I wished to see you alone is to put a propo-

sition to you. Ingham, how would you like the nomination to the State Senate?

DENNIS (*Blankly*): The . . . the . . . Senate?

JUDGE: Yes, Fred, the State Senate!

DENNIS: Very well, thank you—

GOVERNOR: Ah! Good!

DENNIS: And you?

GOVERNOR: We will see that you are swept into office.

JUDGE: Congratulations. A wise decision.

DENNIS: I'm very glad you liked it.

MUSIC: *Light theme—up and out.*

POLLY (*Aghast*): Dennis, after all we've done for you. How could you do such a thing to Mr. Ingham?

INGHAM: The least you could have done, Dennis, was to have told Stearns and the Governor that you wished time to consider the offer.

DENNIS: Is thot so! And would any of the four speeches you told me to use have covered thot emergency? Would it now?

INGHAM (*Helplessly*): I suppose not. (*He starts to laugh.*)

POLLY: Fred, it's no laughing matter.

DENNIS: Indade it's not. Mr. Ingham, it means *you* will be elected to the State Senate, and I'll have to attind all them meetin's.

INGHAM: *I* may be elected, but *you* are going to represent me.

POLLY: Fred, you aren't serious?

INGHAM: I certainly am. Dennis allowed himself to be talked into this. Now let him take the consequence.

POLLY: It will never work out.

DENNIS (*Groans*): Owwww!

POLLY: What's the matter?

DENNIS: I've made a fearful mistake.

POLLY: What?

DENNIS: I'll be elected on one ticket . . . and all me days of

MY DOUBLE AND HOW HE UNDID ME

votin', I've been a mimbir of the opposition party. (*Suddenly*) Ah, but I'll fix thot.

POLLY: How?

DENNIS: I'll vote wit' the opposition party.

MUSIC: *"There'll Be A Hot Time In The Old Town Tonight"— Up briefly under.*

WOMAN: Fred Ingham for State Senator!

MUSIC: *Up briefly and under.*

MAN: Honest Fred!

MUSIC: *Up briefly and under.*

WOMAN 2: Vote for Ingham.

MUSIC: *Up and under.*

MAN 2: Ingham elected.

MUSIC: *Up briefly—hold and out.*

POLLY (*Fading in*): Fred, dear, Dennis has been acting very peculiarly of late. Have you noticed it?

INGHAM: Can't say that I have.

POLLY: Ever since the Legislature has adjourned, he's been avoiding me.

INGHAM: I've been so busy on my book I hadn't noticed.

POLLY: And he's been avoiding you, too.

INGHAM: You're probably imagining things.

POLLY: I'm positive there's something he's hiding.

SOUND: *Door bell rings.*

INGHAM: Wonder who that can be?

POLLY (*Slight fade*): I'll take a look. (*Pause.*)

INGHAM: Can you make out who it is?

POLLY: It's Judge Stearns. (*Slow fade*) I wonder what he wants . . . coming here this time of morning. Must be important.

BRIDGET (*Cross-fading in*): Dinny! Dinny! Where arc ye? (*Pause*) Now lookit, will ye—as usual doin' nothin' but sittin'.

DENNIS: Go way, woman. 'Tis a sick man I am. Oh, Bridget,

lave us git out of here at oncet. Lave us go back to our old home.

BRIDGET: What's eatin' ye? 'Tis the blessin' of the saints thot yez have a good sound roof over your head. And now ye're after wantin' to give it up.

DENNIS: Ow . . . wurra, wurra. 'Twas a bad day we came here.

BRIDGET: Spake up and stop mumblin' to yeself loike an old banshee.

DENNIS: The blow is jest about to fall.

BRIDGET: Come now, Dinny, tell Bridget phat's the matter.

DENNIS: Did yez see who's in conference wit' Mr. Ingham in the parlor?

BRIDGET: I did. Judge Stearns, it 'tis.

DENNIS: Thin you can trace me despondent condition to his visit. (*Fading*) 'Tis the ind, the ind of everything. I should have known better, stupid gossoon thot I be.

STEARNS (*Cross-fading in*): And I really think, Fred, the least you could have done was to answer the Governor. If you'd done so, it wouldn't have been necessary for me to chase up here to see you.

INGHAM (*Stalling*): I'm sorry, Judge. I apologize to you and to the Governor. Fact is I've been busy all summer. Er—just what did the Governor have in mind?

STEARNS: In mind? Fred, are you joking?

INGHAM: Of course not.

STEARNS: Mean to say you've already forgotten the promise you made to the Governor and the State Central Committee?

INGHAM: Governor . . . Committee . . . promise. Oh, yes, I did make a promise, didn't I?

STEARNS: You certainly did!

INGHAM: Yes siree! I promised to . . . to . . .

STEARNS: You promised to run for Congress.

INGHAM: I promised to run for—(*Double take*) *What?* (*Pause*) Congress . . . oh, yes . . . so I did.
STEARNS: You certainly were enthusiastic enough at the time.
INGHAM: I was?
STEARNS: Definitely! Fact is, the Committee is quite enthusiastic about you.
INGHAM: Why?
STEARNS: Because of your spotless record. You're a perfect politician. You've sat for a term in the Senate and not once have you opened your mouth . . . except to vote.
INGHAM: You don't think I'll get the nomination?
STEARNS: Of course you will.
INGHAM (*Hopefully*): But I won't be elected?
STEARNS: With ease! You will be the people's choice.
INGHAM: That can't be so.
STEARNS: But it is. The press says you're the wittiest man ever to hold public office. And they offer as proof your terse answers to their questions.
INGHAM: Oh, my! Terrible! (*Hurriedly*) I mean—fine!
STEARNS: The convention is the first week in September. So be prepared for fireworks.
INGHAM (*Grimly*): Judge, as far as I'm concerned, the fireworks are starting immediately—and right here!
MUSIC: *Comic stuff—Up and under for:*
POLLY: Bridget, Mr. Ingham wishes to see Dennis at once.
BRIDGET (*With dignity*): And Mr. Dennis Shea begs to inform Mr. Ingham that he is not at liberty.
POLLY: Where is he?
BRIDGET: Hiding in the attic.
MUSIC: *Up and under.*
INGHAM: Why . . . why did you do it, Dennis?
DENNIS: Will, when them poly-ticians told me what a foine character I was—I mean *you* was—I started balavin' thim.

And the first thing you know, *you* was a candidate for Congress.

INGHAM: You impostor!

DENNIS: *Me? You're* the impostor . . . not *me!*

MUSIC: *Up and out.*

INGHAM (*Troubled. Fading in*): All right, all right, Polly. I'm listening to you. Give me a chance to think.

POLLY: Of all the predicaments to be in. Fred, you've got to get out of it somehow.

INGHAM (*The light*): I have. Yes, it's all clear.

POLLY: I'm glad you think so.

INGHAM: Listen closely. Dennis appears for me at the convention. Maybe he'll do something . . . or maybe they'll decide not to nominate me.

POLLY: Not a chance.

INGHAM: If I get the nomination, I may not be elected.

POLLY: And if you *are* elected?

INGHAM: Ah, I have that settled. I'll act. I'll have Dennis step out and I'll take my place in Washington.

POLLY: But you've always said you never wanted to live in Washington.

INGHAM: You can't have everything, Polly. What do you want them to do—move the House of Representatives up here?

MUSIC: *"There'll Be A Hot Time In The Old Town Tonight" up briefly and out into:*

SOUND: *Roar of large auditorium crowd—establish and fade for: echo of gavel rapped briskly.*

GOVERNOR (*On echo*): Your attention . . . attention. Will the delegates please come to attention.

SOUND: *The crowd noise gradually subsides.*

GOVERNOR: Thank you. (*Crowd out*) As Governor of this grand and glorious state and chairman of this convention, allow me to pause long enough to say that your last choice—

that of nominating a candidate for Congress—has been an admirable one. The candidate of your choice is an outstanding citizen . . . he is a scholar . . . an author . . . and a family man. . . .

DENNIS (*Whispers fiercely*): Hey, Governor . . . I have no family.

GOVERNOR: He has no fam—(*He catches himself*) He has no familiar characteristics of the average candidate. And now let me close by saying that as true as I am now standing on this platform, come next November, Frederick Ingham will be our party's new Congressman. I thank you.

SOUND: *Applause from huge crowd—as it dies: Crowd noise. "Ingham . . . Ingham . . . Ingham."—Take crowd noise up and drop it slightly for: Following voices heard off mike and slight echo.*

MAN: Hurray for Ingham.

WOMAN: The people's choice.

MAN 2: Honest Fred!

WOMAN 2: Our new Congressman.

WOMAN 3: A job for everyone.

SOUND (*On echo*): *Gavel cutting in over crowd roar—very brisk.*

GOVERNOR: Quiet . . . Order . . . order, please. (*Sound gradually out*) Thank you. Fellow and lady convention members, I know that Fred Ingham, sitting right behind me, did not intend to speak today. But I am sure I can prevail upon him to speak just a few words. I present him, your friend, the party's friend—Fred Ingham.

SOUND (*Crowd noise and cast*): "*Ingham . . . Ingham*"—*up full and gradually out.*

DENNIS (*On echo and as crowd noise dies away*): Ladies and gentlemen, there has been so much said, and, on the whole, so well said, I will not occupy the time. Thank you.

Biz (*Cast off mike*): "Go ahead." "We want more." "More." "Don't stop."

Dennis: I am very glad you liked it.

Man: What are yuh tryin' to give us?

Man 2: What kinda speech is that?

Dennis (*A little desperately*): I'm very glad you liked it.

Woman: Boooooo!

Man 3: You're a big faker! Faker!

Dennis: I agree, in general, with my friend on the other side of the room.

Man 1: How's your mother?

Dennis: Very well, thank you. And you?

Sound: *Crowd background—up full—Fade it long enough to get in jeers, catcalls, "boos."*

Dennis (*Reverts to a rich brogue*): Hold on! Listen! (*The noise dies away*) Now lit me tell all of yez somethin'. Whin I promised to come to this convention, I told a certain party I'd do me best. And mind ye, I have. But let me tell yez all this: A Shea takes insult from nather man nor baste.

Tough Guy: Aw pipe down, lug-head.

Dennis (*Enraged*): Lug-head, is it, now? Will let me tell yez this—ye all a bunch of dawgs and cowards—the hull lot of yez. And I, Dennis Shea, hereby invite anyone in the house who's lookin' fer a fight to step down on this platform. I'll lick any eight men in the house. Who's first! I'm waitin' . . . Step down. Come on! By the blood of me ansistors, I'll lick yez.

Sound: *Roar of crowd—up full . . . hold out. A long pause, then:*

Ingham (*Dead air*): My double . . . had undone me.

Music: *Sneak in whimsically reflective tune—hold under.*

Ingham: We left town at seven the next morning. Not collectively—for Dennis and Bridget were ahead of us by a matter of several hours. And the Convention? The State Central

Committee? They never did learn the truth. They ascribed Dennis' action to a lapse . . . and they went on to pick some other luckless victim for the seat in Congress. And here we are—Polly and I—living a new life in a new and remote section of the country. Polly tends to the house, while I, lucky creature, write to my heart's content. Never more do I hear:
WOMAN 1: Dear Mr. Ingham, won't you speak to the Ladies' Aid Society?
WOMAN 2: We'd love having you for tea.
MAN 1: You must come to the Community Club meeting.
MAN 2: To say nothing of the Boosters' Club.
GIRL (*Shrill voice*): Gee! May I have your autograph?
CAST CHORUS: "Mr. Ingham, won't you join our club . . . and do this . . . and that. . . ."
WOMAN 1: Et cetera.
MAN 1: Et cetera.
WOMAN 2: Et cetera.
MUSIC: *Segue to comic chords and out.*
INGHAM: And dear Dennis? He has retired to his sanctissimum at the beach where first we met. And there, I have no doubt, he regales his beloved Bridget with wild and wondrous tales of days departed, when he, a figurative man in the iron mask, almost became Congressman. (*Pause*) P.S.—Owing to circumstances I have plenty of time to write this account; and any similarity to Dennis Shea is *not* purely coincidental!
MUSIC: *Payoff curtain stuff—up—hold and out.*

THE END

The Sire deMaletroit's Door

by Robert Louis Stevenson

MUSIC: *A strong martial theme. Forte and fade under.*

NARRATOR: This is a story that occurred centuries ago when France presented a turbulent map, as red as her native wine. For months the forces of King Louis have been locked in combat with those of the Duke of Burgundy. It is now the spring of the year. At an outpost, a sentry, wearing the uniform of the Duke of Burgundy, watches as a man advances toward him from the camp of the King.

BURGUNDIAN (*Calling out*): Halt! You, there, halt! (*Pause*) Who are you?

DENIS (*Slightly away*): I am Denis deBeaulieu, soldier in the service of His Majesty, King Louis of France.

BURGUNDIAN: Why do you approach our lines?

DENIS: I have a message for Burgundy.

BURGUNDIAN: From whom?

DENIS: From the King.

BURGUNDIAN: Burgundy is King.

DENIS: I am not here to argue. Tell your captain that my message is to be delievered directly into the hands of your Duke.

MUSIC: *Up and then segue to religious theme, which fades out under.*

NARRATOR: A fortnight's truce is declared. Now the troops from each side mingle in the Paris streets, even frequenting the same taverns. Despite the temporary break in the fighting, there is an air of unrest, a nervous tension present everywhere, except in the great cathedral of Notre Dame. It is Sunday, and a great throng of worshippers streams from its portals.

SOUND: *Sneak in under narration and dialogue. Low ad libs from many people. Hold.*

NARRATOR (*No pause*): In this crowd descending the steps is Blanche deMaletroit and her personal servant, Marie. A handsome young soldier follows them. Suddenly he shoulders his way forward until he reaches the side of Blanche.

SOLDIER (*Low voice*): At last I have discovered your name. I have watched you for the past ten days.

BLANCHE: Please, sir, I do not know you.

SOLDIER: It makes no difference. Here—take this note. (*Insistently*) Take it. (*Fading*) And now farewell for a short time.

MARIE (*Sharply*): Mam'selle should destroy that note.

BLANCHE: It is the same soldier who has been staring at me every morning for more than a week.

MARIE: Destroy that note at once. The Sire is behind us.

SIRE (*Quietly*): Give me that note. (*Sharply*) Blanche, that note the soldier just gave you, give it to me.

BLANCHE: I do not even know him, Uncle.

SIRE: The note! (*Beat*) Thank you. You will meet me in the great hall within the hour.

MUSIC: *Troubled theme. A short bridge. Up and out.*

BLANCHE: I am not lying. I do not know the soldier who gave me this note. You must believe me.

SIRE: But you admit having seen him before this morning.

BLANCHE: Yes, in church. For the past ten days he has stood near me, watching me.

SIRE: Why did you not complain?

BLANCHE: Because I did not wish to cause trouble.

SIRE: A very interesting note, one which would seem to make out my niece to be a liar.

BLANCHE: I do not know him.
SIRE: In his billet-doux, your soldier makes a request. I shall do everything possible to aid his proposal.
BLANCHE (*Frightened*): What do you plan, Sire?
SIRE (*Cunningly*): A small surprise. (*Laughs*) A very simple device.
BLANCHE: You're planning something cruel.
SIRE (*Pleasantly malicious*): Do not be harsh on your old uncle, Blanche. I have your best interests always in mind. That is why tonight I will surprise both you and the soldier who is in love with you.
MUSIC: *Grim theme as a bridge. Up and out.*
JULES (*An old voice*): Let me see, it has been seven—no, eight years since I last saw you, Denis. You're a grown man. How long have you been in the service of the King?
DENIS: Almost five years, Father Jules.
JULES: You are enough like your father to be his twin. How well I remember him.
DENIS: He often spoke of you, Father.
JULES: Then you are the last of the deBeaulieu's?
DENIS: Yes.
JULES: You should carry on the name. It is an illustrious one. But perhaps you are contemplating marriage?
DENIS: No. Not until this war has ended.
JULES: The young lady, she is from your province?
DENIS: There is no young lady.
JULES: You will find someone. (*Transition*) What are your plans? I am referring to this period of truce.
DENIS: I have none.
JULES: Why not remain here at the Abbey as my guest? I can at least promise you a fairly comfortable bed and good food.
DENIS: It will give us a chance to talk, Father Jules.
JULES: Unfortunately this evening I will not be able to pass

time with you. Tomorrow morning is the day we feed the poor of Paris. It requires much work.

DENIS: I shall spend the evening in the city. (*Beat*) Why do you shake your head, Father?

JULES: The streets of Paris are not safe, especially at night.

DENIS: I have my safe-conduct pass.

JULES: A roving band of Burgundians might not respect a scrap of paper.

DENIS: I have my sword.

JULES: Youth and chance, they seem to walk hand in hand.

DENIS: I might welcome a stray adventure.

JULES: Be careful, my son. Remember, danger lies in every dimly-lit Paris alley.

DENIS (*Lightly*): Father Jules, tonight I'll walk the streets of Paris and I'll wager that nothing out of the ordinary happens to me.

MUSIC: *A bridge. Up and out.*

SOLDIER 1 (*Protests*): I'm not walking another step until I rest my feet. All we have done all night is wander the streets.

SOLDIER 2: There is an inn down this lane. We could go there.

SOLDIER 3: Why did we leave the last inn?

SOLDIER 4: Because I didn't like the place. It smelled. Everything smelled. The air, the food, the wine. Even the innkeeper smelled.

SOLDIER 1: We leave an inn simply because it smells. I joined you because I was seeking excitement. And what do I get? Nothing but sore feet.

SOLDIER 3: The evening is young. If it becomes too dull, we can always scare up a street brawl.

BIZ (*Away*): DENIS *humming a ballad. It continues under the following.*

SOLDIER 4: A brawl would suit me. That is why I joined Burgundy—to fight.

SOLDIER 2: Remember, a truce has been signed.
SOLDIER 4: What of it!
SOLDIER 3: Hold your tongues.
SOLDIER 1: What is wrong?
SOLDIER 3: Down there—in the alley. See him . . . walking alone.
SOLDIER 1: A man.
SOLDIER 3: A soldier. See—the light from the inn window shines upon him.
SOLDIER 4 (*Eagerly*): A King's man. Here's our chance.
SOLDIER 2: But we're supposed to be at peace, at least until the armistice is done.
SOLDIER 4: When I give the word, rush him. (*Fading*) We'll do away with him in short order. Quiet now. Walk quietly. (*A pause, then*):
SOUND: *A few steps on cobblestones.*
DENIS (*Hums to himself. Then he stops, yawning*): Oh! Should have remained at the Abbey . . . gone to bed. Fool to be wandering the streets like a beggar.
SOLDIER 3 (*Away*): You there, wait.
SOLDIER 4: We wish to speak to you.
DENIS (*Calling back*): What do you want of me?
SOLDIER 4: You're a Royalist.
SOLDIER 3: Rush him!
DENIS: Thank you, but there are too many of you. Good evening, messieurs.
BIZ: *The* SOLDIERS, *slightly away, continue to yell after* DENIS, *as:*
SOUND: *Running footsteps on cobblestones.*
DENIS (*Panting*): Too many of them. Got to escape. Down this alley . . . around the corner. The nearest door. Here!
SOUND: *Steps out.*
BIZ: *Voices of the pursuing Burgundians get louder.*

DENIS: This doorway.
SOUND: *Door handle turned. Door squeaks open, then closed.*
BIZ: *The voices of the Burgundians die out.*
DENIS (*A sigh of relief*): Thank goodness for such a convenient doorway.
SIRE: Yes, it *is* a convenient doorway.
DENIS: Who's there? (*Pause*) Answer me.
SIRE: No need to be alarmed. I've been expecting you.
DENIS: Expecting me?
SIRE: You're late.
DENIS: I don't understand.
SIRE: Follow me, please.
SOUND: *Door handle rattled vigorously.*
SIRE: No need to try the outside door. It won't open.
DENIS: Then suppose you open it for me.
SIRE: It does not open out; only in.
SOUND: *Door handle.*
SIRE: You are wasting your strength and my time.
DENIS: Let me out of here.
SIRE: Follow me. And be careful, for the stairs are steep and slippery.
MUSIC: *An ominous bridge. Up and out.*
DENIS: Instead of staring at me, suppose you explain matters.
SIRE: Forgive me. I've been studying your face. It has a certain strength of character which I approve.
DENIS: Why are you trying to detain me?
SIRE (*Smoothly*): You are in error. I have been expecting you.
DENIS (*Patiently*): There must be some mistake. I was escaping from a band of soldiers, and finding your door unlatched, I—
SIRE: You stepped inside.
DENIS: It was an accident.
SIRE: We hold different opinions. No matter. You are here, and

that is the important thing. I want you to be entirely at ease.
DENIS: About your door—
SIRE: Oh, yes, my door. A hospitable notion. As you desired to make my acquaintance, but fearing that you might be a bit shy, I cast about for a means to overcome it. Consequently the door that opens in but not out. (*Slyly*) You arrived uninvited, but you are most welcome.
DENIS: There is a mistake. I am a stranger to Paris. My name is Denis deBeaulieu, a soldier in the army of His Majesty. My entering your doorway was an error.
SIRE: Time will prove which of us is right.
DENIS (*Impatiently*): I demand to be let out of here.
SIRE: Sit down.
DENIS: And I refuse.
SIRE: My ingenious door is not the limit of my ability. If you wish to remain a young lad, agreeably conversing with an old man, then sit where you are.
DENIS: You mean I am a prisoner?
SIRE: I state the facts. I will leave the conclusion to you. (*Pause*) Now we shall proceed as I had planned. By the way, it was your note that made this meeting possible.
DENIS (*Puzzled*): What note?
SIRE: You shouldn't have written it.
DENIS: I wrote no note.
SIRE: No matter. And now for our first step.
SOUND: *Hand bell tinkled.*
JOSEPH (*Fading in*): You wish to speak to me, Sire?
SIRE: Yes, Father Joseph. This is the young blade. Not a bad appearing young man, eh? Seems to spring from good stock. (*As an aside*) Where are you from, young sir?
DENIS: Provence.
SIRE: His name is Denis deBeaulieu.
JOSEPH: I have heard of the deBeaulieu's of Provence.

SIRE: I had hoped for a greater name. Still she could do much worse, especially under the circumstances.

JOSEPH: She is rather upset, Sire.

SIRE: She should have thought of the trouble she would cause. It is none of my choosing. Please bring her in, Father.

PRIEST (*Fading*): I shall call her at once, Sire.

DENIS: I demand an explanation of all this.

SIRE (*Chuckles*): Patience, patience, my nephew.

DENIS: I am not your nephew.

SIRE: I can tell that you are contemplating something desperate. May I advise against it. Remember, you must continue to look your best.

BLANCHE (*Fading in*): You have sent for me, Uncle?

SIRE (*Pleasantly*): My dear Blanche. How charming you look. That flush to your cheeks is most becoming. Your white gown is most charming. I have a pleasant surprise for you. See who is here. Your impatient friend.

BLANCHE: Uncle, please believe me—

SIRE: Give him your pretty hand, the exquisite hand he loves. Do not be reticent. (*Grimly*) Greet him tenderly.

BLANCHE: He is not the man.

SIRE: Not the man! You must be wrong. Of course under the strained circumstances, one could not expect you to remember his name nor his face.

BLANCHE: I have never seen this man before. Sir, whoever you are, tell my uncle the truth. Have I ever seen you? Have you ever seen me before this moment?

DENIS: I have never had that pleasure, mam'selle. My Lord, your niece and I are strangers.

SIRE: A pity! I am sorry to hear that. But do not worry about it. Oftentimes impromptu marriages are the best marriages.

DENIS: What nonsense is this?

SIRE: I was discussing marriage, young sir. As the bridegroom, naturally you have some small voice. I will give you not more than thirty minutes either to agree or disagree to it.

BLANCHE: Is it possible that you still think this is the man?

SIRE: Despite your protests, *yes*.

BLANCHE: You are wrong, Uncle.

SIRE: Blanche, when you took it upon yourself to dishonor my family, the great name I have borne so honorably, you lost the right to question my designs.

BLANCHE: But I have done nothing.

SIRE: If your father were alive, he would deal with you more harshly than I.

BLANCHE: Please take my word—

SIRE (*Interrupting*): It has become my duty to get you married without delay. I have endeavored to find the man you love, and I believe I have succeeded. But if I have not, I am not too disturbed. If I were you, Blanche, I would be polite to our young friend, for your next bridegroom may be less appetizing. (*Fading*) And now I shall oversee the necessary arrangements. I shall be back.

BLANCHE (*To* DENIS): Suppose you explain why you are here?

DENIS: I ask you: Why am I here? All I can say is that I seem to be a prisoner in a house of strangers.

BLANCHE: I asked for an explanation.

DENIS: I am Denis deBeaulieu of Provence, a soldier in the army of His Majesty. This evening I went for a stroll; I was pursued by some Burgundians. In seeking escape, I dodged into what now seems to have been your uncle's doorway. Perhaps you can answer this riddle.

BLANCHE: I am Blanche deMaletroit.

DENIS: Then that man, your uncle, is the Sire deMaletroit?

BLANCHE: Yes.

DENIS: Alain, Sire deMaletroit, one of the greatest and wealthiest lords in France.

BLANCHE: Perhaps the most ruthless and scheming man in the entire kingdom.

DENIS: And you are his niece.

BLANCHE: Unfortunately. I have made my home here since the death of my parents. It has been a most unhappy existence. I have had no freedom, have been allowed no friends.

DENIS: Why?

BLANCHE (*Bitterly*): You think you are a prisoner, but if you had led my life for the past five years, you would know your existence to be as free as the rolling French countryside.

DENIS: Why has he forced this cloistered life upon you? What is his motive?

BLANCHE: It is his great pride. A fierce pride of the name he bears; the deMaletroit pride that refuses to link itself with other names. The Sire deMaletroit holds himself greater than even the King of France.

DENIS: What connection has all that with this—our predicament?

BLANCHE: Everything! Some days ago, a young soldier began to stand near me every day in church. I could see he was attracted to me. I shouldn't have encouraged him.

DENIS: But you did.

BLANCHE: I never spoke to him, only smiled This morning he passed a note to me as I was leaving Notre Dame. In it he asked me to leave the door open this evening, so he could come and talk to me.

DENIS: Wasn't the note evidence to your uncle that you didn't know this soldier?

BLANCHE: No. Evidently this unknown soldier had found out who I was. In it he even addressed me by name.

DENIS: Which led your uncle to believe that you had met before.

BLANCHE: Yes.

DENIS: What makes your uncle believe I am that person?

BLANCHE: From a distance, he saw me receive the note. Unfortunately you and the soldier look somewhat alike. Tonight the Sire ordered me to dress myself as you now see me—in bridal costume. And then he waited.

DENIS: And I walked into his trap—the door that opens in but not out. (*Trying to smile it off*) I hardly expected to become a bridegroom.

BLANCHE: Nor I a bride. I have done nothing to deserve such punishment.

DENIS (*Grim humor*): Hardly a compliment to me. (*Abruptly*) I could be in worse straits, I suppose.

BLANCHE: What do you intend doing?

DENIS: You wait here. I'm going to speak again to your uncle.

MUSIC: *An ominous bridge. Up and out.*

SIRE: You will forgive me if I tell you I do not care to listen to you.

DENIS: Very well. Then with no more comment, suppose I say this: I refuse to marry your niece.

SIRE: And she feels the same way?

DENIS: She does.

SIRE (*Softly*): I am afraid, Denis deBeaulieu, that you do not understand the choice I offer. Have the goodness to glance out this window.

DENIS: I see nothing.

SIRE: Observe the iron ring set into the masonry, and reeved through it a very efficacious rope. Understand me correctly: If you still find yourself disinclined to marry my niece I shall have you hanged out of that window before you are an hour older. (*Sotto voce*) Have you ever seen a man hanged? It's an ugly sight.

DENIS: You wouldn't dare do it.

SIRE: You may find out.

DENIS: I have friends. They would search for me.

SIRE: And strangely enough they never would find you.
DENIS: Unbelievable!
SIRE: An unfortunate extremity. I don't desire to take your life, but I do intend to see my niece established in life.
DENIS: But we don't love each other.
SIRE: You could in time.
DENIS: How can I think—
SIRE: Your family may be all right in its way.
DENIS: My family is dead.
SIRE: But even if you sprang from Adam himself, I wouldn't allow you to insult a deMaletroit—not if my niece were as common as the dirt along the Paris road. The honor of my house has been questioned.
DENIS: And you think I am the guilty person?
SIRE: I do. At least you are now in on the secret, and I am holding you to a hard bargain. Remember, I have no real wish to see your lifeless body hanging at the end of a rope.
DENIS: Suppose I were to kill you?
SIRE: I have taken steps in that direction. (*He calls out.*) Jacques!
SOUND (*Slightly away*): *Door open.*
JACQUES (*Away*): You wish something, Sire?
SIRE: Stand from the doorway and allow my doubting friend to observe. (*Beat*) Ah, thank you. (*To* DENIS) There you see six men. Observe them. (*He calls out.*) If I need your services, Jacques, I shall call.
SOUND: *Door closed.*
DENIS: You think of everything.
SIRE: I am no longer young. Those armed men are my sinews, my sword arm. (*Abruptly*) I am offering you but another fifteen minutes to make your decision. (*Fading*) Remember, a great many important problems have been settled in less time, my young friend.

Music: *Agitato. Forte and fade.*

Blanche: But, Denis, you must not be so rash. You have no choice but to marry me. There is no need for you to die.

Denis: You think I am afraid of death?

Blanche: I have no such opinion. I know you are no coward. It isn't a question of bravery. You have no choice. You must marry me.

Denis: I, too, have my pride.

Blanche: Then set it aside.

Denis: This other man, the one who wished to see you.

Blanche: I don't love this other man. I don't even know him.

Denis: There is no need for us to talk any more.

Blanche: Is there nothing I can do to help you? There are but a few minutes remaining.

Denis: I would like to sit beside you as if I were a dear friend, instead of a blundering stranger. If you can make these last minutes go pleasantly, I shall be very grateful to you.

Blanche: I may not be much help, but in me you will find a most friendly listener. I'm too bewildered to cry. (*Pause*) What would it have been like, Denis, if we had met under happier conditions?

Denis: We might have become close friends.

Blanche: You said your parents are dead.

Denis: Yes. I have no ties.

Blanche: Friends?

Denis: A few.

Blanche: I shall never forget you: your courage, the way you spoke to my uncle as no other person has dared.

Denis: And yet I had not planned to die this way.

Blanche: Do you think me beautiful, Denis? (*Pause*) Do you?

Denis: Yes, very.

Blanche: And do you think there are many men who have been asked in marriage by a beautiful woman?

Denis: Please, Blanche—

Blanche (*Continuing*): And who refused, without even considering. Do you?

Denis: It's an unbelievable situation.

Blanche: There is nothing a woman prizes more dearly than love, yet you rejected me without a second thought.

Denis: You asked because you pity me, and I don't want pity.

Blanche: It may sound strange, what I am about to tell you. When I asked you to marry me, it was because I respected and admired you and—yes, perhaps loved you. I loved you from the moment you took my part against my uncle.

Denis: You can't mean all this.

Blanche: I mean every word of it. It is only because I know how indifferently you regard me that I have the courage to speak so plainly. I'm glad that for once in my life I have had the courage to say what is closest to my heart.

Denis: I also must say what is on my mind.

Blanche: If you should go back on your word that is already given, I would no more marry you than I would a beggar.

Denis: You are the one who is proud, Blanche. Now that you have spoken your mind, you refuse to listen to me. (*Beat*) Here, give me your hand. Come with me—over by the window. (*Pause*) Look out across the hills. The moon is beginning to lift. Dawn is not far away.

Blanche: So peaceful and quiet. (*Suddenly*) Look! A falling star. That means—(*She quickly cuts it off.*)

Denis: Why not finish? When a star falls, it means that another mortal has died.

Blanche: I didn't mean to say that. I . . . I . . . don't know what I'm saying. So mixed up.

Denis: The words shape themselves on my lips, but I don't know how to say them. (*Pause*) Blanche! I can't let you go.

Blanche: All I can see is a picture of you being led away.

DENIS: And I can visualize a softer scene. I can see the two of us in the years to come.
BLANCHE: An eternity.
DENIS: The two of us. (*Pause*)
BLANCHE: Go on, Denis.
DENIS: I can't explain it.
BLANCHE: It happens with no warning, so I have heard. Two people fall in love. They cannot explain it.
DENIS: I don't want to leave you.
BLANCHE: Do you have to, Denis?
SOUND: *Door open.*
SIRE: Good morning, my children. I am here for my answer.
DENIS: I have it ready for you. I want to marry Blanche, but it is not a marriage of fear. I'm marrying her because I love her.
SIRE: Is this true, Blanche?
BLANCHE: Yes.
DENIS: You think you have won, Sire, but in reality you have lost. As soon as we are married, Blanche and I are leaving here. While the war lasts, she will follow me; and after it is finished, we shall go to my home in Provence.
BLANCHE: And now what may we expect from you?
DENIS: Further revenge?
SIRE (*Sly chuckle*): I am harboring no such emotions. My tender heart warms at the thought of your marriage. In fact, I am the happiest of men.
MUSIC: *Curtain. Up and out.*

THE END

A Christmas Carol

by *Charles Dickens*

SOUND: *Church clock striking three times.*
CHORUS (*Young voices*): *They sing a chorus of "God Rest Ye Merry Gentlemen." At its climax:*
SOUND: *Door opens.*
SCROOGE (*Barks*): Stop it! Stop it, I say! (*Singing stops*) Get away from here. We'll have no singing around here. Understand me! No singing!
BOY: A Merry Christmas, sir.
SCROOGE: Get away, I say.
2ND BOY: No need to wish 'im a Merry Christmas. That's Old Scrooge.
MUSIC: *A contemporary Christmas ballad. Forte and fade under.*
NARRATOR: Yes, that is Old Scrooge . . . Ebenezer Scrooge. It is the afternoon before Christmas Day in the year of our Lord 1844. Despite the bitterly cold weather, all of London is in a festive mood. But there is no happy expression on Ebenezer Scrooge's lined face, as he closes the front door of his warehouse and returns to his office. (*Music out*) He throws a glowering look at his clerk, Bob Cratchit. Satisfied that the poor wretch is hard at work, Scrooge adjusts his spectacles. Then without warning . . .
SOUND: *Door (away) opens.*
FRED: A Merry Christmas, Uncle. God save you!
SCROOGE: Bah! Humbug!
FRED: Christmas a humbug? Surely, you don't mean that, Uncle.

SCROOGE: Merry Christmas, indeed! What right have you to be merry? You're poor enough.

FRED: What right have you to be dismal? You're rich enough.

SCROOGE: What's Christmas time to you but a time for paying bills without money; a time for finding yourself a year older, and not an hour richer. If I had my way, every idiot who goes about with "Merry Christmas" on his lips should be boiled with his own pudding and buried with a stake of holly through his heart. You keep Christmas in your own way, and let me keep it in mine.

FRED: I came here to ask you to spend Christmas Day with Peg and me.

SCROOGE (*Flatly*): No!

FRED: But we want nothing from you, Uncle, other than your company. (*Pause*) Won't you change your mind and have dinner with us?

SCROOGE: Good afternoon, Fred.

FRED: A Merry Christmas.

SCROOGE: Good afternoon.

FRED: And a Happy New Year.

SCROOGE: Bah! Humbug!

MUSIC: *A brief bridge, up and out.*

CRATCHIT: Er, pardon me, Mr. Scrooge, but there is a gentleman here to see you.

SCROOGE: What about, Cratchit?

CRATCHIT: He didn't say, sir.

GENTLEMAN: Ah, good afternoon, sir. Have I the pleasure of addressing Mr. Scrooge or Mr. Marley?

SCROOGE: Mr. Marley, my former partner, has been dead these seven years. He died seven years ago, this very night.

GENTLEMAN: Then I have no doubt his liberality is well represented by his surviving partner.

SCROOGE: What do you want?

GENTLEMAN: At this festive season, Mr. Scrooge, we try to make some slight provision for the poor and destitute. Many thousands are in want of common necessities.
SCROOGE: Are there no prisons?
GENTLEMAN: Oh, plenty of prisons.
SCROOGE: And the workhouses, are they still in operation?
GENTLEMAN: I wish I could say they were not. How much shall I put you down for, Mr. Scrooge?
SCROOGE: Nothing!
GENTLEMAN (*Puzzled*): Nothing!
SCROOGE: Exactly! Let these deserving people of yours go to the establishments I have mentioned.
GENTLEMAN: Most of them would rather die than do that.
SCROOGE: Then let them do that, and help decrease the surplus population. I'm busy. Good afternoon to you.
GENTLEMAN (*Quietly*): Very good, Mr. Scrooge. Merry Christmas to you.
SOUND: *Door (off) open and close.*
SCROOGE (*Grumbles*): Charity! Pah! Humbug! Plain rot!
CRATCHIT: Er, Mr. Scrooge, sir.
SCROOGE: Well, what is it, Cratchit?
CRATCHIT: I was wondering—
SCROOGE: You were wondering if you could go home.
CRATCHIT: Yes, sir. It's getting late.
SCROOGE: Yes, go on. You'll want all day tomorrow, I suppose?
CRATCHIT: If quite convenient, sir.
SCROOGE: It's not convenient, and it's not fair.
CRATCHIT: It's only once a year, sir.
SCROOGE: A poor excuse for picking a man's pocket every twenty-fifth day of December. I suppose you must have the whole day. But be here all the earlier the next day. Understand?
CRATCHIT: Yes, sir. And Merry Christmas.

SCROOGE: Christmas! Humbug!
MUSIC: *A Christmas theme, up and under.*
NARRATOR: A few minutes later Scrooge leaves his warehouse and makes his way to his melancholy chambers, a gloomy suite of rooms. By the light of a single flickering candle, he eats his cold supper. And then to save lighting his stove, Ebenezer Scrooge retires for the night. (*Music out*) The minutes tick away. Scrooge sleeps uneasily, tossing from side to side.
SOUND: *Chains being dragged across the floor.*
NARRATOR: Suddenly he awakes with a start. Walking toward him, and dragging a heavy chain, is a gray, dim figure of a man. It stops at the foot of the bed.
SCROOGE (*Frightened*): Who are you? What do you want with me? (*Pause*) Who are you?
MARLEY: Ask me who I *was*.
SCROOGE: You're . . . you're . . .
MARLEY: Yes, in life I was your partner, Jacob Marley.
SCROOGE: But it cannot be so. You're dead.
MARLEY: You don't believe in me.
SCROOGE: No. You're nothing but an undigested bit of beef, a blot of mustard, a crumb of cheese.
MARLEY: You are wrong, Ebenezer. I am the ghost of Jacob Marley.
SCROOGE: Why do you come to me?
MARLEY: It is required of every man that the spirit within him should walk abroad among his fellow men and travel far and wide; and if that spirit goes not forth in life, it is condemned to do so after death.
SCROOGE: No, no, I don't believe it.
MARLEY: It is then doomed to wander through the world.
SCROOGE: You are chained, Jacob. Tell me why?
MARLEY: I wear the chain I forged in life. I made it link by link, and yard by yard. I wore it of my own free will. Is its pattern strange to you?

SCROOGE (*Trembling*): I don't understand.
MARLEY: This chain I wear is as heavy as the one you are now forging.
SCROOGE: You talk strangely, Jacob.
MARLEY: For seven years I have been dead—traveling the whole time. No rest, no peace. Only remorse.
SCROOGE: But you were always shrewd, Jacob.
MARLEY: Aye, too shrewd.
SCROOGE: A good man of business.
MARLEY: Business! Mankind was my business. The common welfare was my business; charity, mercy, forbearance and benevolence were all my business. But I heeded none of these. Instead, I thought only of money.
SCROOGE: And what is wrong with making money?
MARLEY: That is your fault, Ebenezer, as it was mine. That is why I am here tonight. That is part of my penance. I am here to warn you . . . to help you escape my fate. You have one chance left.
SCROOGE: Tell me how this chance will come!
MARLEY: My time draws near. I must go. Tonight you will be haunted by three spirits. The first will appear when the bell strikes one; expect the second at the stroke of two, and the third as the bell tolls three.
SCROOGE: Couldn't I take 'em all at once, and have it over with?
MARLEY: No. And heed them when they appear. (*Fading*) Remember it is your last chance to escape my miserable fate.
MUSIC: *A bit ominous. Forte and fade out under* NARRATOR.
NARRATOR: As Scrooge stares in frightened silence, the wraith-like figure of his deceased partner dissolves into space. Then, exhausted by the ordeal, Scrooge drops off to sleep. Twelve o'clock comes. Time passes. Then:
SOUND: *Off in the distance, steeple clock strikes once.*
NARRATOR: The curtains of Scrooge's bed are drawn aside, but by no visible hand. There by the bed stands an unearthly

visitor ... a strange figure—like a child. Its hair is white, and in its hand it holds a sprig of fresh green holly. Scrooge stares and then speaks.

SCROOGE: Are you the spirit whose coming was told me by Jacob Marley?

1ST GHOST (*A gentle voice*): I am.

SCROOGE: Who, and what are you?

1ST GHOST: I am the Ghost of Christmas Past.

SCROOGE: Long past?

1ST GHOST: No. Your Past. Rise and walk with me.

SCROOGE: Where?

1ST GHOST: Out through the window.

SCROOGE: But we are three stories above ground. I am only a mortal.

1ST GHOST: Bear but a touch of my hand upon your heart and you shall be upheld in more than this.

SCROOGE: What are we to do?

1ST GHOST: *I* am going to help reclaim you. Come! Walk with me out into the night ... into the past.

SOUND: *Wind. It sweeps in; hold and then fade out.*

SCROOGE: Tell me, Ghost of Christmas Past, where are we?

1ST GHOST: Look down, Ebenezer, and remember back.

SCROOGE (*Amazed*): Why ... why, of course. The river ... the meadows ... and—why, there's my old school. I went there as a lad. But there is no one about.

1ST GHOST: It is Christmas holiday. Let us look into this study hall.

SCROOGE: Empty, except for a young boy sitting at a desk, his head in his hands. Left behind. He ... he's crying. Poor chap! No place to go at Christmas. Ah, now he's looking up.

1ST GHOST: Do you recognize him?

SCROOGE (*Stunned*): Why, it's—

1ST GHOST: What is his name?

SCROOGE (*Slowly*): Ebenezer Scrooge. (*Pause*) I wish— But it's too late now.
1ST GHOST: What is the matter?
SCROOGE: Nothing, nothing. There were some boys singing Christmas carols outside my warehouse door yesterday afternoon. I drove them away.
1ST GHOST: Let us see another Christmas.
SOUND: *Wind up briefly and out.*
1ST GHOST: It is a year later . . . another Christmas.
SCROOGE: And again there is the school.
1ST GHOST: That boy standing in the driveway, pacing up and down.
SCROOGE: It is I.
1ST GHOST: And what do you see?
SCROOGE: A coach coming up the driveway. Now it has stopped, and a little girl gets out. Look, she is hugging me. It's Fan, my sister.
1ST GHOST: Listen to what she says.
FAN: I've come to bring you home, dear brother. Father's not mean any more, and he says you're never coming back here, and from now on we'll always be together. (*Fading*) Just think, together for the first time in four years.
1ST GHOST: Your sister was a delicate creature . . . kind . . . big-hearted.
SCROOGE: So she was, so she was. She died comparatively young.
1ST GHOST: She left one child behind her.
SCROOGE: Yes. Fred, my nephew.
1ST GHOST (*Mildly*): He was in to wish you a Merry Christmas yesterday.
SCROOGE: Yes. Yes, he did so. Please take me back.
1ST GHOST: Not yet. There is one more shadow.
SCROOGE: No more. I do not wish to see it.

1st Ghost: You must.

Sound: *The wind sweeps in full again, then out.*

1st Ghost: The years have passed. In this house below. Look, there sits a young girl, a beautiful girl.

Scrooge: It's Belle.

1st Ghost: The girl you were to marry. And there you sit next to her, a young man in your prime. Only now your face begins to show the signs of avarice. There is a greedy, restless motion in your eyes. Listen to what she is saying to you.

Belle (*She is about 18*): It matters very little to you. Another idol has displaced me, a golden one. You hold money more important than me or anything else, for that matter. And I'm going to grant your wish: free you from marrying me. (*Fading*) That is the way you wish it, Ebenezer. I feel sorry for you.

Scrooge: Spirit, show me no more.

1st Ghost: Today, Belle is a happy woman, surrounded with her fine children. Those children might have been yours if you hadn't been so selfish.

Scrooge: Take me back. Haunt me no more! I beg of you, don't!

Music: *Ethereal theme. Forte and fade under for* Narrator.

Narrator: The steeple clock has just finished striking the second hour of Christmas Day. Scrooge finds himself back in his bedroom. Slowly his door, though bolted, swings open.

Music: *Out.*

2nd Ghost (*A big, booming voice*): Good morning, Ebenezer. Welcome me. I am the Ghost of Christmas Present. Look upon me.

Scrooge: You're practically a giant. Yet you have a young face.

2nd Ghost: Have you never seen the like of me before?

Scrooge: Never.

2nd Ghost: I have many brothers, over eighteen hundred of them, one for each Christmas since the very first.
Scrooge: And you are here to take me with you?
2nd Ghost: Yes. I trust you will profit by your journey. Touch my robe, Ebenezer.
Sound: *Wind. Up full and out into:*
Chorus (*Mixed voices*): *Singing a chorus of a Christmas hymn. As they near conclusion, fade them under for:*
Scrooge: Those people in this church, they seem very happy.
2nd Ghost: They are, for they are giving thanks for all the joys brought to them during the year.
Scrooge: And the crew of that ship over there. . . . Look, they are shaking hands with the captain.
Chorus: *Out.*
2nd Ghost: Wishing him a Merry Christmas. But come! We have not much time left, and there is still another place we must visit. It is a very poor house in a very poor section of London. This one directly below us.
Scrooge: Indeed it is. Who, may I ask, lives here?
2nd Ghost: An underpaid clerk named Bob Cratchit.
Scrooge: The Bob Cratchit who is employed by me?
2nd Ghost: The very same.
Scrooge: That woman . . . those four children.
2nd Ghost: His wife and family.
Scrooge: Coming up the stairs right now. That's Cratchit. He's carrying a young boy.
2nd Ghost: His fifth child . . . Tiny Tim.
Scrooge: He carries a crutch.
2nd Ghost: Because he is crippled.
Scrooge: But the doctors—
2nd Ghost: Cratchit cannot afford a doctor, not on fifteen shillings a week.
Scrooge: But—

2nd Ghost: Sshhh! Listen.
Sound: *Door opens.*
Cratchit (*Heartily*): Good afternoon, everyone.
Tim: And a most Merry Christmas.
Mrs. Cratchit: Father . . . Tiny Tim.
The Other Cratchits (*They ad lib*): "Merry Christmas," "Welcome," "Tiny Tim, sit next to me," "Father, let me take your muffler."
Mrs. Cratchit: And how did Tiny Tim behave at church?
Cratchit: As good as gold, and better.
Tim: I was glad to be able to go to church. That's because I wanted the people to see that I'm a cripple.
Mrs. Cratchit: Now that's a peculiar thing to say, Tiny Tim.
Tim (*Eagerly*): No, it isn't. That's because I was in God's House, and it was God who made the blind able to see and the lame able to walk. And when the people at church saw me and my crutch, I was hoping they would think of what God can do, and that they would say a prayer for me.
Mrs. Cratchit: I . . . I'm certain they must have prayed for you.
Tim: And one of these days I'm going to get well, and that'll mean I can throw away this crutch, and run and play like the other boys.
Cratchit (*Softly*): You will, Tim—one of these days. (*Heartily*) And now, Mother, the big question. When will dinner be ready?
Biz: *Ad libs from the children.*
Mrs. Cratchit: It's ready right now: just about the finest goose you have ever seen. Martha, you carry it in. Tom, you fetch the potatoes and turnips. Dick, Peter, set the chairs around the table.
Tim: And I'll sit between Father and Mother.
Cratchit: This is going to be the best Christmas dinner any-

one could hope for. (*Fading*) And I'm the luckiest man in the world, having such a fine family.

SCROOGE: It isn't a very big goose, is it? I could eat the whole bird myself, I believe.

2ND GHOST: It is all Bob Cratchit can afford. His family doesn't complain. To them, that meagre goose is a sumptuous banquet. And more important, much more important, Ebenezer.

SCROOGE: Go on.

2ND GHOST: They are a happy and united group. Look at their shining faces. Listen to them.

BIZ: *The* CRATCHITS *ad libbing in happy fashion,*

CRATCHIT: What a superb dinner we have had . . . the tempting meat, the delicious dressing.

TIM: And the plum pudding, Father. Don't forget that.

CRATCHIT: That pudding was the greatest success achieved by Mrs. Cratchit since her marriage.

BIZ: *The children laugh.*

MRS. CRATCHIT: Thank you for the compliment.

CRATCHIT: And now for the crowning touch. The punch!

BIZ (*Ad libs of*): "The punch!" "Good!" "Oh!"

CRATCHIT: Here we are. Get your glasses. You, Peter . . . Dick . . . Tom . . . Martha . . . Tiny Tim . . . and last, but far from least, you, Mother. And not to forget myself. (*With finality*) There!

TIM: A toast!

CRATCHIT: First the founder of this feast, the man who has made it possible. I give you Mr. Scrooge.

MRS. CRATCHIT (*Bristling*): Mr. Scrooge, indeed. I wish I had him here. I'd give him a piece of my mind to feast upon, and I hope he'd have a good appetite for it.

CRATCHIT (*Warningly*): My dear, the children! Christmas Day.

MRS. CRATCHIT: He's a hard, stingy, unfeeling man. You know he is, Robert, better than anybody else.

CRATCHIT (*Mildly*): My dear. Remember, Christmas Day.
MRS. CRATCHIT: I'm sorry. Very well, I'll drink his health. Long life to him! A Merry Christmas to him! To Mr. Scrooge.
FAMILY (*Chorusing*): To Mr. Scrooge!
CRATCHIT: And now a toast to us: A Merry Christmas to us all. God bless us!
FAMILY: God bless us.
TIM: God bless us every one.
MUSIC: *"Noel"—Forte and fade under.*
SCROOGE: Spirit, tell me if Tiny Tim will live.
2ND GHOST: I see a vacant seat in the chimney corner, and a crutch without an owner, carefully preserved. If these shadows remain unaltered by the Future the child will die.
SCROOGE: No, no. Oh, no, kind Spirit! Say he will live, that he will be spared.
2ND GHOST: Why concern yourself about him? Isn't it better that he die and decrease the surplus population?
SCROOGE: But these poor people must be helped.
2ND GHOST: Are there no prisons? And the workhouses, are they still in operation?
SCROOGE: Do not taunt me.
2ND GHOST: It is time for us to go.
SCROOGE: No I wish to remain.
2ND GHOST: I can remain no longer. Touch my robe and we shall go.
SCROOGE: No! No, I say! Spirit, don't desert me. I need your help.
MUSIC: *Up briefly and under.*
NARRATOR: As Ebenezer Scrooge comes to his senses, he discovers himself standing on the street, outside of his lodgings. A heavy snow is falling, blanketing a sleeping London. The wind has died down. It is still early Christmas morning.

MUSIC: *Out into:*
SOUND: *Steeple bell off in distance striking three times.*
3RD GHOST (*Warningly*): Ebenezer . . . Ebenezer Scrooge.
SCROOGE: You are the third and last.
3RD GHOST: I am the Ghost of Christmas Yet To Come.
SCROOGE: You are about to show me shadows of the things that have not happened, but will happen in the time before us. Is that so, Spirit?
3RD GHOST: Yes, Ebenezer, that is correct.
SCROOGE: I tremble at going with you. I fear what I am to see.
3RD GHOST: Come, Ebenezer.
SOUND: *Wind up full and out.*
SCROOGE: Why do we stop here on this street corner, Spirit?
3RD GHOST: Those two men standing there, do you know them?
SCROOGE: Why, yes, I do business with them.
3RD GHOST: Their conversation is interesting.
MAN 1: When did he die?
MAN 2: Last night, I believe.
MAN 1: I thought he'd never die.
MAN 2: What has he done with his money?
MAN 1: I haven't heard. Left it to his company, perhaps. Well, one thing is certain, he didn't leave it to charity.
MAN 2: Are you going to his funeral?
MAN 1: Not unless a free lunch is provided.
MAN 2 (*Fading*): A very good point. Can't say that I blame you.
SCROOGE: Spirit, this dead man they were discussing, who is he?
3RD GHOST: I will show you.
SOUND: *Wind up briefly and out.*
SCROOGE: This room, it's too dark to see.
3RD GHOST: In front of you is a bed. On it lies a man—the body of the man those men on the street were discussing.
SCROOGE: And no one has come to claim this body?

3rd Ghost: No one, for he left not a friend behind him. Come closer and look into his face.
Scrooge: No.
3rd Ghost: Look!
Scrooge: Spirit, this is a fearful place. Let us go.
3rd Ghost: Look at the face of this unclaimed man.
Scrooge: I would do it if I could. But I haven't the power. Let me see some tenderness connected with a death. If I don't, that lonely body in this dark room will ever haunt me.
3rd Ghost: Yes, I know of such a home, one where there is tenderness connected with death. Over here on this poor street and in this dismal house.
Scrooge: But this house— Why, yes, I've been here before. Bob Cratchit, my clerk, lives here. There is Mrs. Cratchit and her eldest daughter, Martha.
Martha: Your eyes, Mother, you'll strain them working in this bad light.
Mrs. Cratchit: I'll stop for a while. I wouldn't show weak eyes to your father when he comes home. It's time he was here.
Martha: Past it rather. But these days he walks slower than he used to, Mother.
Mrs. Cratchit: I have known him to walk with Tiny Tim upon his shoulder very fast, indeed. He was very light to carry and your father loved him so, it was no trouble.
Sound: *Door handle.*
Mrs. Cratchit: There is your father now at the door.
Sound: *Door opens and shuts.*
Mrs. Cratchit: You're late tonight, Robert.
Cratchit: Yes, I'm late.
Martha: I'll get some tea for you, Father.
Cratchit: Thank you, Martha.
Mrs. Cratchit: You went there today, Robert?
Cratchit: Yes. I wish you could have gone. It would have done you good to see how green a place it is.

Mrs. Cratchit: I'll see it soon.

Cratchit: I promised him I would walk there every Sunday. My poor Tiny Tim. At last he got rid of his crutch.

Mrs. Cratchit (*Fading*): Yes, at last he did. Our poor Tiny Tim.

Scrooge: Tell me, Spirit, why did Tiny Tim have to die?

3rd Ghost: Come, there is still another place to visit.

Sound: *Wind. Up and out.*

Scrooge: A graveyard. Why do we pause here?

3rd Ghost: That tombstone . . . read the name on it.

Scrooge: Before I do, answer me one question. Are these the shadows of the things that *will* be, or are they the shadows of the things that *may* be, only?

3rd Ghost: The inscription on the tombstone.

Scrooge: It reads . . . (*Slowly*) "Ebenezer Scrooge." No, Spirit. Oh, no, no! Hear me! I am not the man I was. I will not be the man I must have been but for this lesson. I will honor Christmas in my heart.

3rd Ghost: But will you?

Scrooge: Oh, yes. I will try and keep it alive all the year. I will live in the Past, the Present and the Future. I will not shut out the lesson that all three Spirits have taught me. Oh, tell me there is hope, that I may wipe away the writing on this stone.

Sound: *Wind up strong. Hold and out into: Joyous church bells, tolling Christmas Day. Hold under.*

Scrooge (*Moans, as though coming out of a dream*): Tell me there is hope, that I may wipe away the writing on this stone. (*Coming to*) Eh, what am I holding on to? The bedpost. I am in my own bed . . . home. Those bells! It must be Christmas Day. Christmas Day—I wonder if it really is. We shall see. Open the window.

Sound: *Window being raised.*

Scrooge: You boy, down there.

Boy (*Away*): Eh?
Scrooge: What day is today, my fine lad?
Boy: Today! Why, Christmas Day, of course.
Scrooge: And to think the Spirits have done it all in one night.
Boy: What did you say, sir?
Scrooge: Do you know the poulterer's in the next street?
Boy: I should hope I did.
Scrooge: An intelligent boy! A remarkable boy! Do you know whether they've sold the prize turkey that was hanging in the window?
Boy: The one as big as me?
Scrooge: What a delightful boy. Yes, the one as big as you.
Boy: It's hanging there now.
Scrooge: Go and buy it. I am in earnest. Here is the money. Catch. (*Pause*) Deliver it to Bob Cratchit, who lives on Golden Street in Camden Town.
Boy: But, sir, there will be considerable change left over.
Scrooge (*Chuckling*): Keep it, my boy. Keep it.
Boy (*Delighted*): Oh, thank you, sir.
Scrooge: And, boy.
Boy: Yes, sir.
Scrooge: Don't let Mr. Cratchit know who sent the turkey. It's something of a surprise. And something else.
Boy: Yes, sir.
Scrooge: A very Merry Christmas to you.
Music: *A Christmas hymn. Up and under.*
Sound: *Knock on door. Repeated. Door opens.*
Fred: What is it? (*Pause*) Why, bless my soul!
Scrooge (*Heartily*): Yes, yes, it is I—your Uncle Scrooge. I've come for dinner. Now let me in. I have a present for your good wife. From now on I'm going to be one of your most persistent guests. I've changed, my boy: you'll see!
Music: *Up and under for* Narrator.

NARRATOR: Scrooge was better than his word. He did everything he promised, and infinitely more. He became a persistent visitor to his nephew's home, and even took Fred into business with him. He raised Bob Cratchit's salary to a figure that left that bewildered gentleman gasping; and to Tiny Tim, who did not die, he was a second father. He provided doctors for the little lad, and very soon Tiny Tim will have his wish: he will be able to throw away his crutch and run and play like the other boys. As for the three Spirits, Ebenezer Scrooge never saw them again. That was due to the unchallengeable fact that Scrooge, for the rest of his days, helped keep alive the spirit of Christmas. And so, as Tiny Tim observed, God bless us every one.

MUSIC: *Up full to close.*

THE END